Communities and Social
Policy in Canada

Communities and Social Policy in Canada

BRIAN WHARF

Canadian Cataloguing in Publication Data

Wharf, Brian
 Communities and social policy in Canada

Includes bibliographical references and index.
ISBN 0-7710-8827-2

1. Community organization – Canada. 2. Community
power – Canada. 3. Canada – Social policy.
I. Title.

HN107.W53 1992   361.971   C92-093209-6

McClelland & Stewart Inc.
The Canadian Publishers
481 University Avenue
Toronto, Ontario
M5G 2E9

Printed and bound in Canada by
John Deyell Company Limited.

CONTENTS

DEDICATION

This book is dedicated to my aunt, Margaret Heseltine, a pioneer in Canadian social work. Following her career as a settlement house worker in England, Margaret came to Canada in 1938. Over the next thirty years she held a variety of positions, including directing the Children's Aid Society in Fort William, opening and staffing an office in Geraldton for the Port Arthur Children's Aid Society, and being appointed by the then Department of Indian Affairs as the first departmental social worker in Saskatchewan. Margaret's last position was as the warden of the Prince Albert Jail for Women, where she distinguished herself not only as a humane administrator but as an advocate for prisoners.

She was named Citizen of the Year in Prince Albert in 1959, and in a letter of congratulations to her, the Director of Welfare commented: "I do want you to know how proud we are of you. Your recognition as a community accepted person, I think, is an important lesson to all our staff to take part in local community affairs."

For Margaret Heseltine, involvement in community affairs and in social reform was part and parcel of social work practice.

PREFACE

In a very direct fashion this book continues the work begun in *Social Work and Social Change in Canada* (Wharf, 1990) on the contributions of the profession of social work to social reform. *Social Work and Social Change* focused attention on the connections between social work and three social movements: those of labour, women, and First Nations. The book concluded that the contributions of social work to social reform would be greatly aided if the social work discipline were to establish firm connections with these social movements and thus profit from their knowledge and experience.

While similar in intent, *Communities and Social Policy in Canada* examines the potential of community organizations and the roles of social workers within these organizations to influence social policy. The rationale for this investigation is that while social policies in Canada are largely developed in provincial capitals and Ottawa, their consequences are played out and experienced in local communities. Community organizations, and indeed local governments, have little influence on the design of social policies, and the central issue addressed throughout the book is whether increased involvement on the part of community organizations and municipal governments would improve social policies.

Communities and Social Policy in Canada is, therefore, all about connections: between social work and community work practice, between social problems and social policy, and between communities and provincial and federal governments. However, one important connection is missing: that between the local community and international forces. Certainly, for example, international dictates on the price of lumber affect the economy of British Columbia in such a direct fashion that the budget-balancing efforts of the provincial government pale into relative insignificance. This book not only ignores the impact of the global market and of multinational corporations, but it also neglects what are referred to

9

as the "grand" issues of policy: matters such as the free trade agreement, which has resulted in many thousands of Canadian jobs being lost to the U.S. and to cheap-labour Third World countries.

One can take the position that neglect of the grand issues renders inconsequential any consideration of community-level matters. While not disputing in any way the crucial significance of both international and national forces on the lives of Canadians, the position taken here is that local-level changes can improve the quality of life for citizens. Thus the closure of a hospital school for developmentally delayed children in New Brunswick and the control of child welfare services by the Champagne/Aishihik band in the Yukon have greatly improved services for children and families in these jurisdictions. The argument is strengthened by pointing to the differences between the U.S. and Canada. Although both countries are characterized by a capitalist, free-enterprise economy largely controlled by those who benefit from this economic system, the health and social policies developed in this country have substantially improved the quality of life for Canadians and are demonstrably superior to those in the U.S.

The present work contends that even in countries with neo-conservative national governments and in the face of mounting despair about the impact of the global economy, it is possible to improve the quality of life within communities. To avoid the challenge of doing so on the rationale that there are larger and more fundamental challenges makes no sense for a profession that has been grounded in community from its earliest days. Finally, an admittedly optimistic vein runs through the book: as citizens in their local organizations change conditions and shape social policies, they are better prepared to influence the grand issues of public policy.

CHAPTER I

Introduction: Communities
and Social Policy

This book has two objectives. The first is to examine the capacity of community organizations and community work strategies to confront and ameliorate significant social problems. All of the case studies presented in the book address such problems and the social policies developed to deal with them: deinstitutionalization and the development of community support systems; poverty and the reform of income security programs; the emergence of First Nation control of child welfare; the struggle to gain control of abortion policy and services; and the growth of the healthy community movement. While five swallows do not a summer make, these case studies were selected because they possess the potential to examine the connections between community work and social policy. Several crucial questions are addressed throughout the book. Can such policy issues be dealt with at the community level? Can community organizations make a distinctive contribution to the resolution of problems, given that the community is the locale in which these problems are experienced? Since most social policies are conceived at the national or provincial levels but implemented in local communities, are the present linkages and connections between different levels of government sufficient to ensure that social policies meet the needs of local communities? Should the role of local communities be strengthened? Is the community a viable base for governing the social services?

The initial plan for the book was to examine the capacity of voluntary agencies to engage in social reform and to influence social policy. Thus conceived, the inquiry would have focused on the efforts of the voluntary sector to influence the public sector. However, the decision to include a chapter on healthy communities altered the initial plan since municipal governments are heavily involved in healthy community projects. The book is then concerned with the capacity of community-based organizations, whether public or voluntary, to influence the social policies of provincial and federal governments.

The second objective is to examine the connections between community work and social work. The profession has made many distinguished contributions to the theory and practice of community work, but its commitment to and interest in community work have declined in recent years. One important reason for this decline is the lack of priority assigned to community work by both the public and private sectors. A second reason concerns the compatibility between social work and community work practice. While this is a long-standing and much discussed issue, changes in the structure of social work education in Canada over the past two decades lend a new and distinctive dimension to the debate. These changes are outlined in a later section of this chapter.

Thus the book is all about connections: connections among social problems, social policy, and community work and between social work and community work practice. This introductory chapter sets the stage by describing community work practice and introducing the connections noted above. These connections are examined in detail in Chapters 2 to 6. Chapters 7 and 8 consider the challenging task of assessing whether community organizations can address social policy issues and whether social work's commitment to community practice might be reawakened.

A brief note on the research approach used in the book is in order at this point. One of the most perceptive books on the case study as a research approach claims that:

> As a research endeavour, the case study contributes uniquely to our knowledge of individual, organizational, social and political phenomena. . . . The distinctive need for case studies arises out of the desire to understand complex social phenomena. In brief the case study allows an investigation to retain the holistic and meaningful characteristics of real life events – such as individual life cycles, organizational and managerial processes, neighbourhood change, international relations and the motivation of industries. (Yin, 1984: 14)

Given that the policy process and attempts to influence this process represent complex social phenomena, the case study approach is particularly appropriate for this book. In addition, a distinct advantage of this method is that case studies capture the interest of students. Many social work students have an instinctive dislike of social policy, viewing it as boring and unconnected to practice. Many years ago a colleague and I discovered that one way to overcome this problem was to connect policy to practice through the medium of a case study (Callahan and Wharf, 1982). Nevertheless, despite the considerable contributions of the case study approach in yielding rich and detailed information, it is based on a small number of cases. The findings of case studies are therefore suggestive rather than conclusive.

DEFINING SOCIAL POLICY

Two important terms – social policy and community – need to be defined. Definitions of social policy abound in the literature. The following is most appropriate for this book, given the objective of connecting social policy and community.

> Social policy is all about social purposes and the choices between them. The choices and the conflicts between them have continuously to be made at the governmental level, the community level and the individual level. At each level by acting or not acting, by opting in or contracting out, we can influence the direction in which choices are made. (Titmuss, 1974: 131)

There are three important components of this definition: purpose, choice and the conflict between these choices, and participation. Purpose represents a direction – institutional or community care, traditional or First Nation approaches to child welfare, Pro-Choice or Pro-Life positions on abortion, to name but three possible directions for social policy; choice emphasizes that the direction for policy is frequently far from clear and that firmly held values and ideologies compete for attention; participation reminds us that there are opportunities to influence the policy process.

Social policy is viewed here as a statement of intent by government and social reform as activities designed to influence these statements. However, the case studies also examine whether governments engage in reform: whether, as in the case of municipal governments, they attempt to change the policies of senior levels of government, and whether provincial and federal governments engage in reform by changing the policies of their predecessors.

The distinction between "ordinary and grand issues of policy" is of pivotal significance for this book. Lindblom defines grand issues as "those pertaining to the fundamental structure of political-economic life. These grand issues include those on distribution of income and wealth, on the distribution of political power and on corporate prerogatives" (Lindblom, 1979: 523). By contrast, ordinary issues include such topics as those covered in this book – the governance of child welfare services, deinstitutionalization and the development of community support programs, the emergence of the healthy community movement, the struggle to raise social assistance rates in Ontario, and the debate about abortion politics in Nanaimo.

Yet, some ordinary issues touch on and are affected by the grand issues, as exemplified by the case studies on income security and abortion. Raising social assistance rates in Ontario would not have required a fundamental restructuring of income and wealth, but it made questioning of the existing distribution unavoidable. Similarly, the abortion struggle in Nanaimo reflected a larger power struggle on the dimension of values rather than wealth.

For a number of reasons this book is concerned with the ordinary issues of policy. First, these issues affect the lives of those served by community workers and social workers in a very direct fashion. Indeed, for those affected, ordinary issues are vastly more important than the grand issues of redistributing wealth and power on a national scale. Second, it seems reasonable to assume that these issues can be altered by community-based organizations; for example, the potential of these agencies to shift the governance of child welfare is greater than their ability to affect the distribution of income or the power of the corporate sector. Third, some problems experienced by consumers of services are the consequence of earlier reforms. For example, reformers assumed that the combination of public sponsorship and professional expertise would resolve many social problems. However, as a number of writers have pointed out, the consequence of these reforms has been the creation of large public-sector organizations and a new set of problems for consumers (see, among others, Carniol, 1991; Davies and Shragge, 1990). A much needed reform at the present time is the restructuring of public agencies to increase the benefits provided, to strengthen connections to community, and to reduce agency size and rigidity.

DEFINING COMMUNITY

In a review of the literature some thirty-five years ago, Hillery discovered ninety-seven definitions of community, and without doubt many additions could now be made to the list. However, it is not the intent here to engage in a protracted discussion of definitions. "Community" is defined here as a network of individuals with common needs and issues. This directs attention to the two essential characteristics of communities – relationships and needs. These characteristics can be expressed by a group living in a defined geographic area, as the example of the the healthy community movement illustrates. In the case study of deinstitutionalization the community consisted of developmentally delayed children and adults in southern New Brunswick. In the chapter on reforming income security the community was the province of Ontario. The communities in the child welfare chapter are First Nation children in Vancouver and the Champagne/Aishihik community in the Yukon. The latter community represents a classic example of the "traditional" community. It is characterized by geographic boundaries, shared values, history, an economic base, and a governing structure. By contrast, the First Nation children in Vancouver come from many bands across the province and have only their Indian ancestry and a variety of needs in common. Thus communities range from small, self-contained groups to large and diverse populations. Despite size and complexity, the essential common denominators of a community are a pattern of relationships among people and the existence of needs shared by these individuals.

"Community work" is used in this book as an umbrella term encompassing all of the following: locality development, community development, community organization, social action, social reform, and social planning. It is not unusual to find these terms being used interchangeably; in particular, the first three typically refer to efforts to mobilize residents of a neighbourhood or a larger geographic unit to take action and resolve an issue or problem facing them.

In an effort to introduce some clarity and precision into community work practice, Rothman developed a conceptual framework that identified three approaches to community work: locality development, social planning, and social action (Rothman, 1974). Since the distinctions between these approaches are important for the discussion of practice throughout this book, it is necessary to describe them briefly. Locality development refers to developing the capacity of local areas to confront and resolve problems that face them. The basic assumption underlying this approach is that Canadian society is essentially benevolent, and that once problems are identified they can be tackled by residents working together in a co-operative fashion. Social action is rooted in completely opposite assumptions. The essential premise is that society is governed by an elite few who rule in their own interests. The existence of poverty and other social problems is the direct consequence of this imbalance of power, and oppressed groups seek to realign the distribution of power and wealth through strategies of confrontation. Social planning represents a rational, technocratic approach to practice and requires the application of research and other methodologies to social problems. Once identified, measured, and described, appropriate solutions will be evident and put into place.

Rothman also identified a fourth approach, social reform, which is an amalgam of social action and social planning.

> Assumptions concerning the community situation include both substantive and social programs (inadequate housing), and disadvantaged populations (poor people who cannot afford decent housing) .... Change techniques utilize in large measure campaign tactics, the employment of facts and persuasion to apply pressure to appropriate decision-making bodies. (Rothman, 1974: 30)

It should be noted that social reform receives only scant mention in the Rothman classification. It is not included in the title of the article and only briefly referred to in the discussion of objectives, assumptions, and strategies in community work. However, as will become apparent as the discussion proceeds in this and other chapters, social reform is viewed here as the primary objective of community work.

Despite Rothman's contribution in introducing some much needed precision into a murky and confusing field of practice, an unintended consequence has been to divert attention from identifying a set of overarching objectives for community work. O'Brien criticizes the Rothman framework in the following terms:

I believe the Rothman framework invites the creation of practice enclaves which reinforce the tendency to partialize and segment. Can anyone not be impressed with the frequent and often bitter exchanges among community practitioners over the past decade as to which brand of practice is most relevant. . . . My opinion is that any approach which contains the potential of reinforcing the already existing tendency in the field toward fragmentation is an undesirable one. (O'Brien, 1979: 234)

Since the principal concern in this book is to discover connections – between social work and community work practice, between theory and practice, and between social policy and community work, the Rothman approach is not used as the organizing framework for the case studies. A more useful conceptualization of community work practice is provided by Perlman and Gurin, whose review of theory and practice led to the conclusion that two themes have dominated community work practice from its beginnings – "strengthening social provisions and improving peoples' problem-solving capacities and relationships" (Perlman and Gurin, 1972: 58). The first theme has been pursued by organizations such as social planning councils, governments, and social movements. The latter theme has been the object of attention for a wide variety of social welfare agencies, and in the community work arena by neighbourhood organizations and self-help groups. To recast this slightly, the following themes represent the overall objectives of the profession of social work: a concern for social policies that attend to public issues and provide social and health programs; a concern for the private troubles of individuals; and a concern for the connections between public issues and private troubles.

These themes also bear a striking resemblance to the development of conceptual frameworks on prevention in mental health. Recognizing that primary prevention, entailing as it does basic changes in the distribution of income and power, is beyond the immediate scope and mandate of mental health professionals, Emory Cowen has argued the case for "baby steps toward prevention." Cowen's suggestions for some appropriate "baby steps" are altering negative environments (strengthening social provisions) and enhancing competence (improving people's problem-solving capacities) (Cowen, 1977).

A somewhat reworked version of these conceptualizations is used in this book to define the mission of community work: the overriding purpose of community work is social reform, which is achieved mainly by improving social policies and programs and by enhancing the competence of consumers, staff, and others affected by social welfare programs. This statement of mission is consistent with a definition advanced in a recent text.

> The foremost objective of community work is to increase the capacity of consumers to use and influence institutional-relations organizations to better meet their needs and protect their interests. There are three professional goals that may be pursued singly or in combination that follow from this statement: (a) increasing the competence of users of social services; (b) increasing the responsiveness of social service organizations to consumer needs, wants and rights and (c) bringing about alterations in institutional policies and programs that impinge on consumer interests. (Brager, Specht, and Torczyner, 1987: 70)

It is not clear why Brager, Specht, and Torczyner chose to focus on "institutional-relations organizations whose major function is to mediate the relations between individuals and institutions. Examples are trade unions, professional associations, civil rights groups, social planning councils and parent-teacher associations" (Brager, Specht, and Torczyner, 1987: 64). While some of these organizations are in the very forefront of reform, as will be seen in the chapter dealing with the Metropolitan Social Planning Council in Toronto and the reform of income security programs in Ontario, others may be in need of reform. And certainly in Canada community work is not primarily mediated through these organizations. As will be seen in the following chapters, community work can be undertaken by public-sector organizations, by First Nation band councils, and by local interest groups.

SOCIAL POLICY AND COMMUNITY WORK

As emphasized in the preceding pages, the distinguishing characteristic of this book is the focus on the connections between community and social policy. This represents a marked departure from most Canadian books on community work, which deal with ɘ of community workers in enhancing the capacity of resi-ᴅᴜᴜᴛɪ of a local area or members of an interest group to deal with issues and problems of concern to them. Typically, but by no means always, these issues are local, such as the need for improved playgrounds and streetlights. However, the most serious social problems of poverty, the lack of affordable housing, alcoholism, drug addiction, prostitution, crime, and delinquency know no boundaries and are to be found in all communities across the country. In an effort to deal with these cross-community issues, federal and provincial governments have developed social policies and programs. For their part, most municipal and regional governments have been content, if not pleased, to pass the responsibility for social policy to senior levels of government. Their reasons have included lack of funds, the recognition that social problems are contentious, complicated, and seemingly impervious to effective resolution, and a conviction that these cross-community problems are the responsibility of national and provincial governments. This conviction had its origins in the Great Depression when municipal governments clearly lacked the capacity to respond to the devastating effects of nation-wide unemployment. Somewhat reluctantly, the federal government assumed responsibility for coping with the impact of the depression, but this initial stance was gradually replaced by one of leadership in developing Canadian health and social welfare programs. Recently, the reluctance has returned and the federal government is now abandoning its role as a leader in social policy.

The paradox is that while responsibility for social policy has largely been passed to senior levels of government, social problems are experienced and played out in local communities. For example, the vexing problems of street kids and juvenile prostitution that currently plague many Canadian cities are most visible on city streets and to local merchants and residents. While senior levels of government have and should retain a responsibility for social policy, the argument developed in this book is that when these governments plan *for* communities, not *with* them, the programs developed are frequently ineffective and inappropriate. The argument is convincingly supported by the complete failure of child welfare programs established by the federal and provincial governments without the involvement of First Nations peoples. This example is discussed at length in Chapter 4.

A pointed comment on the lack of congruence between the plans of federal bureaucracies and the needs of local communities comes from one of Paul St. Pierre's stories of ranching in the Chilcotin area in B.C.

> Without time to consider and without having asked for anything the Namko Cattlemen's Association was informed that Namko was to become an Agricultural Redevelopment Area. There would be a major range improvement program, the draining of wet meadows and the irrigation of dry ones by damming creeks. They would be employed by their governments to do this work, on their own lands at staggering rates of pay.
>
> The ranchers responded gravely, softly, even courteously, but in a manner totally unexpected. They voted an absolute and unequivocal rejection of the offer on the principle that governments knew bugger all about ranching and were best kept far away from where anything worthwhile was to be done. (St. Pierre, 1985: 4)

To be sure, the argument that social problems such as poverty are not only national in scope but in large measure are caused by the basic structures of Canadian society is plausible and defensible. The adherence to and active support of the institutions of capitalism, private property, and wealth by a succession of federal governments have resulted in a society where an elite few prosper, a large middle class fares well, and no less than a fifth of the population lives in poverty (Ross, 1987; McQuaig, 1988). Altering such basic and fundamental arrangements will require governments committed to democratic socialism, and even they will face formidable obstacles from those who, because of their wealth and connections, exercise considerable influence on the grand issues of social policy. As noted earlier, such issues are not the primary concern of this book, but the connections between ordinary and grand issues are discussed further in the final chapter.

The position taken here is that senior levels of government have the clear responsibility for resolving what is, after all, the most fundamental social problem – poverty. However, their continuing reluctance to attack the problem in a serious and committed fashion places a particular responsibility on social reform organizations, and the efforts of one such organization are explored in Chapter 3. Other social policy issues, such as child welfare, deinstitutionalization, and the development of healthy communities, require the active participation of people and organizations at the community level. These issues cannot be dealt with by senior levels of government in isolation from communities.

Hence the focus of this book is on the community as the meeting ground between social problems and social policies. It seeks to determine the viability of community organizations and community work strategies for addressing social problems, and the potential of communities for assuming a larger role in social policies than has occurred in the past. Support for an expanded role for communities comes from a variety of sources. Common sense suggests that those closest to a problem should have some way of contributing information about the problem – its scope, impact, and the effect of current programs. This common-sense view is reinforced by the literature on the implementation of policy. A main message from the literature (see, for example, Williams, 1980; Pressman and Wildavsky, 1984; Lipsky, 1980) is that a potentially powerful way to improve the effectiveness of social policy is to concentrate attention on local delivery units – to provide sufficient resources to these units, to delegate appropriate responsibility and authority to them, and to include the staff and consumers of these units in the policy process.

Support also comes from municipal governments, which have recognized their inability to influence the social policies of provincial and federal governments. A task force report of the Canadian Federation of Municipalities states that municipal governments are:

> responsible for protecting and fostering the social and economic well being of their communities. This includes policies which promote and capitalize on the natural assets of the community, countering the undesirable consequences of urban growth, anticipating the consequences of public decisions on the lives of citizens and resolving conflicts and maximizing

opportunities for the community as a whole. (Federation of Canadian Municipalities, 1986: 115)

In the Federation's view, municipal governments must become active partners with provincial and federal governments in establishing social policies that affect the lives of citizens. Evidence of the emerging interest of municipal governments in social policy comes from the healthy community projects. In a comparatively short span of time over 100 municipalities have launched such projects, and their broad mandate includes activities designed to improve environments, to reduce inequities, and to promote the capacity of citizens and communities to take charge of health and social issues. The healthy community projects are discussed in detail in Chapter 6.

Municipal interest in social issues is also reflected in the development of social planning departments at the municipal level. For example, in B.C. alone ten municipalities have hired social planners to take on the task of identifying community needs and suggesting ways of meeting these needs.

First Nation band and tribal councils are equivalent to municipal governments and, as noted in Chapter 4, many councils across the country have taken a leadership role in child welfare and other human services. Thus, both municipal governments and First Nation councils are transforming their former passive role in social policy into one of innovation and leadership.

If the interest by municipal councils in social policy is relatively new, the same cannot be said of voluntary organizations in Canada. Various organizations, ranging from those with very specific concerns (the Association for Community Living) to those with a broad spectrum of interests (social planning councils), have been a conspicuous feature of the social policy and community work scene for many years. Including examples of these agencies in this book was deemed necessary not only because of their historical significance but also because their attempts to bring about change represent useful examples of the exercise of influence. Voluntary organizations do not possess power to affect change and hence must rely on persuasion or other avenues in attempting to convince policy-makers of the need for change.

Although most Canadian texts on community work have been

principally concerned with local issues, two recent books – *Community Organization and the State* (Ng, Walker, and Muller, 1990) and *Bureaucracy and Community* (Davies and Shragge, 1990) – are important exceptions. *Community Organization and the State* is anchored in a belief that Canadian society furthers the interests of a powerful few rather than the interests of the majority of Canadian citizens. But as the authors acknowledge, "The state is not a neutral body, but neither is it completely controlled by the dominant classes. . . . The authors in one section begin to identify ways in which space can be created to respond to the needs and demands of subordinate groups" (Ng, Walker, and Muller, 1990: 23). This work is concerned with the struggles of class, race, and gender-based groups to change the ways in which the state oppresses them. A theme that pervades *Community Organization and the State* is the struggle to understand "how the state transforms class issues and political disaffection into problems that can be dealt with through an expanded social problem apparatus of professionals and bureaucrats" (Ng, Walker, and Muller, 1990: 18).

In a series of essays concerned with the management of and services provided by social welfare agencies, *Bureaucracy and Community* examines the fit between the promise and the reality of social policies in selected jurisdictions in Canada and the U.K. The essays reveal a large gap between objectives and outcomes. The failure is attributed in part to the unrealistic expectation that the social welfare enterprise could offset the serious dislocations caused by economic and fiscal policies of capitalist, free enterprise countries. In addition, the social welfare agencies designed to aid and help consumers have become large and remote bureaucracies governed by managers preoccupied by accountability to policy-makers. In the process the needs of consumers and of staff have been neglected, if not disregarded.

In his introduction to *Bureaucracy and Community*, Peter Leonard describes the focus of the book in the following terms:

> The social democratic/liberal welfare state proved not to be the democratic and participative vehicles for progressive social change that many of us had hoped. Its remote bureaucratic and controlling features made it especially vulnerable to attack from

the radical right and came to be subjected to severe criticism from the left for their sexism and racism. (Leonard, 1990: 12-13)

There are many similarities between these books and the work at hand. All are concerned with the connections between community organizations, community work, and social policy. All share disaffection with the lack of responsiveness of large-scale public-sector organizations, disappointment at the unfulfilled promise of the welfare state, and dismay about the continued concentration of power in the hands of a relatively few men who largely control Canada's economy.

The similarities notwithstanding, *Communities and Social Policy in Canada* departs from the other books in three ways. First, it includes an examination of the connections between social work and community work practice. Second, it inquires into the capacity of "the problem-solving apparatus of professionals and bureaucracies" to determine if some professionals and some bureaucracies can participate in social reform. Third, *Communities and Social Policy in Canada* focuses attention on the ordinary issues of policy. It is important to remind the reader that this focus was selected because of its impact on consumers and its relevance to the practice of front-line social work and community work practitioners. The interest is then to place social reform squarely on the agenda of community work and social work practitioners.

Three matters are of particular importance in social reform: power and the initiation and implementation phases of the policy process. Definitions of power and arguments about the differences between power, influence, and authority occupy a prominent place in the social science literature. Brager, Specht, and Torczyner define power "as the potential for influence as well as its exercise" (1987: 245). This definition departs from one of the classic views: "power is the process of affecting the powers of others, with the help of (threatened) severe deprivations for non-conformity" (Lasswell and Kaplan, 1950: 76). Bachrach and Baratz (1970: 21) agree with the latter position and argue that "the threat of sanctions is what differentiates power from influence."

Power is defined here as the capacity to alter policies and decisions. This capacity may be exercised through persuasion, rewards, or other means of securing compliance, but where these strategies fail policy-makers can bring about change on a unilateral basis. Influence is viewed as an attempt to convince policy-makers of the need for change. These definitions are employed throughout the book; policy-makers have power, even though their ability to secure compliance may at times be slender because of the pitfalls in implementation. On the other hand, social reform organizations possess varying degrees of influence, but not power. Given this important limitation, the exercise of influence to have reforms placed on the policy agenda and then approved is of fundamental importance to social reform organizations.

In previous studies in community work and social policy, the notion of the convergence of interest has proven to be a useful explanation of how issues emerge on the agenda. The concept was first described by Christopher Sower and his associates as a consequence of their work in analysing the emergence of a community health council in rural Michigan.

> There are two crucial conditions for the initiation of an action, both of which will play an important role in determining the probability that the proposed action will move from the stage of initiation to that of legitimation. The first condition is related to who the initiators are. What is the relationship, for instance, between the identity of the initiators in the community structure and the possibility of favourable acceptance? The second condition is concerned with the extent to which the idea of the proposed action is compatible with existing conceptions of "community welfare". (Sower et al., 1957: 64)

The concept of convergence of interest represents a beginning attempt to explain how issues are placed on the community agenda. However, other factors besides the legitimacy of the initiators and the congruence of the "proposed action with existing conceptions of community welfare" may be important in the initiation phase (ibid.: 66). A matter of keen interest in this book is to determine if the concept of convergence can be refined and made explicit for use by practitioners.

Once placed on the policy agenda, issues compete for attention, only some are approved, and even these are rarely given sufficient attention in the implementation stage. Social reform organizations have typically neglected the implementation phase on the confident but mistaken assumption that the quality of their research and the compelling logic of their proposals for change will ensure not only acceptance on the policy agenda but approval of the proposal. Indeed, "implementation is the Achilles Heel of the policy process" (Williams, 1980: ix), and it receives close attention in the case studies and in Chapter 7.

CONNECTING SOCIAL WORK AND COMMUNITY WORK PRACTICE

The connections between the practice of social work and of community work are also considered in this book. Community work was at one time a well-recognized specialization in social work education, but such is not the case in Canada in the 1990s. The profession of social work began to take shape in the early years of this century, but it was not until 1939 that community organization was formally accepted by the profession as a form of social work practice. In that year the Lane Report submitted to the National Conference on Social Work in the United States developed the case for inclusion on the grounds that the values and principles underlying community organization were the same as those on which the established approaches of case work and group work rested. These values included the right of clients, and in the case of community organization, residents of a particular neighbourhood, to self-determination and respect for the innate worth and dignity of individuals.

Implementing the Lane Report required that new specializations in community organization be developed. Since social work education in Canada was restricted to seven schools of social work and since all were somewhat peripheral units on their respective campuses, establishing these specializations was far from an easy task. However, a number of factors aided the development. First, the already established sequences of case work and group work included courses on the history of social work and social welfare, social policy, human growth and behaviour, and research.

Such core content was deemed eminently appropriate for community organization, and hence the essential task was to develop the specialized courses and practicum placements.

Second, the two-year structure of the MSW programs in place at that time was conducive to the development of community organization sequences. New courses did not have to be squashed into an already crowded curriculum but could be organized in a coherent fashion over the full two-year period. Typically, the core content was provided during the first year together with an introductory course on the theory of community organization, leaving the second year for the specialized courses.

The third factor facilitating the inclusion of community organization into social work came from the early conceptualizations of practice. The most influential book on the theory and practice of community work argued that the overall objective was to assist residents of a particular area to confront and resolve the problems facing them (Ross, 1967). This early definition largely ignored the political process, the issues of power, and the social policy responsibilities of government – issues that in recent years have been at the forefront of community work. However, as noted earlier, the competence-building theme has remained one of the dominant themes in community work practice. The distinct advantage of this approach to practice in the early years was its similarity to group work. In effect, communities were simply large groups and hence the skills and knowledge required were not dissimilar from those needed by group workers.

For all of the above reasons, community organization fitted neatly into the curricula of schools of social work. It was not until the sixties that the fit began to fall apart; and today it has still to be reconstructed. Some reasons for the separation are discussed below, but first it is necessary to acknowledge that social work has never been the only profession with an interest in community work, which has attracted attention from a wide variety of practitioners in urban and community planning, adult education, sociology, and political science. In addition, many community workers have graduated from the "school of hard knocks," having acquired their skills and knowledge from working as trade union organizers, political activists, and as members of social movements.

For some, the first signs of the impending separation between social and community work became evident when community work was at its zenith, particularly in the U.S. during the sixties and early seventies. In this era both government and large foundations were enamoured of the notion that the solution to the significant social problems of poverty and delinquency lay in the hands of local communities. Nicholas Lemann provides a succinct summary of the War on Poverty in the U.S. "The Vietnam War did not represent nearly as great a departure from the usual activities of a world power as did the attempt to eliminate poverty in a capitalist country without giving poor people either money or jobs" (Lemann, 1988: 49). Lemann's comment neatly captures the position already staked out here – that problems of national scope and origin cannot be solved by local action.

Regardless of outcomes, the emphasis on community work in these decades provided a boost to community work. Employment opportunities became available both in government departments and in a variety of newly created local organizations. The dramatic increase in the number and diversity of programs drew attention to the need for new conceptualizations of practice and revealed the limitations of the locality development approach. Community work required both planners with research and policy analysis skills and social activists, who eschewed the co-operative strategies of locality development in favour of the conflict tactics espoused by Saul Alinsky. The range of community work approaches, each with its distinct objectives, assumptions, and strategies, was well captured by social work educator Rothman. And just as Rothman responded to the challenge of conceptualizing different approaches to practice, so, too, did schools of social work restructure their curricula to prepare graduates for a range of practice roles. To be sure, the conflict model of practice presented schools with some difficulty, given the tradition of consensus and co-operation that characterized social work education.

In my view the separation between social work and community work practice cannot be attributed to the explosion of community work activity in the sixties. In Canada, two other factors account for the separation: the decline in government support and the development of undergraduate education.

Since community work is essentially concerned with social reforms to improve health and social services, it is not difficult to understand why it has been neglected in the past two decades. In these years social policy in most Western democracies has been dominated by a neo-conservative political philosophy. "The neo-conservative argument is premised on the values of individualism, liberty and property rights and on inequality as the natural outcomes of the workings of the market" (Mishra, 1984: 61). In the view of neo-conservatives, such as Margaret Thatcher and Ronald Reagan, the welfare state should be diminished if not dismantled since its provisions interfere with the market economy and rob individuals of their innate ability to take care of themselves and their families. Hence, the neo-conservative approach to social policy is interested in preserving only those services required as a last resort to protect children from neglect and abuse or to aid individuals in desperate need of counselling and other support services. Policy-makers of this persuasion have no interest in organizations and associations that have as their mission the further development and expansion of social services and benefits. Thus, support for community work in recent years has been slender and casual at best.

The lack of interest in and funding for community work by government has had two consequences. First, employment opportunities in community work have been drastically reduced and the message to students in schools of social work and other programs preparing students for community practice has been clear: specialize in community work at your peril, for there may well be no employment opportunities for you after graduation. Second, professional schools have to pay close attention to the needs and demands of their constituencies, such as professional associations and employers. If these groups accord low priority to a particular field of service or methodology, schools must take this into account when designing curricula and establishing fieldwork placements. A low ranking by constituencies results in few courses being developed and offered, few fieldwork placements being organized, and low priority within the school. The combination of a low ranking and a scarcity of employment opportunities for graduates has resulted in a withering of interest in community work in schools of social work in Canada.

A second reason for the decline in interest is that social work education in Canada has changed dramatically over the past twenty years. Prior to the late sixties, there were only seven schools in the country; today there are twenty-three. These twenty-three schools offer a total of forty-one programs: five at the doctoral level, sixteen master's, and twenty bachelor programs. Not only have the number of schools increased but the new schools have largely eschewed the previous model of social work education, which consisted of two-year graduate programs built on a general baccalaureate degree. The new schools have combined professional training with general university studies at the undergraduate level. These schools also rejected the traditional specializations in social work practice and sought to unify social work practice using the conceptualizations of generalist practice based on systems and ecological theory. Of the sixteen master's programs in Canada, only four currently advertise a specialization in community work.

The establishment and objectives of the School of Social Work at the University of Victoria will serve as an example of the argument being developed here. The School was founded in 1975 with the specific objective of preparing practitioners for practice in rural communities. The faculty were committed to developing a curriculum that would prepare graduates to be just as competent in dealing with community issues and problems as in working with individuals and families. A follow-up study of Victoria graduates suggests that this objective has been largely achieved. Reviewing the careers of 329 graduates of the School, John Cossom found that "two-thirds of these practitioners define themselves as generalists as opposed to specialists, and they provide strong evidence in support of this in that they report using a variety of intervention strategies and methods in their work" (Cossom, 1988: 305). However, the responses from graduates also showed "a steady decline in the proportion of graduates who reported involvement with change at system levels as these levels became larger and more complex" (ibid.: 306). Ninety-six per cent of respondents reported working with individuals, 81.9 per cent with families, 68.3 per cent with groups, and 53.3 per cent with neighbourhoods or communities (ibid.: 305).

The conclusion emerging from the Victoria experience would, I suspect, be confirmed by that of other undergraduate programs across the country. It suggests that generalist practice is more concerned with direct intervention with the personal troubles of individuals and families than it is with the public issues of communities. Additional support for this emerging conclusion comes from the interests of social work students. The great majority of students enter the field with a desire to help individuals and families in distress, and tailor their studies accordingly. Given a succession of cohorts of students with very specific interests in individual and family work, it is not surprising that curricula in schools of social work favour these interests.

A third reason is that in its heyday community work was the radical arm of social work. As noted earlier, it held promise of effecting significant social change. It attracted and was supported by some of the most radical theorists and practitioners in social work. However, in recent years these supporters have deserted community work, finding it too professional, too exclusive, and too cautionary for their liking. Many of these erstwhile advocates have found solace in and have identified with the writings of Freire and Gutierrez (see, for example, Carniol, 1991). Essentially, these writers argue that change can come only from the oppressed, and the potency of their message has been dramatically illustrated by the changes in the governing structures of countries in Eastern Europe. However, it may be that this message is not applicable to Western democracies, where conditions of extreme oppression do not exist. In any event, a relevant and practical focused translation of the Freirian position to community work in Canada remains an unfilled challenge.

The final reason is that the theoretical base of the generalist approach to practice was provided first by systems theory and more recently by ecological theory, and in the view of the writer both provide only slender support for community work practice. These theories stress the importance of connections between people and the systems that affect them, and the differences between the two theories are slight. Perhaps the principal difference is that systems theory has tended to focus on the change process, whereas ecological theory has given major attention to understanding the relationships between people and their social environment. Since systems theory has been expanded by ecological theory as the base for integrated practice, the following discussion refers principally to it rather than to the systems approach.

The distinguishing characteristic of ecological theory is its insistence on viewing and understanding individuals within the family, community, and social context in which they live. Thus researchers operating from this framework have examined the impact of poverty on the lives of families (Pelton, 1981), of the significance of the lack of support from families and friends (Pancoast, 1981; Whittaker, 1983), and of neighbourhoods characterized by poor environmental conditions (Garbarino and Sherman, 1981; Warren, 1971). The results of these and other investigations are rich in detail and convincing in their support for the argument that family, community, and societal environments affect individuals and, in particular, the ability of parents to care for their children.

The attractiveness of ecological theory for a generalist approach to social work practice is that it appears to hold the promise of "allowing practice to occur on a micro level (individuals and families), on a macro level (community and society) or on both levels simultaneously" (Germain and Gitterman, 1980). At first and even second glance, it is difficult to quarrel with a theory that seems to provide an appropriate base for practice with individuals, families, communities, and society. However, a number of social work educators and practitioners have criticized ecological theory on the grounds that while it allows and indeed pushes practitioners to consider the impact of societal and community factors on the lives of individuals and families, it fails to come to grips with how change occurs at the community and societal levels (Carniol, 1991; Gould, 1987; Wharf, 1990). The consequence is that individuals and families must adapt to or otherwise cope with their environment rather than the reverse.

A number of interconnected reasons account for the failure of ecological theory to address social and community change adequately. First, it largely neglects the importance of power in the change process. Ecological theory assumes a largely benevolent stance toward change and how it occurs: a problem is identified, agreement is secured on the cause and dimensions of the problem and on the strategies required, and the process of change unfolds in a relatively smooth fashion. To be sure, ecological theory allows for resistance to change, but it does not squarely address the crucial issue of who holds the power and whether the change proposed will receive the approval of those in power. A recurring theme in this book is that community work practice requires an understanding of the concept of power and how it is distributed in a society, community, and organization.

Second, ecological theory ignores the issue of auspices. It assumes that practitioners are independent of organizational constraints and therefore can select a change strategy based solely on its appropriateness to address the problem at hand. However, in community work as in many other fields of human service, the policies of organizations that employ practitioners influence practice. Among other authors, Mayer Zald has addressed the importance of organizational auspices in community work. Zald argues that "whether the practitioner facilitates, fund raises, foments or fumes – whether he plans, serves as a resource expert, counsels or agitates he is guided by the structure, aims and operating procedures of the organization that pays the bills" (Zald, 1967: 4). The issue of organizational auspices is addressed in the case studies and in Chapter 7.

A third set of criticisms of the ecological approach has come from feminists. Ketayun Gould expresses her dissatisfaction with ecological theory in the following terms: "Being a woman in a sexist society introduces such a potent intervening variable that any assumption of confluence between individual and societal good is an unwarranted conclusion" (Gould, 1987: 348). For Gould and other feminist social work educators, women are an oppressed group and explanations of society and proposals for change that do not recognize this status are by definition invalid.

The ecological framework constitutes the theoretical base of many undergraduate social work education programs in Canada. Given that BSW programs provide the majority of professionally prepared practitioners at the present time, the question can be raised whether social workers are well equipped for community work practice. This question is examined in the case studies to determine if the generic approach embraces community work. Are the theories, values, and principles that guide community work and social work similar or at least compatible? Alternatively, does community work require a distinctive theoretical base and set of skills?

These questions are pursued in the case studies and then reviewed in the final chapter with the intent of making suggestions for changes in social work education. However, while these are important questions, they are secondary to the primary purpose of the book, which is to examine the potential of community organizations and community work strategies to address the social issues and problems affecting all communities. Can community organizations engage in social reform activities and influence social policy?

CHAPTER II

Planning for
Deinstitutionalization and the
Development of Community
Support Programs in
New Brunswick

The closing of large hospitals for the mentally ill and handicapped and the placement of former patients in the community have been important aspects of social policy in the past four decades. The overall objective of deinstitutionalization has been widely praised by professionals in mental health and social services and by organizations such as the Association for Community Living, but implementation of this laudable objective has been criticized by municipal politicians and members of the general public. Perhaps the major reason for this criticism has been the failure of those responsible for deinstitutionalization to provide sufficient resources for community-based programs. Other reasons include concerns about the behaviour of discharged patients, the perception that group homes will adversely affect property values and the quality of life in neighbourhoods, and the nature of the planning process, which has typically excluded municipalities and voluntary organizations.

Closing institutions and developing community support systems represent large-scale social planning ventures. Such a project requires tough decisions at the policy level and poses equally difficult dilemmas for practitioners in communities. For example, policy-makers must decide whether institutions should be closed prior to, parallel with, or subsequent to the development of community support programs. Should all patients be discharged, including those who have lived in the institution for many years and who show little interest in or capacity for living and working in the community? Which agencies should take on the responsibility of developing a community support system? When these policy issues have been decided, practitioners in the community must contend with the difficult tasks of developing new services and introducing or returning former patients to neighbourhoods and communities, as well as the ubiquitous challenge of co-ordinating community services on behalf of the clients.

Deinstitutionalization represents a virtually perfect example of the connections between social policy and local communities. Decisions to close or reduce the size of provincial institutions clearly can only be taken by provincial governments, yet the consequences of these decisions are felt and experienced in communities. In addition, the contribution of community organizations in pushing the government to make decisions is often considerable.

Hence the issue of deinstitutionalization affords an opportunity to examine the role of community organizations in the initiation and implementation of social policy.

The province of New Brunswick was selected for two reasons. First, a study by the National Institute on Mental Retardation revealed that New Brunswick

> has clear and official policies for deinstitutionalization. It has a track record of being true to these policies. Attempts to redesign the system in New Brunswick, although far from complete and open to extensive criticism, have many qualities that hold promise for success. (National Institute on Mental Retardation, 1985: 3)

Second, it was desirable to include case studies from as many provinces as possible. British Columbia, Ontario, and the Yukon had earlier been selected.

THE WILLIAM F. ROBERTS HOSPITAL SCHOOL AND THE CENTRACARE PROJECTS

Two projects are examined in this chapter. The first concerns the development of a community support system for children with special needs and the simultaneous closing of the William F. Roberts School. The second involves the placement of seventy-two individuals from the Centracare Psychiatric Hospital into communities in southern New Brunswick. Both projects came into being as a consequence of the efforts of the New Brunswick Association for Community Living. Both projects occurred during the same time period and the structures established to guide the planning processes were virtually identical. A brief description of the two projects and a chronology of events will provide a context for the analysis of the planning process.

The William F. Roberts Hospital School was built in 1965 to provide services for the developmentally delayed and handicapped children of the province. The intent was to provide specialized medical treatment, dental services, rehabilitation therapies, and educational services, but in the opinion of many individuals interviewed by the writer it was neither a hospital nor a school. Rather, the School provided accommodation (described by some as warehousing) for children who were developmentally delayed or who exhibited behaviour problems. Located in Saint John, it was at first the administrative responsibility of the Department of Health; later, responsibility was shifted to the Department of Social Services.

> As of September, the WFR was providing care for three groups of children: a small number (17) with multiple handicaps and profound retardation; a second small group (16) that was severely retarded and had some related disabilities; and, a substantial group who were called "behaviourally disordered". While some of this latter group had a history of considerable disruptive behaviour, many of the behaviour problems appeared to us relatively modest and situational in nature which could have been handled in normal community service contexts given some specialized support services. Of the 131 children admitted to the WFR in 1982, 50% came from respite care. Only 8 of the children admitted spoke French as their mother tongue. More detailed examination of data shows that the WFR essentially serves those people closest to it, with the largest user being the Saint John region. The francophone communities remain virtually unserved. (Applied Research Consulting House, 1983: i)

An appreciation of the concerns of the Department of Social Services about the care provided by the W.F. Roberts School and its cost can be found from the fact that the six previous reports had been commissioned by the department. All had raised questions about the characteristics of the children admitted. Why, for example, were such a high proportion from the Saint John area and why were so many deemed to be in need of respite care? However, none of these reports were as explicit as that of the Applied Research Consulting House, which completed its review with the following statement:

> One of the most fundamental questions we addressed throughout this whole exercise was "Why, in 1983, should any child be admitted to an institution?". The evidence from experience elsewhere and in the literature, as well as our observations in this

study, suggest this practice is only of limited help at best and positively harmful at worst. On the other hand, there is considerable evidence that properly supported services in or near the child's home, in a normal environment, have a much higher likelihood of success. In the final chapter of this Report we outline a Three-Phase Plan whereby New Brunswick might move from a dependence on institution-focused to child-focused services in the community. (*Ibid.:* iv)

The deputy minister of the Department of Social Services, Georgio Gaudet, was a key figure in the decision to close the Roberts School. Gaudet expressed his views as follows:

In my three years as deputy minister I discovered that we were not doing anything for kids at the William F. – just locking them away – hiding them – anything could happen and no one would know – communities are open systems and institutions are closed. (Interview with Georgio Gaudet, October 17, 1990)

Concerns about the school were not restricted to senior staff of the department or members of the Association for Community Living. Many social workers in regional offices were critical of the school and the care it provided. For example, the Fredericton regional office of the Department of Social Services commissioned a study by the National Institute on Mental Retardation in 1983. At that time there were twenty-one children from the Fredericton region in the school: "the most important statement that can be made about these children is that there is no inherent, clinical, educational, or medical reason for them to be in the W.F. Roberts" (Cawthorpe, 1983: 3). The report concludes with the recommendation that these children be returned to the jurisdiction of the regional office and that appropriate programs be developed to support them in the community. Hence, the social work staff, community associations, and parents in some regions not only agreed with the decision to close the school but were already engaged in the process of developing community-based programs prior to its closure.

A final factor in the decision to close the William F. Roberts

Hospital School was that expensive repairs to the building were required at the time the report of the Applied Research Consulting House was submitted. The policy question was then framed in the following terms: Why spend money on an institution that serves only a portion of the provincial population of children with special needs and does so in an inappropriate and unsatisfactory fashion? As noted by the assistant deputy minister in a speech given in Sweden in 1988, "The William F. Roberts stood as an archaic monument to a bygone age" (Doucet, n.d.: 20).

The report of the Applied Research Consulting House was submitted to Gaudet in December, 1983, and its findings and recommendations came as no surprise to him and his colleagues. In fact, Gaudet acknowledged that the report was used to justify and to defend a decision that had been forming in his mind and those of senior staff for some time. This was no royal commission report slated for extensive discussion, delays, and a final resting place on the shelf. Rather, the report served as the "launching pad" from which to take a recommendation to cabinet that a community support system for children with special needs be developed and the Roberts School be closed. Cabinet approved this recommendation in April, 1984, and a public announcement was made the following month.

It should be noted that despite initial fears regarding the employment of staff, the relocation process proceeded quite smoothly. Staff can and do become institutionalized and require almost as much assistance in being relocated to employment in the community as do patients. A staff member of the central steering committee located appropriate employment for most employees of the school.

The decision to close the school and the commitment to preserve this decision in the face of considerable opposition in the legislature and in the community of Saint John were key factors in the development of community support programs. There was simply no institution in which special needs children could be placed, and the ability of the department to reallocate funds from the school to the development of a community support system proved to be another crucial factor in the success of the Roberts project. However, this development was barely in place when the predictable occurred. The existence of community-based services resulted in the surfacing of "mirror children" – children with special needs who had not been placed in the school but who were in need of the same support services. By the time the needs of this expanded population, and not only those released from the Roberts School, generated a demand for increased funding, the commitment to these programs was firmly in place.

Centracare is one of two psychiatric hospitals for adults in New Brunswick. It is located in Saint John and, like its counterpart, Restigouche, is managed by a non-profit corporation but funded by the provincial government. Parts of the Centracare buildings are believed to be the oldest psychiatric hospitals in continuous use in North America. The population of Centracare has fluctuated around 360 and has included adults with intellectual impairment as well as those suffering from mental illness.

Like the William F. Roberts School, Centracare has been the subject of a number of inquiries and reviews. One of the most influential reports, the *Southern New Brunswick Mental Health Planning Study* (1982), recommended restructuring mental health services in southern New Brunswick. The report was based on the principles of regionalization, appropriate level of care, and continuity of care and recommended the following direction for mental health services:

> The model developed consists of three levels of service delivery: COMMUNITY, OUT PATIENT, and IN PATIENT. Patients in need of mental health services would be assessed and cared for in the most appropriate and least restrictive levels. The emphasis on this model, and one which seems eminently consistent with the provincial approach to health care is placed on community and extramural services. All services would be provided on a regional basis as close as possible to the patient's home. The essence of this model is that an appropriate range of services be provided in each region depending on psychiatric and physical care needs, and that the mentally ill person no longer be segregated from the general health and community service system.
>
> . . .
>
> For Centracare the implication of implementation of the model is that patients currently residing at Centracare who do not

require twenty-four-hour intensive medical, psychiatric, and nursing care would be transferred to appropriate community settings within their home regions. During the transition period, patients must be individually assessed and discharge plans developed which would prepare patients for community living and transfer to more appropriate community settings which have support services.

Similar concerns, therefore, were being expressed in the late seventies and early eighties about both the William F. Roberts Hospital School and Centracare. But while these concerns resulted in a decision to close the school, Centracare remains open to this day. Closure was considered in 1979 when provincial Minister of Health Brenda Robertson announced that a new, small institution would be built to replace Centracare. However, the cost implications of this plan were considerable, and it failed to win the support of the board and staff of Centracare. While the Association for Community Living pushed for closure during the 1980s its arguments fell on deaf ears. Some reasons for the decision to keep Centracare open are suggested below.

First, Centracare is operated by a corporation and the board of directors consists of citizens from Saint John. According to some members of the Saint John branch of the Association for Community Living, the businessmen on the Centracare board are acutely aware and appreciative of the economic importance of Centracare to Saint John. Indeed, closing the Roberts School did arouse the opposition of the business community in Saint John, and as a smaller institution its economic impact was not as substantial as that of Centracare. Second, at the time the project was initiated the corporation reported to and was funded through the Ministry of Health. However, the project was initiated by the Department of Social Services and managed by a steering committee co-chaired by the deputy ministers of Health and Social Services. Thus the Department of Social Services did not exercise direct and exclusive control over Centracare. In contrast, administrative control over the Roberts School allowed the deputy minister to relocate a director of the school because he disagreed with and blocked plans to close the school.

Table 1
Planning for Deinstitutionalization – Summary of Events

	Centracare	W.F. Roberts School
Objectives	To provide to handicapped adults who are or who have been long-term residents of Centracare and who do not require in-patient treatment in an active treatment facility with a range of support services in the community to enable them to transfer from the facility with a minimum of disruption and to achieve a maximum of self-sufficiency in the community.	To develop a community care system for children with special needs. To close the school.
Principal Actors	Centracare Inc./staff of the Department of Social Services/Canadian Association for Community Living/Canadian Mental Health Association.	Political leaders, particularly Health Minister Nancy Teed. Senior staff of the Department of Social Services. Canadian Association for Community Living.
Structures for Planning and Managing Program	Centracare Project Steering Committee composed of staff from Centracare, the Departments of Social Services and Health,* and representatives of the Association for Community	Central Steering Committee composed of deputy ministers of Health, Education, and Social Services, and representatives from the Premier's Advisory Council on Persons with Disabilities,

Table 1 (continued)

	Centracare	W.F. Roberts School
	Living (ACL) and the Canadian Mental Health Association (CMHA).	ACL, and Canadian Rehabilitation Council for the Disabled.
	Regional transfer teams (same composition as steering committee).	Regional project teams charted by regional directors.
	Individual treatment team.	Interdisciplinary teams.
	Role of the case manager a key aspect.	Role of the case manager a key aspect.
Outcomes	Seventy-two patients discharged and living in community. Population of Centracare remains the same. Budget for outpatient care is $1,353,834.	School closed in December, 1985; 135 children placed in community; 679 children now being served. Budget expenditures: Roberts 6.7 M; Community care 17.1 M.

*Mental Health Division was principally involved, not the Division of Hospitals.

THE OUTCOMES OF THE ROBERTS AND CENTRACARE PROJECTS

As indicated by the outline of events in Table 1, the policy decision to develop a community support system for children with special needs and to close the W.F. Roberts Hospital School was made by the New Brunswick cabinet following recommendations from senior civil servants. In turn, these recommendations were formed as a consequence of a long campaign conducted by the Association for Community Living in New Brunswick and of a number of reviews of the school and its program. These decisions have been implemented with considerable success. Staff of the Department of Health and Community Services and the executive director of the New Brunswick Association for Community Living agree that while some specialized resources are still not available, community-based programs have been established for developmentally delayed children. The current budget is 2.5 times the 1985 budget of the school and 679 children, compared to a school population of 135, are being served. The project has also had very considerable spinoffs, helping, for example, to set the climate for an Integrated Schools Act (1986) that provides for the education of developmentally delayed children in regular classrooms. Hence an outmoded institution, which served in an unsatisfactory fashion only a third of the children requiring attention, has been replaced by community-based programs that reach the vast majority of developmentally delayed children in New Brunswick.

Yet reforms are never without critics. Because of the difficulties experienced in integrating these children into regular schools and the lack of professional services in some areas, some educators in New Brunswick have been forthright in their criticism of the closure of the Roberts School.

> A report prepared for School District 20 (Saint John) released this week paints a distressing picture of what has happened to the mentally retarded, physically disabled and behaviourally disturbed youngsters who were discharged from the school. . . . The problems were especially acute for behaviourally disturbed boys, many of whom were repeatedly suspended for various offenses. They also got into trouble with the law on charges ranging from robbery and assault to arson, manslaughter and even murder. (*New Brunswick Telegraph-Journal*, March 2, 1991)

Supporters of the closure of the school will doubtless respond by acknowledging difficulties in integrating some children into regular schools and by admitting that a full array of services is still not available. Above all, however, they will argue that the W.F. Roberts Hospital School did not provide effective treatment for any children, particularly the behaviourally distressed, and that community care is far preferable to institutional care for many reasons, not the least of which is that inadequate and ineffective programs can be more easily identified.

There are three outcomes of the Centracare project. Seventy-two patients have been placed in community settings at a cost slightly lower than the amount required for institutional care. The second outcome is that fifty-two "Centracare-like" patients (i.e., individuals similar to those discharged from Centracare) are receiving the same range of services and programs as the former patients of that institution. The third and most significant outcome has been to demonstrate that mentally ill and handicapped patients who had been institutionalized for many years can be cared for in the community.

In retrospect, it is clear that if institutions remain open they will be used – and to the fullest extent. Despite the success of the Centracare project, the institution's population remains the same. While those involved in the Roberts project were convinced that residential care for children with special needs was unnecessary, no such unanimity obtained with respect to mentally ill adults. As a number of people interviewed for this study pointed out, children with special needs can be cared for in communities more easily than can mentally ill adults. Children can live with parents or foster parents and can attend school. Adults require accommodation and employment, both of which are difficult to locate. In addition, deinstitutionalization has pushed patients whose strange appearance and bizarre behaviour were formerly hidden from view onto city streets. A not uncommon reaction from many citizens, including municipal politicians and businessmen, has been a mixture of fear and revulsion.

While Centracare remains open, it should be emphasized that the objective of the Centracare project was to place a particular group of patients in community settings. This objective has been realized. The recidivism rate for project patients is 30 per cent opposed to 75-80 per cent for other patients. The project has demonstrated the viability of the concept of community living for mentally ill and handicapped adults, and like the Roberts project it has shown that allocating dollars to individual service plans controlled by case managers in local offices is an effective method of implementing deinstitutionalization.

The Centracare project had a budget of $1,391,200 for 1989-90, but these funds were required to support the seventy-two individuals discharged over the past seven years. The number of placements and the annual budgets are listed in Table 2.

Table 2
Centracare Placements and Expenditures, 1983-84–1988-89

Year	Placements	Expenditures
1983-84	—	$ 101,438
1984-85	29	562,606
1985-86	27	859,691
1986-87	9	1,050,568
1987-88	4	1,223,337
1988-89	3	1,353,834

NOTE: Expenditures do not cover all costs, such as the salaries of case managers. The cost per person per day of the Centracare project is approximately $150.

There is no commitment to expand the project in its current form. One reason is that a Mental Health Commission was established in 1990. The Commission has the mandate to reduce the number of patients in Centracare and Restigouche by developing a community support system for adults, and it has the authority to redirect funds from institutions to community-based programs. However, funds for the Centracare project and individuals like Donna Gordon, a senior program consultant who provided much of the leadership, remain in the Department of Health and Community Services.*

THE PRINCIPLE OF NORMALIZATION

For the Association for Community Living the closure of the W.F. Roberts Hospital School, the development of a community support system, and the Centracare project represented the culmination of years of effort to secure appropriate care for children and adults with special needs. The philosophical base for the Association's work is the principle of normalization, which calls for children with special needs to live at home, to be educated in the regular public school system, and to enjoy the same recreational and

*In 1986 a structural reorganization resulted in the Community Services division being transferred to the Department of Health. The title of the new department is Health and Community Services.

cultural activities as other children. However, because they have special needs they and their parents require a range of supportive services.

The Association first attempted to establish the principle of normalization through a project called COMSERV, designed to establish community-based services for developmentally delayed children and adults. COMSERV represented a sophisticated and detailed approach for identifying needs and developing and evaluating community programs. After several years of experimentation COMSERV was rejected as being too ambitious and too insensitive to the particular needs of particular communities. The next attempt to implement normalization resulted in the notion of individual service plans, and for at least two reasons implementation in New Brunswick has been successful.

In the first place, Gordon Porter and Lorraine Silliphant, the representatives of the Association for Community Living on the steering committee and the branch representatives in Saint John, were committed to normalization and to individualized service plans. Porter and Silliphant were well respected in the province for their diligent work on behalf of children with special needs, and at the time Porter had the added prestige of being national president of the Association. In addition, the Saint John branch was and remains the most radical segment of the Association for Community Living in New Brunswick and has consistently advocated the closure of institutions and the establishment of programs that are both community-based and community-owned. Ken Ross, now the director of administration and planning for the New Brunswick Mental Health Commission and formerly the executive director of the New Brunswick division of the Canadian Mental Health Association, was a member of the steering committee for the Centracare project. Ross acknowledged that the ACL "had their act together," and had a philosophy that provided a rationale and direction for the Minister of Health and Community Services, Nancy Teed, Deputy Minister Georgio Gaudet, and other senior members of the department. The legitimacy of the ACL in New Brunswick and national acceptance of the principle of normalization proved to be potent forces for change.

The philosophy of the ACL is expressed in a brief sent to the Premier in 1983:

1. All people who are mentally retarded, regardless of the degree of their handicaps, can and must be supported to live in the community, preferably in their home communities.
2. The supports and services available in the community must be planned on the basis of the known strengths and needs of individuals, in the context of the communities in which they live.
3. In planning and developing supports and services, first consideration should be given to using the normal services and opportunities (generic services) available to the rest of the population.
4. Institutions have no legitimate or necessary role in the lives of handicapped people.
5. The community, as the only place where the lives of handicapped people can be appropriately improved, must be the level at which supports and services are planned, developed, implemented and coordinated. (Canadian Association for the Mentally Retarded, 1983)

Not only did the ACL have a philosophy, but no other visions for change were advanced. While Ross and others in mental health were sceptical that community support programs could be developed on the basis of individual service plans, they had no feasible alternative to offer. Their view was that the key to deinstitutionalization was to address the revolving door syndrome – to build up a community support system so comprehensive that, once discharged, patients are only infrequently, if ever, readmitted and that all first-time admissions are absolutely essential. However, such a plan requires either a substantial amount of new funds or a reallocation of existing funds. The latter option is now possible with the establishment of the Mental Health Commission but was not feasible when the Centracare project was launched because of the structural arrangements then in place, which divided budgetary responsibilities between the departments of Health and Social Services.

The principle of normalization was implemented by developing individual service plans as a way to connect the policy level work of the steering committee and the community development work of the regional and local committees. At the policy level the principle contained a strong value base and a vision for change. At the practice level, normalization was established in both projects in the form of individual service plans. These plans contained a thorough review of the individual's mental and physical health, and on the basis of these assessments case managers and local committees were then responsible for identifying and developing the resources required for community living. The individual service plan is described in the program design for the Centracare project in the following terms.

> An ISP is a service plan developed on behalf of an individual client that is goal-oriented and time-limited. It must take into account all facets of the individual's situation that have or may have relevance in the drive to goal achievement. As it is holistic in approach, it will take into account the interrelationship between the component parts and adjust the ISP accordingly. The client's needs should correspond to the plan outlined in the ISP and it should be achievable; for example:
> – an ISP developed in Centracare for potential project clients will have as its goal transfer from Centracare to a community service system by a specific time;
> – it will include: an individual profile of the client encompassing the person's functioning level as characterized by the physical, mental and social aspects, a description of the strengths and weaknesses;
> – the supervision, physical care and other services required by the client;
> – client/patient and family expectations;
> – the relationship with family, friends, staff and other patients;
> – the treatment being received including a drug therapy plan. (Centracare Community Placement Project, 1985, Appendix A)

Developing services required for the discharged children and adults demanded an interdisciplinary approach, and establishing and maintaining interdisciplinary teams within local offices of the department was an essential aspect of both projects. For the children discharged from the Roberts School, regional interdisciplinary teams (I teams) were created to ensure that these children would receive the range of services the school had attempted to provide. Staffing these teams with the requisite specialists in disciplines such as speech and physiotherapy proved to be difficult because of the shortage of these professionals in New Brunswick. In addition, problems inevitably occur when consultants, located in head offices, attempt to assist locally based direct service providers. Typically, consultants provide advice and assistance with regard to assessment, leaving practitioners with the more difficult task of implementing the assessment. Not surprisingly, practitioners often come to resent this division of responsibility. Hence, the use and the usefulness of the I team have varied from time to time and from region to region. The teams remain in place as a backup resource for direct service providers who encounter unusual or difficult family and child situations.

As indicated by the views of those in the mental health system, normalization and the consequent development of individual service plans were not without critics. Indeed, staff members of the Department of Health and Community Services who were involved in the Roberts project acknowledged some discomfort with a bottom-up planning approach centred on individuals. At the time, and indeed in retrospect, it seemed unsystematic, particularly when compared to a research-based approach. Such an approach might have taken the form of a province-wide inventory to identify the needs of special needs children and mentally ill adults and the resources required to meet these needs. However, as Georgio Gaudet noted, the individual service plans allowed resources to be developed in accordance with actual needs rather than those identified through a survey.

We placed the kids in the community at the same time as we developed the services. The theory has it that one plans, develops the services and then places the children. Well, it would never have happened if we followed the theory. If the system has to be put in place there is a duplication of cost, and until you have the real people to deal with you are not sure what you need to deal with them. (Gaudet interview, October 17, 1990)

The approach was eminently pragmatic and the combination of individual service plans and the closure of the Roberts School was a powerful strategy for change. The G. Allan Roeher Institute (formerly the National Institute on Mental Retardation) has continued to refine the notion of individual service plans on the rationale that programs based in communities but controlled by government staff can, like institutions, become closed systems. A recent publication of the Institute outlines a refined version of individual service plans whereby the individual client with the help of a "broker" develops his or her personal service plan. These individualized service plans are funded by government and payment is made directly to the individual, who then purchases the services required. The concept is based on a pilot project designed and implemented by a group of Vancouver families and is intended to empower individuals and enhance accountability in the social services. I return to a discussion of this concept as a strategy to connect policy and practice in Chapter 7.

THE CONVERGENCE OF INTEREST

The concept of convergence of interest was introduced in Chapter 1. It was developed by Sower and his associates to explain the development of a health council in a rural county in Michigan (Sower *et al.*, 1957). It is interesting to note the salience of the concept for a province like New Brunswick where relatively few people are engaged in any particular episode of social reform. The following story illustrates how interests can converge when politicians, civil servants, and citizens interact in an easy and informal fashion. As noted above, the policy thrust of the Association for Community Living in the seventies was COMSERV, which called for the establishment of community-based services. One vehicle to implement this thrust was Community Living Boards, which would have the responsibility for placing developmentally delayed individuals into community settings.

In 1981 Gordon Porter met with Premier Richard Hatfield, who represented Porter's constituency of Woodstock, to acquaint him with the Association and its interest in normalization, COMSERV, and Community Living Boards. Some months later Porter had a more formal meeting on the same topic with Georgio Gaudet and other senior staff of the Department of Health. According to Porter, the reception at the latter meeting to the notion of Community Living Boards was far from enthusiastic. Porter then literally bumped into the Premier in a Saint John hotel and brought him up to date on the discussions with the department. Porter explained: "The Premier said, 'Get the deputy to call me.' I did, and the next meeting was very helpful and resulted in the Community Living Board concept being approved" (Porter interview, January, 1991). The impact of the story is only slightly lessened by the final outcome since, although approved, the Community Living Boards were never established. The Association then turned its attention away from COMSERV and Community Living Boards and concentrated efforts on closing the school and on developing community support programs on the basis of individual needs.

While the Roberts project ultimately became a cause, the Centracare project has been from the beginning and remains a demonstration project. It demonstrated that patients of a psychiatric hospital could be discharged and live in communities across the province. Rein and Miller have analysed the pros and cons of the demonstration project as a strategy of change. They conclude a somewhat sceptical review by stating: "Although we believe more attention should be given to alternative means for achieving action goals we recognize that demonstration projects can contribute to the development of effective modes of action by testing various kinds of policies and programs" (Rein and Miller, 1967: 185).

The Centracare project supports this conclusion. The project did not seek major changes, but its impact has been considerable. In a very real sense the project has paved the way for the work of the New Brunswick Mental Health Commission. While it faces many challenges in its mandate to develop a community support system at the expense of institutional budgets, the Commission does not have to demonstrate the viability of the concept of community living for mentally ill and handicapped adults.

In both projects the policy was set by a relatively small group of people and was designed to improve the quality of life for two very specific populations – children with special needs and adults with mental handicaps. Neither population is confined to a particular geographic community and hence community work was concerned with a constituency rather than a geographic area. Indeed, one of the interesting aspects of the Roberts project was that the political and business communities of Saint John objected vigorously to the closure of schools. The objections were based not on the familiar "not in my backyard" syndrome, but on economic factors.

INFLUENCING SOCIAL POLICY

The study of deinstitutionalization in New Brunswick provides a convincing example that community organizations can engage in social reform and can influence social policy. To be sure, the Association for Community Living is a large and influential organization with national and provincial offices and local branches. Nevertheless, the Association's efforts over a period of years convinced policy-makers to close the Roberts School, to develop community programs for children with special needs, and to launch the Centracare project.

The factors that accounted for these successful outcomes are identified below and are discussed in detail in Chapter 7. The essential ingredients identified from this case study are the possession of accurate information, connections with policy-makers, the capacity to develop a well-conceived vision for change, sufficient credibility to have this vision accepted on the policy agenda, and tenacity. The vision for change developed by the Association was anchored in the principle of normalization, and as will be discussed in Chapter 7, advocacy of this position resulted in redefining the social role of developmentally delayed children and adults.

CONNECTING THEORY AND PRACTICE IN COMMUNITY WORK

Both the policy-makers and practitioners interviewed for this study reported that they practised their craft without reference to theories or a set of concepts. Indeed, as noted earlier, some of the senior staff in the Roberts project viewed their approach as unsystematic and somewhat haphazard. To be sure, others, such as Gaudet, voiced an opposing view and took pride in the essentially pragmatic stance that dominated the planning process. And members of the Association for Community Living were so rooted in the principle of normalization and individualization that they took for granted that an approach based on these principles made sense and would work.

The individualization approach is not only supported by the Association and consistent with the values of the profession of social work; it is also consistent with two explanations of policy-making – disjointed incrementalism and backwards mapping. The notion of policy-making as disjointed incrementalism, or more kindly put, muddling through, has been around for some time. First advanced by Charles Lindblom, muddling through rejects a planned, comprehensive, and fact-based approach to the development of policy. Rather, Lindblom claims that policy-making consists of a series of small steps, each built on the last. In this view policy-making is never finished but a continuing process, with implementation and evaluation endlessly altering the official policy (Lindblom, 1968).

The concept of policy-making as muddling through is supported by the relatively recent notion of backwards mapping, which emerged as a consequence of attention being given to the implementation phase of the policy process. From this focus emerged the contention that one way to improve the policy process, and hence the product of policy, is to concentrate attention on the back end – hence the term "backwards mapping."

> The logic of backward mapping is, in all important respects, the opposite of forward mapping. It begins not at the top of the implementation process but at the last possible stage, the point at which administrative actions intersect private choices. It begins, not with a statement of intent, but with a statement of the specific behaviour at the lowest level of the implementation process that generates the need for a policy. Only after that behaviour is described does the analysis presume to state an objective; the objective is first stated as a set of organizational operations and then as a set of effects, or outcomes, that will result from these operations. Having established a relatively precise target at the lowest level of the system, the analysis backs up through the structure of implementing agencies, asking at each level two questions: What is the ability of this unit to affect the behaviour that is the target of the policy? And what resources does this unit require in order to have that effect? In the final stage of analysis the analyst or policymaker describes a

policy that directs resources at the organizational units likely to have the greatest effect.

Forward mapping assumes that organizational units in the implementation process are linked in essentially hierarchical relationships. This assumption has two corollaries: the closer one is to the source of the policy, the greater is one's authority and influence; and the ability of [a] complex system to respond to problems depends on the establishment of clear lines of authority and control. Backward mapping assumes essentially the opposite: The closer one is to the source of the problem, the greater is one's ability to influence it; and the problem-solving ability of complex systems depends not on hierarchical control but on maximizing discretion at the point where the problem is most immediate. (Elmore, 1982: 21)

The backwards mapping approach represents a radical alteration of the policy process and of the roles of those involved in that process. Taken to its logical conclusion, backwards mapping argues that practitioners in local service delivery units should control the policy-making process. They are closest to the source of the problem and have the greatest ability to influence it. The argument is attractive in many respects but it ignores the reality that practitioners are, to use a truism, so close to the trees they cannot see the forest. Frequently oppressed by very hierarchical structures, surrounded by complex rules and regulations and besieged by crises, practitioners haven't the time, imagination, or inclination to take charge of the policy process.

A division of responsibility is suggested by the New Brunswick experience. In the Roberts and Centracare projects, the decision to make changes came from politicians and senior bureaucrats. But the responsibility for implementing these decisions was awarded to regional offices, in particular to case managers. This arrangement exemplifies the position taken by Williams, Berman, and Elmore in the policy literature. Williams calls for delegating responsibility for implementation to local units (Williams, 1980). Berman distinguishes between programmed and adaptive approaches to implementation (Berman, 1980). The former is appropriate when the programs or procedures to be implemented are clear and straightforward. The adaptive approach requires the exercise of discretion and judgement, and is particularly relevant to implementing policy in the human services. Clearly the Centracare and Roberts projects exemplify the adaptive approach, and the successful outcomes of these projects suggest that the adaptive approach has considerable relevance to the human services. The principle of normalization provided direction for policy-makers, while the spinoff notion of individual service plans guided the work of practitioners. In the words of one senior bureaucrat, both policy-makers and practitioners "sang from the same hymn book."

For practitioners, the individual service plan represented a way of making community work real. Rather than community work being seen as a daunting proposition involving the development of programs and services on a community-wide basis, the individual service plan provided a starting point and a continuing frame of reference. What will it take for "George" to live in a community setting? What kind of home, employment, recreation, friends, medical care, counselling does he require? Are these programs and services available? If not, can existing agencies develop the needed programs, or should new agencies be developed?

The focus on the individual and the service plan connected policy and practice in a second and important way. Funding was provided through these plans, and hence the resources necessary to build community support programs were acquired on the basis of the needs of individuals and were controlled by the case managers. Although case managers reported to senior staff in the regional offices, and although their budgets required annual approval, the extent of delegation was extensive. In both projects, the function of case management included developing and co-ordinating services on behalf of individuals and assembling and monitoring budgets. The role of the case manager is discussed in detail below.

The contrast between the New Brunswick approach and that of Ontario, which relied on a classical top-down approach to deinstitutionalization, is striking. A report from the National Institute on Mental Retardation, *Missing the Mark*, comments on the Ontario experience in the following terms.

The 5-year plan turned on the machinery of the Ontario system to respond to a challenge. The machinery failed to work. It failed because it was not prepared to assume responsibility. Those organizations assigned responsibility for planning and development lacked the authority and the means to act. Major and necessary components had never been implemented including (a) case management and contracting mechanisms which make planning, development and resource use efficient, (b) quality control and (c) focused advocacy. (National Institute on Mental Retardation, 1984: 25)

The Ontario approach represented a programmed approach to implementation. Authority and budgets were not delegated to local units, nor were professional staff allowed to exercise discretion and judgement. Such approaches also typically neglect the contribution of outside groups.

In the Centracare and Roberts projects, representatives of the CMHA, the ACL, and the Canadian Council for the Disabled were included as members of the policy committees for both projects. While partnerships between government and representatives of the business community in planning new industrial ventures are not unusual, such partnerships are rare in the social policy arena. Typically, governments establish policy as a result of deliberations confined to departments or after considering the recommendations of task forces and royal commissions. Rarely are representatives of outside organizations included as full members of the policy-making process. However, New Brunswick's experience indicates that these representatives can make valuable contributions, and these contributions can then be captured in and become part of the policy product. A more usual and unproductive pattern is for governments to restrict membership in the policy-making process only to see the contributions of outside organizations confined to criticizing policy outcomes.

The study conducted by John Lord and Cheryl Hearn on the closing of Tranquille in Kamloops, B.C., in 1983 confirms the importance of involving outside groups in planning for deinstitutionalization.

The fact that [the B.C.] government did not involve outside groups in any kind of consultation process, either before or after the announcement, is consistent with previous closures in Ontario where the province decided on the direction, the resources and the implementation strategies. . . . Data from this study suggests that there are important roles for these groups in terms of planning and implementing an institutional closure. (Lord and Hearn, 1987: 61)

In New Brunswick these key contributions included the leadership taken by the Association for Community Living in public education and in developing new programs such as respite care and group homes. The Association's extensive network of families in communities throughout southern New Brunswick greatly facilitated the development of such resources. Conceivably, the Association would have been a willing participant in the development of community support systems even if it had been excluded from the policy process. But inclusion guaranteed not simply participation but leadership and commitment.

CONNECTING SOCIAL WORK AND COMMUNITY WORK PRACTICE

In the view of the case managers interviewed, their role represents the epitome of the generalist approach to social work practice. The functions of the case manager included the following:

1) *Client assessment* – what supports are needed to reinforce community placement; determining the role of the client, family, peer supports, advocates and service providers through discussion and agreement.
2) *Individualization* – clients are dealt with separately, needs are assessed independently and services are packaged to meet the special needs of the clients, contracting for service provision and contracting with the client regarding goods.
3) *Advocacy* – leveraging the system to make more services available and guarding against use of inappropriate services.
4) *Follow-up* – monitoring for continuing appropriateness of the service mix, responsiveness to changes in the client or the milieu to restabilize or enhance the situation.
5) *Resource locater* – information about options and accessibil-

ity, facilitating utilization, lessening of disjointedness and randomness.

6) *Information provision* – to both client and family, provide appropriate information and choices and advice.

7) *Consultation* – to the Transfer Team and other service providers on how the service system can be manipulated to serve the client population, provide a holistic view of service needs and quality of services.

8) *Public educator* – purpose of community services that have community living as a viable alternative to long-term care in an institutional setting.

9) *Data collection* – based on individual case plans, identification of service gaps, capacity of the existing system, areas requiring emphasis, linkage or access problems. (Centracare Community Placement Project, 1985: 12)

The case managers began with the individual, listened to him/her and his family for an identification of strengths and problem areas, developed a service plan, assessed the appropriateness of programs and services in the community, and then guided the placement process. The unique aspect of the case manager's responsibility was and remains the matching of community resources to the needs of individuals, coupled with control over funds required for the development and maintenance of community programs. The latter point should be emphasized. The task of matching resources and needs is frequently assigned to social workers, but without the funds required to make the match work. Thus, matching depends on the co-operation of other professionals and service providers. However, in these projects, assigning a budget to individual service plans and allocating responsibility for this budget to case managers meant that they were in charge and could deliver.

It should be added that the Roberts and Centrecare projects occurred at a time when resources for social programs were, if not plentiful, more adequate than has since been the case in New Brunswick. Relatively adequate budgets were established for both projects, and case managers could and did advocate for additional resources on the basis of the requirements of individual service plans. As a consequence, these projects did not result in dumping the responsibility for caring for deinstitutionalized patients on mothers and wives for little or no pay. This kind of offloading has occurred in many jurisdictions (see, for example, Bullock, 1990; Guberman, 1985). Preventing offloading requires an explicit and formal guarantee of an adequate budget for a suitable staff complement to community living arrangements, and for ongoing monitoring to ensure that the funding guarantees have been honoured.

It is apparent that the community work aspect of the case manager's role involved developing services on behalf of individuals. The type of work is similar to that described by Rothman as "locality development." However, rather than developing resources with and for a particular neighbourhood, case managers worked to establish programs and services needed for individuals.

At least from the experience in New Brunswick, the generalist approach to social work practice seems ideally suited to a style of community work that can be described as resource development. Indeed, most of the case managers in the Centracare and Roberts projects were social workers with BSW degrees. They were frequently young, full of enthusiasm, worked long hours, and quickly became committed to these innovative projects. They welcomed the range of responsibilities, from working with individuals to chairing meetings, arranging contracts with service providers, and developing resources. Those interviewed could not think of a better match between the generalist approach to social work practice and the role of case manager.

As noted above, both projects were successful and it is difficult to argue with success. But whether the extent of control vested in line social workers of a provincial department by these projects represents a sound foundation for future practice is now being questioned by the Association for Community Living. As noted earlier, the Association is now advancing the case for client empowerment and service brokerage. I return to this issue and its implications for governing the social services in Chapter 7.

CHAPTER III

Reforming Income Security
in Ontario

This chapter examines the efforts of the Social Planning Council (SPC) of Metropolitan Toronto to influence social policy in Ontario. As most readers will know, social planning councils do not provide income security, child welfare, or other social welfare programs, and hence their attempts to improve these programs are designed to convince federal and provincial governments of the need for change. The particular focus of this chapter is the Council's efforts to influence the provincial government in Ontario to improve its general welfare assistance and family benefit programs. While social reform is not the objective of all social planning councils in Canada, many, including the Council in Metropolitan Toronto, have declared this as their central objective. As well, the social problems of poverty and the adequacy of programs developed to address poverty are at the very crux of social policy in Canada. Hence, a review of a community-controlled organization seeking to reform income security is eminently appropriate.

Founded in 1940, the SPC has built an enviable reputation in the country for the quality of its research and the excellence of its reports. It is governed by an elected board of thirty-six directors, is staffed by nine professional and eight support staff, and has an annual budget of approximately $1 million. The budget is derived from a variety of sources, but the principal contributor is the United Way of Toronto, which provides about 65 per cent of the budget. The grant from Metropolitan Toronto amounts to 18-20 per cent, with the remainder coming from membership fees, sale of publications, and fees for services.

The Council is one of six voluntary social planning councils in Metro Toronto. The other councils are located in the municipalities of York, East York, North York, Scarborough, and Etobicoke. The Metropolitan Council is the oldest and largest and has encouraged the development of the other councils, which are organized on a municipal rather than metropolitan basis. However, the growth of social planning councils and the associated costs occasioned some concern among elected officials of Metropolitan Toronto, and in 1986 a study was commissioned to examine the roles and functions of social planning organizations. The Mackay Report concluded that local/municipal and metro-wide social planning organizations had distinctive and complementary roles, and that both types should receive funding from municipal governments. The Mackay Report concluded that the core functions of the Metropolitan Council were:

- public and community advocacy;
- project research to support selected advocacy topics;
- human services planning regarding trends, research and information;
- support to local councils regarding research and methods. (Mackay & Associates, 1986: 22)

The mission statement of the Council reads as follows:

A United Way member agency, the Council is an independent voluntary, community organization dedicated to research, planning, policy analysis and advocacy in the area of social development. The Council supports social and economic policy initiatives which join and promote the shared interests of individuals and families in Metropolitan Toronto with all Canadians across the country. (Child Poverty Action Group, 1991)

In carrying out this mission, the Council relies heavily on research:

one of the Council's most important functions is the use of research to drive and shape policy analysis and development.... Increasingly the Council is actively sought out by decision makers for comment and critique. Invitations to submit briefs, to provide in-house consultations and to participate actively in policy development have increasingly characterized the Council's work over the past year. (Social Planning Council of Metropolitan Toronto, 1989: 1)

Earning the right to speak and commanding a hearing on community issues is not an easy matter. It requires that an organization not only produce high-quality work but that it present a point of view that is not necessarily and not always in its own interests. Indeed, the Council does not seek to promote its own interests, but rather has as its overriding purpose the development of social policies that will improve the quality of life for citizens of Metropolitan Toronto. In the following discussion it will become evident that the Metropolitan Council is viewed as a legitimate and credible organization, albeit with a particular policy position. Since the Council's research into and analysis of existing social policies have revealed that these fail to provide adequate employment, income, housing, and other health and social services, the Council has become an advocate of social reform.

THE COUNCIL'S POLICY AGENDA

The issue of poverty and of the inadequate efforts of all levels of government to eliminate or reduce poverty has been on the agenda of the SPC for as long as any current staff and board members can recall. Dr. Brigitte Kitchen, a professor of social work at York University and a long-time board member, pointed out that Leonard Marsh used the Council's guides for family budgeting in his pioneering and influential report on social security for Canada in 1947. In order to place boundaries around the analysis of the Council's activities in influencing social policy, the decade of the 1980s and, in particular, the Council's work in setting the stage for and in encouraging the implementation of the recommendations of the Social Assistance Review have been selected for attention. The following list of publications indicates the attention given to poverty by the Council in the 1980s:

- 1981 *And the Poor Get Poorer*
- 1982 *The Underfunding of Social Assistance Programs in Ontario*
- 1982 *Poverty Among Ontario's Older Women*
- 1983 *With No Stigma Attached: Family Allowances and the Question of Universality*
- 1983 *And the Poor Get Poorer* (revised edition)
- 1984 *The Adequacy of Welfare Benefits: Responding to the Recession*
- 1986 *Child Poverty Rediscovered*
- 1986 *Welfare Benefits: An Interprovincial Comparison 1985*
- 1986 *Monetary Policy: Its Employment and Social Policy Implications*
- 1986 *Debating Canada's Future Social Policy Agenda*
- 1986 *A Guaranteed Income: A New Look at an Old Idea*

1986 *Living on the Margin: Update of the Poor Get Poorer*
1987 *Hunger – In Canada?*
1987 *The Cost of Raising a Child in the Toronto Area in 1986*
1987 *Housing Affordability in Metro Toronto*
1987 *Minimum Wages and Adequate Income*
1987 *Guides for Family Budgeting*
1989 *The* SARC *Report: Investing in Ontario's Future*
1989 *Reforming Ontario's Social Assistance*
1990 *A Look at Poverty Lines*

It is pertinent to point out that while the Council's commitment to social reform is well known in Metro Toronto and indeed throughout Ontario, formal statements such as annual reports and the mission statement do not make explicit reference to social reform. How, then, did the issue of poverty and the mission of reform come to occupy such a central place on the agenda of the Council? One significant reason has already been mentioned. The Council has been compelled to attend to social reform issues because of the conclusions of its research. An additional and equally important reason is to be found in the composition of the membership of the board of directors. In some earlier times in its history the board of directors had been heavily influenced by an elite and business perspective, but this is no longer the case. Indeed, in the late sixties and early seventies radical organizations and activists in Toronto organized campaigns to alter composition of the boards of a number of agencies, including the SPC. Since that time, the predominant perspectives within the board have come from faculty members in schools of social work and social science departments of the universities located in Toronto, from left-of-centre professionals, and from the clergy. These individuals have shaped the policy agenda of the Council to focus on working with and/or on behalf of the disadvantaged. Without altering official statements of purpose, the Council has adopted a critical, if not radical, perspective in following its purpose of exercising an independent voice in developing social policies and services. Besides being independent in setting its mission and course of action, the SPC is also decidedly committed to the cause of the poor and the powerless.

SETTING THE STAGE FOR THE SOCIAL ASSISTANCE REVIEW

The reports prepared in the early eighties can be viewed as setting the stage for the work of the Social Assistance Review Committee established in 1986 by the Liberal government then in power in Ontario. The report of the Committee, *Transitions*, was published in 1988. Several related and consistent themes emerge from a review of these earlier reports, including demystifying who receives social assistance and the adequacy of the amount paid to recipients. A *Globe and Mail* editorial commenting on *And the Poor Get Poorer* stated:

> Much of the Council's report is devoted to a statistical characterization of just who is on welfare and how well they are surviving. The purpose is twofold: to shake the persistent public image of welfare recipients as malingerers and work dodgers and to put the case for increases in aid. (September 23, 1983)

And the Poor Get Poorer reported that "the overwhelming majority of people receiving social assistance are sick, disabled or elderly adults and their dependents and women raising children alone." The majority of the reports noted above speak to the same point and with the same purpose. The myth of the employable male who refuses to work as the typical welfare recipient is just that – a myth that must be shattered. The extent to which the Council succeeded in debunking this myth among the citizens of Toronto is difficult to estimate, but certainly Toronto's newspapers showed a considerable amount of interest in the issue, and it received further attention in the work of the Social Assistance Review Committee. *And the Poor Get Poorer* documented the incidence of poverty among children, and reported that 42 per cent of the beneficiaries of social assistance are children.

> If parents are maintained in poverty because of the inadequacy of public programs their children will suffer directly. Indeed, these children will have a greater likelihood of being poor when they become adults. The cost to society of keeping children in poverty is a significant loss of human potential. (Social Plan-

ning Council of Metropolitan Toronto and Ontario Social Development Council, 1983: 62)

This 1983 report captured a good deal of attention in Metro Toronto. The *Globe and Mail* devoted most of the editorial cited above to the number of children living in poverty. As a consequence of its research into child poverty, the Council assisted in the formation of the Child Poverty Action Group. The group has developed proposals designed to eliminate child poverty, has peppered provincial and national governments with these proposals, and has organized national conferences.

Another fondly cherished myth is that social assistance rates are generous, and the Council has documented that the precise opposite is in fact the case. In *The Underfunding of Social Assistance Programs in Ontario* (July, 1982), the Council reported that:

Measured in relation to median Ontario incomes social assistance recipients have total incomes which are only 22-32% of those experienced by average households of comparable size. The real incomes of social assistance recipients have declined significantly since 1975, and their incomes fall well below any acceptable community standard of adequacy – often by as much as 30-50 percent.

Two reports by the Council examined the benefits paid by all provinces to recipients and ranked the provinces in terms of their relative generosity. The term "relative" is used advisedly since no province provided benefits sufficient to allow recipients to live above any of the accepted poverty lines. The major findings of the 1984 report were as follows:

As a provider of welfare incomes to families Ontario's performance rivals New Brunswick's as the worst in Canada. In six of the categories of assistance Ontario ranked 9th or 10th.

In Ontario and B.C. the incomes of families on welfare in relation to median provincial incomes were the lowest in the country. (Social Planning Council of Metropoliton Toronto, 1984)

One year later the interprovincial comparison report revealed similar conclusions. Along with New Brunswick and Prince Edward Island, Ontario provided the lowest benefits to families (Social Planning Council of Metropoliton Toronto, 1986a).

In its reviews of the adequacy of benefits the Council did not ignore the cost issue. Recognizing that recommendations for adequate benefits would require additional resources, the Council took pains to place the added expenditures in proper perspective. In *The Underfunding of Social Assistance Programs in Ontario*, the Council notes that:

> To restore income maintenance to the same share of government spending as in 1975 would require an additional 100 million. The direct provincial revenue needed to finance this additional increase would be about 42 million. Federal transfers and municipal payments would cover the remainder. This amount represents less than 1/5 of one percent of total provincial spending. Ironically, this is about four times the cost of the premier's personal jet.

The Council's work in reporting on income insecurity in Ontario was aided by similar studies of poverty at the national level by the National Council of Welfare and the Canadian Council on Social Development (e.g., National Council of Welfare, 1975, 1979; Canadian Council on Social Development, 1978, 1983). During the 1980s, these councils produced work of comparable quality and virtually identical results. The research studies at the national level complemented and aided the work of Metro Toronto's Social Planning Council in setting the stage for a full-scale review of Ontario's social assistance programs.

In 1986 the Council released *Living on the Margin*, an update of *And the Poor Get Poorer* that focused on the need to reform social assistance programs over the next decade. In a very real sense, *Living on the Margin* represented the culmination of the Council's work over the previous five years – work that emphasized the inadequacy of Ontario's income maintenance programs.

There is no doubt in the minds of the SPC board and staff members interviewed that the SPC was influential in preparing the ground for the reform of social assistance programs in Ontario. As noted above, the SPC spent much of its energy and resources on documenting the extent and impact of poverty in Ontario. In particular, the two editions of *And the Poor Get Poorer, The Underfunding of Social Assistance Programs in Ontario, The Adequacy of Welfare Benefits, Welfare Benefits: An Interprovincial Comparison,* and *Living on the Margin* received widespread publicity and acclaim. In the opinion of some Council staff members, pointing to Ontario's record as the stingiest province in the amounts provided to recipients wounded the pride of a newly elected Liberal government and some sections of the business community. How could Canada's wealthiest province be so niggardly in assisting the poor? How could it possibly lag behind the prairie and maritime provinces! However, Patrick Johnston, who served as a senior adviser on policy and research to the Social Assistance Review Committee, is of the view that at least some MLAs and members of the business community saw this record as demonstrating fiscal responsibility!

Two members of the Social Assistance Review Committee differ in their views of the influence of the Council in setting a stage for reform. Johnston reported that the Council's work paved the way for the reform of social assistance in Ontario, noting that the Council's work was influential in affecting the social policy climate. Poverty was a problem in affluent Ontario; children were living in poverty and the stereotype of the unemployed male as the typical welfare recipient was without foundation. "I'm convinced that the Council was very important over the years in helping create the climate for reform. When I began work with the Social Assistance Review Committee the first document I ordered and read was *Living on the Margin*" (Johnston, 1990). However, John Stapleton, also a senior adviser, attributed no special influence to the Council. Stapleton noted that the provincial government tends to disregard Metropolitan Toronto organizations as representing only the views of Ontario's largest and richest city rather than those of the province as a whole. This difference of opinion will be explored.

The terms of reference of the Social Assistance Review Committee were based on the following questions:

What should be the guiding principles and objectives of social assistance and related programs?

To what extent is the present system meeting these objectives?

What overall strategies for change should the province adopt?

What parameters should the province accept as it moves to change its legislation? (Social Assistance Review Committee, 1988: 1)

The Committee worked for two years, held twenty-three public hearings, and received 1,500 submissions and reports. Its 624-page report, *Transitions*, contains 274 recommendations and has been widely hailed, not only for its comprehensiveness, but for its indictment of the philosophy, policies, and benefits of social assistance in Ontario and for its recommendations for change. *Transitions* received widespread support from social policy and social reform groups in Ontario. While it is not the purpose of this chapter to present a thorough review of *Transitions*, it is necessary to provide a brief outline in order to assess the influence of the SPC. Some appreciation of its orientation and vision can be found from the following statement and listing of major recommendations.

All people in Ontario are entitled to an equal assurance of life opportunities in a society that is based on fairness, shared responsibility, and personal dignity for all. The objective of social assistance, therefore, must be to ensure that individuals are able to make the transition from dependence to autonomy, and from exclusion on the margins of society to integration within the mainstream of community life. (*Ibid.*: 8)

Table 1
List of Major Recommendations

Stage One
- increase monthly benefit levels, including eliminating the disparity between Gains-A (seniors) and Gains-D (disabled)
- reimburse shelter costs more adequately by covering full utility costs, and 100 percent of rents up to existing subsidy ceilings

- commission a study to identify a "basket of goods" the cost of which would provide the basis for future benefit rate increases
- begin the process of reducing the 22 benefit categories based on a "hierarchy of deservedness" to 3 categories based solely on need
- extend eligibility to many groups currently excluded including some refugee claimants and those without permanent shelter
- introduce a series of proposals designed to improve work incentives
- elimination of a host of long-standing inequities and anomalies in the treatment of particular recipient groups

Stage Two
- merging of General Welfare and Family Benefits into one piece of Legislation covering all social assistance recipients
- completing the process of reducing to three benefit categories, with new definitions of disability, and of adequacy based on a "market basket" approach, and greater safeguards of procedural fairness during appeals
- develop and expand support services to disabled and other recipients through mainstream programs, including a new province-wide training program
- complete consultation process around several elements of a new social assistance system, including: 1) provincial criteria to devolve administration to municipalities; and 2) the staffing and support services that would make up "opportunity planning", including the role of the voluntary sector in delivering services

Stage Three
- detailed implementation of the new delivery system, including the "opportunity planning" component, as well as further improvements to both work incentives and employment supports
- further improvements in adequacy by covering shelter costs up to 100 percent of the average rent level in the community
- the transfer of many items handled as special needs and subject to discretion to mainstream programs in other Ministries

Stage Four
- implementation of full income adequacy based on a "market basket" approach

– introduction of an income supplementation program for the working poor, to be developed in conjunction with improvements in the minimum wage

Stage Five
– integration of social assistance reforms with other broader income security reforms including a Children's Benefit and a Disability Insurance program, both to be cost-shared with the federal government

SOURCE: Social Assistance Review Committee, 1988: 519–20.

Recognizing the scale and potential cost of the recommendations, *Transitions* set out a five-stage plan for implementation. Stage One called for improving benefits for the costs of shelter and reducing the disincentive to employment. One year following the release of the report the government announced a $290 million package of improvements and an additional 6 per cent living adjustment to monthly benefits to take effect January 1, 1990. The principal effect was to increase benefits substantially to recipients with high housing costs.

In May, 1990, the Minister of Community and Social Services established an advisory group to "provide him with ongoing strategy advice on the development of new social assistance legislation for Ontario" (Advisory Group on New Social Assistance Legislation, 1991: 23). However, in the fall of 1990 the Liberal government was defeated and the newly elected New Democratic Party assumed the responsibility for implementing *Transitions*. Thus the recommendations of the advisory group's first report, *Back on Track*, were presented to a new government and a new minister.

Back on Track states that while "the Minister was committed to reform the government was not, and in the summer of 1990 the government declined to provide the project of social assistance reform with the funding it required" (*ibid.*: vii). *Back on Track* notes that the new minister has made a commitment to reform on behalf of the NDP government, and in January of 1991 the government announced an increase for recipients of social assistance.

Back on Track contains eighty-eight recommendations designed to improve the inadequacies in benefits, to resolve the inequities in the treatment of people, and to change unnecessary complexities. It proposes giving people who receive social assistance a formal role in the decision-making process through a council of consumers. The cost estimate of the package of reforms is approximately $450 million (*ibid.*: 1).

Some important indices of the influence of the Social Planning Council on the work of the Social Assistance Review Committee can be identified. First, after reviewing all of the various approaches to establishing poverty lines the Committee adopted the use of the family budget guides developed by the Council in *Transitions*. "These guidelines consist of a basket of goods and services intended to be sufficient to provide a modest but adequate standard of living. This approach lies "between the relative and absolute definitions of poverty and includes elements of both" (Social Planning Council of Metropoliton Toronto, 1990). A second way of assessing impact is to compare the principles adopted by the Review Committee with those developed by the Council in *Living on the Margin*. *Transitions* identifies seven principles and *Living on the Margin* five.

Living on the Margin	**Transitions**
Adequacy of Benefits	Adequacy of Benefits
Equity and Fairness	Respect for Diversity
(including Diversity)	Accessibility
Independence	Personal Responsibility
Personal Development	Personal Development
Accountability	Accountability
	Respect for Family Life

Living on the Margin was released in October, 1986, almost two years prior to the publication of *Transitions*. The extent to which *Transitions* relied on the principles enunciated in *Living on the Margin* is striking.

A third contribution by the Council was to organize the participation of citizens. As noted at the beginning of this chapter, one objective of the Council is to "facilitate citizen involvement in the analysis of social issues, the development of social policies, and the planning and delivery of human services" (Social Planning

Council of Metropolitan Toronto, 1989). During the preparation of *Transitions* and during the period between its release and the government's response, the Council gave extensive attention to this objective. The activities included pulling together some of the advisory groups of business, labour, church, and consumers formed by the Social Assistance Review Committee into a working group that met over a period of two years to prepare a joint reaction to *Transitions*. This benchmark document outlined minimum expectations for an appropriate government response to the recommendations of the Committee. Arriving at agreement was no easy task. Eight drafts were prepared by Council staff before the document was approved.

The Council also assisted poor people's organizations to organize their campaign against poverty. One direct outcome of this campaign was a march against poverty from the cities of Toronto, Sudbury, and Ottawa in 1989. Some 3,000 people participated in the finale of this march, which represented one of the most visible outpourings of outrage against poverty in Ontario ever witnessed at Queen's Park. The Ontario Campaign Against Poverty is now a largely independent movement.

A final contribution of the Council during the process of the review was that of public education. Council staff gave literally scores of presentations and seminars on poverty, and *Transitions* was first presented to the public in a forum organized by the Council.

As noted above, policy advisers John Stapleton and Patrick Johnston differ in their evaluation of the impact of the Council. Stapleton reports that he could not distinguish its contribution from those of other groups ("They all sang from the same hymn book"), while Johnston has no difficulty in recognizing the distinctive contributions of the SPC. Johnston indicates that the quality of the Council reports was recognized by the Committee; indeed, David Thornley, the Council staff member responsible for much of its work in income security, was hired to write the introductory chapter of *Transitions*.

In part, the difference in these evaluations can be attributed to the backgrounds of Stapleton and Johnston. The former is a senior bureaucrat whose views have been shaped by a lifetime of service within government. Typically, senior civil servants view policy-making as the prerogative of government. Although the careful and considered plans of bureaucrats are often upset by political considerations and bargaining, it is the particular predilection of civil servants to pursue a rational course and to resist attempts by special interest and pressure groups to influence the policy-making process. Thus, bureaucrats like Stapleton tend to dismiss the efforts of organizations such as the SPC. By contrast, Johnston has spent most of his career as a social worker/community organizer in the voluntary sector and is aware of and interested in the work of community-based organizations.

This discussion would not be complete without mentioning the contribution of the Laidlaw Foundation, which developed an overall plan for groups to follow and funded community groups across Ontario to push for implementation of the recommendations. The plan identified the Treasurer of the Ontario government as a key figure and urged the involvement of business leaders in pushing for reform. A pivotal part of this action plan was a letter to the Premier signed by leaders of social policy and religious organizations, the business community, including Conrad Black, Adam Zimmerman, and members of the Bronfman family, politicians, including Toronto Mayor Art Eggleton, and several prominent citizens, such as Pierre Berton and June Callwood.

INFLUENCING SOCIAL POLICY

Three insights emerging from this case study are explored in the next section of the chapter: the influences on the implementation stage of the policy process, the need for connections between reformers and policy-makers, and the issue of the cost of reforms.

Assessing the influence of the SPC in implementing the recommendations of *Transitions* is extremely difficult; indeed, the following discussion is not limited to the Council but rather reviews the process of implementation of the report and identifies some lessons both for government and for social reform groups.

Viewed from one perspective, the prospect for implementing *Transitions* could not have been more favourable. The Minister of Community and Social Services hailed it as a blueprint for reforming income security programs in Ontario. Despite initial reservations on the part of the Treasurer, the report was unanimously endorsed by cabinet. As noted earlier, social policy groups gave the report rave reviews and, as a deliberate strategy designed to enhance the likelihood of implementation, muted their criticisms. The provincial economy was buoyant and there was widespread recognition both inside and outside government that the time had come to bring about substantial changes in income security programs. As Patrick Johnston points out in a letter to the writer:

It is important to keep in mind that during the implementation stages not only was I in the Premier's office but George Thomson, Chair of the Social Assistance Review Committee, had been appointed a Deputy Minister first of Citizenship then of Labour. He was highly respected by politicians and civil servants alike and is a close personal friend of the Secretary of Cabinet, Peter Barnes. He could not have been in a much better position to exercise influence. In addition, the Vice-Chair of SARC, also highly respected, had been appointed as Chair of the Social Assistance Review Board (SARB). She was also "on the inside" and in a position to bring whatever influence to bear she could on the implementation. (Johnston, 1990)

Seen from other perspectives, however, implementation faced formidable obstacles. *Transitions* recommended eradicating poverty through a variety of measures at a time when the first rumblings of the intentions of the federal government to reduce expenditures for social programs were being heard. Viewed from a class and Marxist perspective, the likelihood of a comfortable, middle-class Liberal government actually eradicating poverty was not only dim but a contradiction in terms.

Two interesting and hitherto unknown aspects of the implementation process were revealed during the interviews conducted for this chapter. According to Johnston, the cabinet had decided to implement some Stage One and Stage Two recommendations prior to the launching of the advocacy campaigns described above. While the campaigns may have been useful in ensuring that the government's commitment to implementation did not erode, their primary purpose had already been achieved.

The second aspect also concerns the campaign. Persuading leaders of the business community to endorse *Transitions* was seen as one of the principal factors in the decision of the government to implement Stage One. However, as noted above, the government made this decision prior to the campaign, and in addition the backing of the business leaders was viewed by the Premier as something of a joke. According to Johnston, the Premier questioned the interest in and commitment to the reform of income security by businessmen such as Conrad Black. The Premier saw Black's action as an empty gesture and one made in response to the mayor of Toronto "calling in some markers," rather than as genuine support for social reform.

A slightly different version of the involvement of Conrad Black is contained in a *Globe and Mail* column by June Callwood in October, 1989. Callwood states that "the crucial telephone call was made by the buttoned-down Mayor of Toronto, Art Eggleton, who told Conrad Black that he was needed to speak on behalf of the poor. Conrad Black did not hang up." Callwood goes on to say that the task of convincing Conrad Black to speak out was given to an assistant of the mayor who believed in the merits of the SARC report and devoted considerable time and effort to explaining the report to Black. Callwood's description of events suggests that Black did not simply respond to a telephone call but was provided with sufficient information about *Transitions* and its recommendations that he could give an informed endorsement. Yet these differing accounts speak mainly to the issue of Black's knowledge of and subsequent commitment to *Transitions*, and in the last analysis Johnston may well be correct in believing that Black's support counted for little with the Premier. Nevertheless, the endorsement of *Transitions* by the business community in the open letter to the Premier may have enhanced the credibility and legitimacy of the proposed reforms. In any event, it is clear from the foregoing that the Council and other community groups did succeed in bringing *Transitions* to the attention of individuals and associations not usually involved in social reform issues. *Transitions* has become a much discussed and well-known report in Toronto and indeed throughout Ontario and Canada.

The above speculations aside, the principal question is: Why, given the favourable climate, were only some recommendations in Stage One and Stage Two implemented? Two reasons are suggested here, and both have implications for the implementation of reforms from the perspective of government and of social reform organizations. First, the attention of governments is always and inevitably focused on the initiation stage or the front end of the policy agenda. Like child welfare workers who are so busy dealing with new complaints of child abuse and neglect that they can rarely find time to provide counselling and other support services to families already known to them, governments are constantly dealing with crises. Their attention is consumed by the new items on their agenda. Thus, after deciding to move on Stage One recommendations, the government was diverted to new and equally pressing issues. The attention given by governments to the initiation stage is reinforced by the corresponding interest of the media in covering announcements of new initiatives. By contrast, the media typically show little interest in implementation, which is, after all, old news.

Second, in recent years all governments have faced severe fiscal constraints. Despite the fact that the provincial economy in Ontario was booming when *Transitions* was released, the provincial debt was substantial and the Treasurer was extremely concerned about the costs of the proposed reforms. When governments or outside lobby groups propose reforms that require additional funds some consideration has to be given to the source of these funds. If financing for a new program is found by reducing funds to existing programs, resistance can be expected from the beneficiaries and supporters of those programs. If funds are to be obtained by increasing taxes, howls of protest can be expected from the general public. If the proposal is to be financed by restructuring the tax system and forcing corporations to pay more than their current tax share, the corporate sector will exercise all of its considerable influence to ensure that the reform is blocked.

These two factors exert a powerful influence in the implementation stage and both governments and social reform groups must begin to pay particular attention to the implementation stage of the policy process. Traditionally, social planning councils have concentrated their attention on the first two stages of the policy process – the documentation of needs and the development of proposals to meet these needs. In a very real sense, social planning councils and governments must recognize that these are the easy tasks.

Implementation must be included in the terms of reference of special committees, task forces, and royal commissions. Whether established within government or as project committees of social planning councils, the presentation of findings should be seen as the first and, arguably, the simplest part of the policy process. The policy agenda is crowded and contentious and the conspicuous failure of many royal commissions and other research groups to gain approval for their recommendations can be attributed in large part to the fact that their job is finished at the point a report is completed.

A recent inquiry into services for children and youth in British Columbia by the Office of the Ombudsman provides an example of including implementation as an integral part of a report (Ombudsman, 1990). After assembling the facts the author of the report met with senior officials in the provincial ministries and worked out a plan for action. The published report not only contained the results of the investigation but a strategy for change sanctioned by the ministries whose policies and programs were deemed to require change. The Ombudsman reports directly to the legislature and has considerable power to investigate and recommend change, and therefore is a force to be reckoned with in the provincial government. Social planning councils do not possess the same "clout" and thus must work harder to persuade provincial ministries to agree to a plan for implementation. Nevertheless, including implementation as an integral component of reviews is preferable to the traditional practice of preparing a report, presenting it to the ministries concerned, and then taking no further responsibility. To be sure, such a strategy is most appropriate in situations where agreement on an action plan can be secured without undue difficulty. Other strategies are required when governments have to be convinced or coerced into making changes.

It should be emphasized that the chair of the Social Assistance Review Committee, George Thomson, many members of the committee, and staff members were seasoned and astute bureaucrats and gave attention to implementation when preparing their final report. In a deliberate and conscious fashion they organized their recommendations in "bite-sized chunks" to facilitate ease of implementation. The rationale for this strategy is outlined in *Transitions*:

Why Proceed in Stages

A "staged" reform process might seem to signal a disappointingly slow implementation of our recommendations. However, the income security system in Ontario and Canada is costly, large, and complex, and any attempt to introduce major change must take this reality into account. Some experts have advocated abolishing the current system and replacing it wholesale with a new, adequate, and rational system. We believe that this deal is impossible. Accordingly, we propose a reform process that would incrementally transform the present system, in orderly and understandable steps, into a better one.

Our objectives for the staging process are as follows:
- to make substantial improvements to the social assistance system at each stage;
- to achieve at each stage measurable milestones in the move towards a fully integrated and harmonized system;
- to pave the way to more comprehensive reforms in a manner that builds upon the progress made at each earlier stage;
- to implement the reforms with some recognition of the overall cost; and
- to adopt a time frame that reflects the urgency of change but also takes into consideration the enormous amount of work involved in achieving all that we have proposed. (Social Assistance Review Committee, 1988: 515)

While reasonable and thoughtful, this strategy did not take into account the short-time horizon of governments, and in a curiously perverse fashion it may have guaranteed that only Stage One recommendations would be implemented.

A different strategy would recognize and build on the short-term horizon. Such strategy would refrain from making over 200 recommendations but would instead concentrate on the issues needing immediate attention. Following this strategy, the SARC report would have folded all recommendations calling for increased benefits to recipients into Stage One rather than reserving many of these for Stages Three and Four. Surely the inadequacy of benefits was the primary reason for establishing the review in the first place, and strategies for ensuring that recipients of social assistance and the working poor would not live below the poverty line should have formed the core of the Committee's recommendations. Proposals for further research and study, such as the case for developing new legislation to combine the General Welfare Assistance Act and Family Benefits Act, are by their nature long range and can be appropriately dealt with in a more leisurely fashion.

The crucial dilemma faced by all investigatory bodies, whether commissioned by government in the form of royal commissions and parliamentary task forces or established by social reform groups, is whether to call for extensive or incremental change. In part, of course, the dilemma is resolved by the nature of the investigation. Some social and political problems require only minor changes and the dilemma is thus avoided. But in other investigations the changes required are extensive and those in charge of the inquiry must then decide whether to recommend incremental steps leading to long-term reform or to push for immediate and sweeping change. If they decide in favour of incremental change they will in all likelihood be derided by critics for their timidity and conservatism. If they opt for comprehensive reform their recommendations may well be dismissed as the product of fanciful imaginations.

The Social Assistance Review Committee attempted to resolve this dilemma by being both credible in recommending short-term changes, and visionary in exposing the myths that supported the social assistance system in Ontario and by proposing new policies based on such principles as adequacy, accessibility, accountability, and respect for personal responsibility and development. While some social policy analysts viewed the vision as too narrowly restricted to reforming the social assistance system, the Committee did achieve a balance between the two extremes. Some changes have been achieved, and *Transitions* still stands as the most complete and comprehensive report in the country on the case for reforming social assistance.

Social planning councils have become acknowledged leaders in identifying needs, in proposing new policies and programs, and in public education. However, this case study has confirmed the appropriateness of the observation that implementation is the most difficult stage of the policy process. Social planning councils might extend their expertise by giving particular attention to analysing how the difficulties that typically beset implementation can be overcome. Are lobbying and public education the only strategies? Is the redefinition strategy employed by the Association of Community Living a viable course of action? Is the strategy employed by the Ombudsman's Office in British Columbia useful? This focus might enrich the already valuable contributions of the social planning councils across the country in the cause of social reform.

CONNECTIONS WITH GOVERNMENT

Another lesson is that social reform organizations can benefit from connections with governments in order to be able to identify the crucial points in the implementation process. As already mentioned, it appears that the efforts to convince government to implement Stage One were largely unnecessary since this decision had already been made. The campaigns waged with respect to Stage One recommendations were extensive and expensive in terms of both energy and resources. The government's announcement was hailed as a victory by the social reform groups, and just as *Transitions* then began to fade from the government's agenda so did the energy and resources of the outside reform groups.

The advantage of having a board of directors and a staff dedicated to the mission of social reform is clear and compelling. Board and staff meetings are focused in a very explicit fashion on this mission, thereby precluding lengthy debates on organizational objectives and on the projects the social planning council should address. There are, however, some disadvantages. A mission of social reform attracts left-leaning individuals who tend to view the world and the problems through the same lens. Thus, in studying issues and solutions the council misses the contributions of individuals with a different perspective.

The range of contacts and connections possessed by board and staff members is inevitably limited when these members are recruited from essentially the same ideology and background. The difference between the Social Planning Council of Metropolitan Toronto and the Association for Community Living is striking. The mission of the latter organization is to improve the quality of life for developmentally delayed children and adults. Board members are usually attracted to this mission because an immediate family member is developmentally delayed, but apart from this common denominator members come from all walks of life and with a range of ideologies. Thus the Association can often find from within its membership individuals who know politicians, senior bureaucrats, and staff members of funding agencies. They can usually arrange meetings with these influential individuals, and at the national level the Association can gain the ear of prominent politicians.

The mission of reform should not result in an automatic exclusion of the business community. I recall from my days in social planning in London, Ontario, a businessman who, as the vice-president of social planning for United Community Services, would contact the social planning office for an update when he returned from out-of-town business before he called his office for a similar report.* Social planning councils will not find it easy to recruit board members from the business world, but their contributions (a different perspective and connection to government) might make the effort worthwhile.

It is also difficult to recruit members from poor people's organizations. Such representatives typically yearn for direct action and find research and analysis much too tame for their liking. Recruiting and keeping activists requires that they appreciate that while the mission is reform, the strategies used are research, public education, and assisting community groups.

SOCIAL REFORM AND THE ISSUE OF COST

A third lesson emerging from this case study, the issue of cost, has already been alluded to. A typical response of governments to recommendations for improved social programs is "where will the money come from?" One response is to reallocate funds, and here the New Brunswick experience provides a helpful illustration. In that province the initial funds for a community support system for children with special needs became available when an institution for these children was closed. However, this option is not always open, and reform groups must be able to counter the inevitable response of conservative and even moderately progressive govern-

---

*Al Cohen is now a professor of sociology at the University of Western Ontario.

ments that new funds are simply not available. As a beginning, two arguments are suggested. The first is based on the statement of the Toronto Daily Bread Food Bank in August, 1990, and reported in Michael Valpy's column in the *Globe and Mail* (Valpy, 1990):

> An Ontario community of 190,000 people has been cut off by a forest fire. There is only enough food to last two days. The federal government refuses to respond, maintaining that it is a provincial responsibility. The provincial government has produced a report on the issue but refuses to follow through on its recommendations. According to the municipal government, its ability to respond is related to property taxes (which it says) is a more serious problem right now ....

Valpy's comments on this "announcement" were as follows:

> So began a public announcement put out last August by Toronto's Daily Bread Food Bank, the central depot for 147 food distribution agencies in the city. It was a desperate act to draw attention to a crisis. Last summer, Toronto's charity food shelves were virtually bare. We know that if a real city of 190,000 people had been cut off from food the federal or provincial governments – and probably both – would have declared an emergency and triggered the armed services and every available instrument of government to assault the problem. We know that Prime Minister Brian Mulroney would have hurried off to the site by armed forces helicopter and had himself captured by the television cameras against a backdrop of billowing smoke, concern stamped across his forehead as he told officials his government would leave no stone unturned in getting people fed. But when the people who are hungry are the poor in Toronto – 190,000 who use food banks in the city on an annual basis, more than 90,000 a month – where is Mr. Mulroney?

Although hypothetical, the statement and the comment are provocative. Why should one community with no food evoke an immediate and sympathetic response while the second elicits no reaction? One reason for the difference is surely that the first example is the consequence of natural disaster, while the reasons for the plight of the hungry and homeless of Toronto are more difficult to discern. But at least one compelling reason is the commitment of federal governments to economic and fiscal policies that result in high levels of unemployment. Given this commitment, is not a logical consequence the provision of adequate and continuing benefits for the unemployed?

A second response begins to connect the ordinary to the grand issues of policy. As will be recalled from Chapter 1, some ordinary issues can be addressed without reference to the grand issues of policy. Others, like the reform of income security, bump into larger issues involving the collection and distribution of income. A clear answer to the response that there are no funds available is to note that more can and should be collected – and collected from the corporate sector.

The inequities of the Canadian tax system were first identified by the Royal Commission on Taxation and are the focus of the recent best-seller, *Behind Closed Doors* (McQuaig, 1988). The conclusion of the book is that representatives of large corporations have influenced a series of federal governments to develop a tax system that largely benefits the corporate sector. The following quotation from McQuaig establishes the point in a convincing fashion.

Among the group of companies enjoying tax-free status in 1986 were some of Canada's most profitable corporations. Hees International, a holding company for the sprawling corporate empire of Edward and Peter Bronfman, was one of those corporations, as was another Bronfman holding company, Carena-Bancorp Incorporated. Yet these two had combined profits of $111.3 million that year. Don Blenkarn, chairman of the Commons finance committee, was shocked by these numbers. As he told Jacquie McNish of *The Wall Street Journal*: "It's unconscionable that they (Hees and Carena-Bancorp) pay so little tax."

And the Bronfmans were not alone. A number of prominent Canadian firms managed to go tax-free in 1986, on profits ranging in the tens of millions of dollars. Alcan Aluminium Limited, for instance, paid no income tax on a profit of $220 million (U.S.); in fact, Alcan chalked up a credit of $32 million to reduce its future taxes. And Brascan Limited, with its massive resource and manufacturing interests, also avoided income taxes entirely that year, despite a profit of $186 million. It qualified for a credit of $2.3 million. Xerox Canada, a subsidiary of the U.S. photocopy giant, reported a profit of $115 million, but paid no income tax and ended up with a $10 million credit. Real estate developer Cadillac Fairview had a profit of $95 million, paid no income tax and managed to qualify for a credit of $12.4 million. The list goes on. (McQuaig, 1988: 335-36)

The crux of this argument is substantiated by a recent Statistics Canada study. In the June, 1991, edition of *Economic Observer*, Statistics Canada reports that "It was not explosive growth in program spending that caused the increase in the deficit after 1975 but a drop in federal revenues relative to the growth of the Gross National Product . . . and the biggest drop was in the amount paid by corporate taxes" (Statistics Canada, 1991).

Taxes are primarily set at the national level, but understanding of the system and how it works against the poor and middle classes can begin at the local level. Canadians need to know, for example, that "when compared with the tax systems of twenty other western industrial companies, Canada has the lowest overall tax on wealth" (McQuaig, 1988: 40), and that for many years the very richest Canadians have paid no income tax at all. Social planning councils have developed a capacity to demolish myths and to educate the public and might turn their attention to the revenue side of the social policy debate. The Metro Toronto SPC demonstrated a beginning interest in this side of the debate when it pointed out that raising social assistance rates in 1982 would have cost the taxpayers about four times the cost of the premier's personal jet (Social Planning Council of Metropoliton Toronto, 1982). The National Council of Welfare has published several reports on the tax system and has consistently pointed out that the present tax system allows both wealthy individuals and corporations to defer and evade taxes (see, for example, *The Hidden Welfare System*, 1976). Councils in Hamilton and Metropolitan Toronto are now turning attention to this issue and to the impact of forgiven taxes on communities. Such comparisons, highlighting as they do government priorities, need to be made often and repeated in a relentless fashion.

CONNECTING POLICY AND PRACTICE

The term "policy" is intended here to refer to setting a council's agenda and to determining overall directions and objectives. Given this interpretation, policy becomes virtually synonymous with objectives and mission statements. Practice is seen as a vehicle for implementing policy. As noted at the beginning of this chapter, a social planning council has two principal objectives, the facilitation of citizen involvement in the development of social policies and the exercise of an independent voice in social policy. However, in pursuing these objectives the council develops a distinctive position for reforming social policies in order to improve the lot of the poor and the powerless. This policy position represents a clear statement to those who wish to become involved in the work of the council as a board or staff member. It integrates the work of staff and board in a very compelling fashion: let there be no mistake whose side the Council is on; it is on the side of social justice and equality of treatment for all citizens. At first glance this position appears to contradict the suggestion that a mission of social reform should not, by definition, exclude representatives of the business community. Some business leaders may welcome the challenge of presenting their point of view in an organization dedicated to reform, and their arguments would add depth and vitality to the policy debates.

The clarity of the council's policy position provides direction for the practice vehicles selected to implement policy. Both the research and community work functions are dedicated to improving social policies and programs. Hence policy and practice at Metro SPC are virtually indistinguishable.

A second reason for the close integration is that the research activities are carried out by a project committee of board and staff members. The board members assume the responsibility of reporting to the board while staff are charged with the tasks of data collection, analysis, and report writing. This structure involves both board and staff in policy issues (which projects should be approved, what resources are to be assigned to them, what action should be taken with respect to committee reports) and in practice (collecting and analysing data, and determining the conclusions to be drawn).

CONNECTING THEORY AND PRACTICE

Theory is viewed here as explanations that assist community workers in their day-to-day practice. Are there theories that provide some insight into the causation and possible remedies of the social problems faced by community workers? And are there useful concepts on the process of policy-making, on the planning of change, and on interorganizational relationships that can aid community workers?

Some theories and concepts exist, and are briefly described below. But, like their counterparts in the other case studies, the staff of the Metro Toronto SPC practise their craft in a highly pragmatic fashion, without conscious and explicit attention to theory. However, some basic theories about society have become an integral part of the consciousness of Council staff. Essentially, they view society in terms of structure and power, thus assigning a disproportionate amount of power and influence to a relatively small group of businessmen and conservative politicians. The consequence of the exercise of influence is that the top 10 per cent of the population own more than half of the country's wealth (McQuaig, 1988: 38). Council staff view the conditions of poverty, homelessness, unemployment, and delinquency as being in large measure created by the structure of Canadian society and only in part by individual and family behaviour. This theoretical orientation coincides completely with the mission of the Council and contributes to the harmony between policy and practice.

Given this degree of harmony, is there any reason to suggest that more extensive reference to concepts and theory would benefit staff and bring about further improvements in the Council's work? The work of the Council is captured best by the social reform approach identified by Rothman and perhaps even more appropriately by Perlman and Gurin as "strengthening social provisions and improving people's problem-solving capacities" (Perlman and Gurin, 1972: 5a). Perlman and Gurin also point to the importance of organizational auspices in community work. The Council's mission of social reform has to be viewed and understood in relation to its organizational auspices as a voluntary agency. The Council cannot compel any level of government to change its policies and programs and must therefore rely on strategies of persuasion.

At least three conceptual frameworks might assist social planning councils in selecting strategies. Roland Warren (1971) identified a simple but nonetheless useful breakdown of strategies. Essentially, Warren argued that proposals for change will be supported, ignored, or resisted. If there is support, the agency or person proposing the change can work in a co-operative and harmonious fashion with the "target of change." If the proposal for change is viewed as not particularly important, the agency or person must organize campaigns to convince the target organization that the proposal is indeed significant and deserving of attention. If the proposal is resisted, then all stops have to be pulled out: those proposing the change may have to transform the campaign strategies into those of contest. Such tactics include demonstrations and marches.

The notion of matching strategies to the particular situation has been developed by a number of writers. Morris and Binstock argue that many if not most proposals will be resisted and that planners must therefore analyse carefully the resources they possess and determine whether any of these resources will be sufficient to overcome the resistance. According to Morris and Binstock (1966: 119) the resources available to planners include:

- money and credit
- personal energy
- professional expertise
- popularity
- social standing, political standing
- control of information
- legitimacy.

To this list might be added the capacity to undertake research and produce credible reports and the mobilization of energies. The second part of this conceptualization of change is that policy-makers can be influenced in a number of ways and that the resources must match these pathways of influence, which include:

- obligation
- friendship
- rational persuasion

- selling
- coercion
- inducement. (*Ibid.*: 117)

Morris and Binstock conclude with the rather dismal observation that the resource usually available to staff of social planning councils is professional expertise, which is most appropriately matched with the pathway of rational persuasion. Unfortunately, while policy-makers lay claim to rationality their decisions often result from obligations, friendships, and the compelling need to be re-elected. Nevertheless, the discipline of applying a resources and pathways of influence framework may assist staff members of social planning councils to analyse their ability to influence and to find out whether additional resources can be acquired.

The work on implementation of policy by such writers as Walter Williams (1980), Richard Elmore (1982), and Michael Lipsky (1980) is not well known in community work but has considerable potential. Given its importance in all of the case studies, the issue of implementation receives considerable attention in the final chapter.

CONNECTING SOCIAL WORK AND COMMUNITY WORK PRACTICE

Council staff are required to be proficient in both the research and community work facilitation functions. Both staff and board members are convinced that these functions complement each other and should not be compartmentalized. Thus council staff are specialists who possess the skills to carry out research studies and to work with community organizations. They are expected to interpret the results of research studies as part of their work with community groups and to bring an awareness of the problems being experienced by the members of these groups to their work as researchers.

In the sixties and seventies most of the professional staff of social planning councils were social workers, and much of the early leadership in social planning came from the social work profession. However, this leadership is waning for a number of reasons. First, as noted in Chapter 1, most undergraduate programs prepare students for the general practice of social work and typically give little attention to research, which has been identified in this chapter as a crucial skill in community work. Undergraduate programs prepare graduates who are skilled in working with individuals and families, who can take into account and appreciate the influence of community and social environments on individuals, and who can develop resources for and with their clients. As a general rule, then, BSW graduates are not viewed as appropriate staff for social planning councils.

At the graduate level most schools of social work depart from a generalist model and provide specializations. In recent years the most popular specialization has been family therapy, and there is little doubt that community work and research are contenders for the least popular specialization. It is easy to understand, therefore, why social planning councils do not require an MSW as basic for staff. Rather, SPCs seek staff members who by virtue of a combination of education and experience are competent researchers and community workers.

If social work wishes to reclaim its former pre-eminence in staffing social planning councils the challenge is clear. Schools of social work must prepare students to become proficient in research and in community work. Indeed, in developing curricula for these skills, schools would profit from the experience of social planning councils that have fused these two functions in a way that enriches both.

The essential knowledge and skills required for the community work function of social planning councils can be briefly summarized as follows. At a macro level community work requires knowledge of Canadian society, of how it is governed and the patterns of power that affect its governance, of social problems, and of the policy responses developed to meet these problems. At a middle-range level community work requires knowledge of communities, their history, and governance and in particular of the human service organizations that provide social and health services and of the problems typically encountered in trying to connect these services in a coherent fashion. In terms of skills, community work requires the ability to carry out surveys, to identify needs and resources, to analyse and evaluate programs, and to develop new services. Finally, community work requires the communication skills common to all social work practice.

It will be readily apparent that this set of knowledge and skills differs from those identified in the previous chapter to develop services for children with special needs. The commonalities and differences between the sets of knowledge and skills required for the various kinds of community work practice identified in this book are discussed in the final chapter.

CHAPTER IV

First Nation Control of Child
Welfare Services

The profession of social work has a long and distinguished connection with child welfare. Indeed, social workers were in the forefront of the reform efforts that resulted in the legislation, programs, and agencies that protect children today from neglect and abuse. Schools of social work have developed curricula to prepare graduates for practice in the field of child welfare and social workers, whether prepared by formal training in schools of social work or through practical experience, have formed the majority of the staff of child welfare agencies. The profession has also provided theorists, researchers, policy-makers, and administrators.

A brief review of the development of societal concern for the welfare of children will help to set the stage for the discussion on community work and child welfare. At the outset it should be emphasized that not until the early years of this century was neglecting and abusing children deemed to be a problem or a concern. In earlier times, children were the property of their parents, particularly of their fathers. Parents treated their children as they wished, and intervention to deal with neglect and abuse, if it occurred at all, was limited to the efforts of relatives and friends. Reframing child neglect and abuse from a purely private family matter into a public issue requiring the intervention of society was the first and most formidable obstacle faced by the early social reformers. In recent years we have seen this reframing questioned by those who favour a residual approach to social policy. This perspective holds that families are by and large capable of caring for their children without any assistance, particularly without assistance from government agencies. Only when this capacity has broken down, only when the resources of relatives, friends, neighbours, the church, and other local, informal helping resources have been exhausted, should government agencies intervene. When one is reminded that Margaret Thatcher, Ronald Reagan, and many politicians in Canada believe in and vigorously pursue a residual approach to social policy, it is apparent that our commitment to social responsibility for the care of children is fragile.

Reluctantly and tenuously, child neglect and abuse have been recognized in legislation as socially intolerable. Various responses have been developed during this century. The first was to build orphanages to take care of abandoned and orphaned children, and this institutional approach characterized the early days of child welfare. The inappropriateness of these institutions was eventually recognized and they then became targets of reformers and were gradually phased out.

Both the institutional approach and the second-stage response of foster care were based on an assumption that parents who neglected and abused their children were evil or at best inadequate, and could not be trusted with the important task of caring for children. This assumption represented a complete reversal of the earlier view that children were chattels and owned by their parents. With child neglect and abuse established as the proper business of the state, the pendulum swung to a view of neglecting parents as villains or inept individuals. Hence the only appropriate response was to remove children from their homes.

The child welfare field has devoted much energy and imagination to the task of developing foster care as an appropriate and satisfactory response to caring for children removed from parents because of neglect and abuse. Foster parents have been recruited and trained; standards for foster homes have been developed and monitored; the role of foster parents in the child welfare system has been examined; valiant efforts to establish payments for foster care at a reasonable level have been made; and specialized foster homes for children with special needs have been established.

Despite these diligent efforts, foster homes have proven to be almost as inadequate as their predecessor. The inadequacy first became manifest because of the difficulties experienced in providing continuity in foster care. For many reasons, some unavoidable, foster children were moved from home to home. The absence of continuity was documented by nation-wide studies in the U.S., such as *Children in Need of Parents* (Maas and Engler, 1959), and replicated in many jurisdictions by local reviews.

A second serious flaw in foster care, long known to practitioners but established without question by the work of Maas and Engler, Fanshel and Shinn (1978), and others, was that the longer children remain in foster care, the more remote the chance of eventual reunification with their natural parents. Hence, these studies revealed two endemic problems in foster care: those children who experienced permanence in their foster home were unlikely to be reunited with parents, and those lacking permanence were neither returned home nor assured continuity in care. For both of these substantial groups of children, the foster care response was, like its predecessor, more a failure than a solution.

A significant attempt to shore up the foster care system emerged from the Oregon Project, a federally funded demonstration project to arrange a permanent plan for all foster children (Lahti *et al.*, 1981). The primary objective of permanency planning was to ensure that children would be returned to their natural parents. The secondary objective was to ensure continuity in care within the foster home system, thereby avoiding all but absolutely essential moves. The principle of permanency planning made eminent sense to child welfare professionals, and in the U.S. it formed one of the cornerstones of the federal Adoption Assistance and Child Welfare Act of 1980. However, Elizabeth Robinson concluded her review of permanency planning with the observation that "while there have been spasmodic attempts, permanency planning is not a matter of provincial or national policy in Canada" (Robinson, 1985: 165).

The most recent response of the child welfare theorists has been to reframe the issue of child neglect and abuse. Rather than focusing attention on the child, these recent efforts conceptualize child welfare as a family matter. Thus, one leading writer in the field claims that "three interwoven sets of ideas" will be central to future child welfare work:

1. The idea of the family as the ideal developmental context for the child
2. The notion of child welfare services as family supportive and strengthening
3. The primary focus on meeting the basic developmental needs of the child as opposed to identifying and treating child-family pathology. (Whittaker, 1983: 174)

A similar position is expressed in a respected U.S. child welfare text.

Family-centered practice brings with it a conviction that the greatest proportion of time, energy and financial resources of the child welfare system must be devoted to preserving families. Child welfare is then defined as a service primarily geared to the enhancement of the welfare of children within their own homes or to the prompt reunification of families when temporary placement is required. (Laird, 1985: 363)

This response of preventing out-of-home placements has been implemented in many jurisdictions in the U.S. and has been aided by funds made available to state and private child welfare agencies through the Adoption Assistance and Child Welfare Act. The response has typically taken the form of demonstration projects that provide a wide range of services to families to prevent out-of-home placements. The results have been uniformly positive. For example, my review of twenty-seven projects conducted in the U.S. revealed that all but one were successful in preventing out-of-home placements. One project reported a 100 per cent success rate, twelve reported success rates in the 80–90 per cent range, and an equal number indicated success within a 60–80 per cent range. These projects were characterized by a range of comprehensive and accessible services; a focus on the family; an administrative arrangement that separated preventive services from the investigation of complaints of abuse and neglect; a commitment to preventive services and a respect for the clients being served (Wharf, 1991).

Despite the success of projects designed to prevent out-of-home placements they retain the status of demonstration projects in the U.S. and have yet to be incorporated as an integral part of child welfare programs in that country. In Canada they have been implemented in a very limited fashion. Only two provinces, Ontario and New Brunswick, plus the Yukon have included prevention in legislation, and even in these jurisdictions the lack of adequate funding greatly restricts the range of preventive programs that can be provided.

This brief review of responses to the problem of child neglect and abuse would be incomplete without emphasizing that the most comprehensive response developed to the present time, that of preventing out-of-home placements, falls far short of a satisfactory social policy for child welfare. An adequate response would begin with the recognition of "the strong relationship between poverty and child neglect and abuse. Every national survey of officially reported incidents of child neglect and abuse has indicated that the preponderance of the reports involves families from the lowest socio-economic levels" (Pelton, 1981: 4). Pelton's conclusions are supported in Canada by the work of the National Council of Welfare. In its report, *Poor Kids*, the Council reported that "one fundamental characteristic of the child welfare system is that its clients are still overwhelmingly drawn from the ranks of Canada's poor" (National Council of Welfare, 1975: 276).

Formal and official acknowledgement of the impact of poverty on the health of children is contained in the report of the federal government, *Achieving Health for All*. On November 26, 1989, a motion to eliminate child poverty in Canada by the year 2000 was passed unanimously in the House of Commons, but according to the leader of the New Democratic Party, Audrey McLaughlin, "a year later the government of Canada has made little progress and 1.1 million children still live below the poverty line" (McLaughlin, 1990).

A comprehensive response to child neglect and abuse would begin by eliminating child poverty. It would continue by addressing the issue of housing, by ensuring safety for children in their neighbourhoods, and by providing day care and a variety of support services for all families. Such a comprehensive response requires action by the federal and provincial governments with respect to the national issues of poverty and substandard housing, and the commitment of resources to community agencies so they can modify negative environments, enhance the competence of parents, and provide supports to all families in the often difficult task of caring for children. In summary, a satisfactory response to child welfare would consist of a national strategy to end child poverty, a community strategy to create healthy communities, a family strategy to enhance the capacity of families to care for children, and a crisis strategy to provide temporary protection for children. A discussion on reforming child welfare and the development of an appropriate set of social policies for child welfare is continued in Chapter 7.

THE CONVERGENCE OF INTEREST

In all of the case studies in this book the concept of the convergence of interest has proven to be a useful way to analyse the emergence of an issue on the policy agenda. Despite its utility as a way of understanding community change, this concept only implicitly includes the larger societal context. In this chapter I make the societal context explicit since the knowledge and awareness of what is happening elsewhere influences conceptions of "community welfare." Certainly this is the case vis-à-vis child welfare and First Nation families.

The inability of the Canadian child welfare system to respond to the needs of First Nation families and children was established beyond doubt by the publication of a national study on *Native Children and the Child Welfare System* (Johnston, 1983). This study documented that the dominant response of the child welfare system to the condition of child neglect and abuse was to apprehend children and place them in some form of substitute care. The consequence for First Nation children was foster care in white families and communities. An appreciation of the damage done to First Nation families by the child welfare system can be found from the following:

In 1955 there were 3,433 children in the care of B.C.'s child welfare branch. Of that number it was estimated that 29 children, or less than one percent of that total, were of Indian ancestry. By 1964, however, 1,446 children in care in B.C. were of Indian extraction. That number represented 34.2 percent of all children in care. Within ten years, in other words, the representation of Native children in B.C.'s child welfare system had jumped from almost nil to a third. It was a pattern being repeated in other parts of Canada as well.

One longtime employee of the Ministry of Human Resources in B.C. referred to this process as the "Sixties Scoop". She admitted that provincial social workers would, quite literally, scoop children from reserves on the slightest pretext. She also made it clear, however, that she and her colleagues sincerely believed that what they were doing was in the best interests of the children. They felt that the apprehension of Indian children from reserves would save them from the effects of crushing poverty, unsanitary health conditions, poor housing and malnutrition, which were facts of life on many reserves. Unfortunately, the long-term effect of apprehension on the individual child was not considered. More likely, it could not have been imagined.

Nor were the effects of apprehension on Indian families and communities taken into account and some reserves lost almost a generation of their children as a result. (*Ibid.*: 63)

The Sixties Scoop has been labelled cultural genocide by Native leaders. A graphic example of the Sixties Scoop is the personal experience of Chief Wayne Christian, reported in *Toward First Nation Control of Child Welfare*:

Much of Chief Christian's concern about child welfare practices were as a result of his own experiences as a child in the care of Human Resources from age 12 until 18. He was removed from his mother's care along with his nine brothers and sisters and was profoundly influenced by the dissolution of his family. Chief Christian went through several foster homes, separated from his siblings, and finally settled in one for a number of years.

Chief Christian stated that his mother was almost destroyed by being without her children, and as a result developed a sense of worthlessness and turned to alcohol as a release. Chief Christian was able to make the change back to living on the reserve when he was 18 years old. One of his brothers was not as successful and committed suicide after being unable to cope with the transition from foster home to reserve life.

Chief Christian clearly expressed the belief that the most valuable resource Indian people have is children. He also stated "without having children understanding where they're coming from and knowing who they are, you are going to end up with a whole population eventually that has no real purpose or has no focus in their life". He further stated his belief that child welfare services in the past served to destroy Indian families and that what was needed was a holistic approach to working with children and their families to maintain them as a unit. (Wharf, 1989a: 10)

By the late 1970s leaders and elders of First Nation communities and some child welfare professionals were not only aware of the cultural insensitivity and the barrenness of the child welfare response to First Nation families and children, but they were beginning to take action to correct matters. To the writer's knowledge, no comprehensive account of the development of First Nation responsibility for child welfare has been written, but some of the first stirring of interest in governing child welfare services came from the Blackfoot nation in Alberta, from Big Grassy and Big Island reserves in the Rainy River area of Ontario, from the Dakota Ojibway tribal council in Manitoba, and from the Spallumcheen band in B.C. The chief of the Spallumcheen band at the time was Wayne Christian, whose views on the non-Native child welfare system have been expressed above. In 1980, convinced that only direct social action would get results, Chief Christian led a Children's Caravan from Enderby in the Okanagan area of B.C. to the home of Grace McCarthy, the Minister of Human Resources, in Vancouver. The caravan camped on the minister's lawn until the minister signed the following agreement:

> The Minister of Human Resources agrees to respect the authority of the Spalamacheen [sic] Band Council to assume responsibility and control over their own children. The Min. of Human Resources further agrees to the desirability of returning Indian children of the Spallumcheen Band presently in care of the Min. of Human Resources to the authority of the Spallumcheen Band and both parties agree to work out an appropriate plan in the best interests of each child presently in care, assuming that the Spallumcheen Band will develop necessary resources in negotiation with the Federal Government. (McCarthy and Christian, 1986: original text of agreement)

Such direct action was no longer required by the mid-eighties. By that time federal and provincial politicians agreed that participation in the provision of child welfare services by First Nation communities was an "idea whose time had come." In the terms of Sower *et al.* (1957: 64), the actions to establish a Native child welfare unit in Vancouver and the child welfare project in the Yukon were "compatible with existing conditions of community welfare."

Native child welfare services in Vancouver and among the Champagne/Aishihik band in the Yukon are the focus of the ensuing description and analysis. These projects are concerned with community issues, with developing new and culturally sensitive programs, with improving the environment for children and families, and with empowering consumers. In so doing, the projects extend the boundaries of child welfare work from a focus on families to include the community. They can be seen as middle-range responses, more comprehensive than child- and family-centred responses but less inclusive than a national social policy response.

THE NATIVE CHILD WELFARE UNIT IN VANCOUVER

Claude Richmond, provincial Minister of Social Services and Housing from August, 1986, to November, 1989, was personally convinced of the necessity to transfer responsibility for child welfare services to First Nation communities and was involved in the discussions leading to agreements with the McLeod Lake band, the Carrier Sekani band, and the Nuu'chah'nulth tribal council. The senior bureaucrats in the ministry, R.K. Butler, the deputy minister, Leslie Arnold, superintendent of child welfare, and Terry Pyper and Bob Cronin, assistant deputy ministers, were in complete agreement with the minister. For example, the ministry seconded a child welfare supervisor to the Nuu'chah'nulth tribal council and assigned a senior staff member in the Family and Children's Service Division the task of aiding First Nation band and tribal councils to bring about First Nation ownership of child welfare.

On April 7, 1989, Richmond and Jack Weisgerber, Minister of Native Affairs, met with First Nation leaders in Vancouver to discuss how social service programs could be changed to meet the needs of Native people in the city more appropriately. The First Nation leaders present at the meeting included Ron George and Ernie Crey of the United Native Nations. Following this meeting a committee composed of staff of Region B, the regional office of the ministry, which serves residents of the core area of Vancouver, and members of First Nation organizations who were knowledgeable about social service programs in Vancouver was established. The mandate of the committee was:

To identify the guiding principles, objectives of the Family and Child Service Act and the programs and services which are implemented under this legislation;

To identify the problems and to examine current research regarding the program;

To what extent are the current programs, services and delivery structures serving the needs of the native community?

What changes are recommended to meet the objectives? (Working Committees, 1989: 1)

This committee established three groups: Family and Child, the Guaranteed Available Income for Need Act, and Housing. All groups were chaired by regional staff and all were assisted in their work by Cal Albright. A First Nation citizen from Saskatchewan, Albright was placed in Region B for his final fieldwork placement in the Master of Social Work program at UBC.

As a first step in gaining input the working committee invited representatives of fifty-two organizations in the downtown Vancouver area to a community forum held on July 6, 1989. Seventeen presentations were made at the forum, and all commented on the absence of programs designed to meet the particular needs of First Nation families, and on the need for Native social workers and for the involvement of First Nation citizens in programs that affect them. Aided by these presentations and by the knowledge and experience of the members of the working group, the Family and Child group completed its report by August, 1989. The report echoes and extends the thrust of the presentations made at the forum: "The theme of the committee's recommendations is that Native child welfare services are best delivered by Native people to Native people and that Native people must be given and take more responsibility and control over Native child welfare services" (Working Committees, 1989: 1).

A particular circumstance made the creation of a new child welfare unit possible. During 1988-89 the ministry had undergone a significant reorganization that resulted in the separation of the income assistance and child welfare functions. One consequence of this reorganization for Region B was the recognition by the ministry that its child welfare caseload was excessive when compared to other regions. Permission was then given to establish a new unit. A child welfare unit typically consists of a supervisor, four or five social workers, plus support staff.

However, the ministry did not direct Region B to use these resources to establish a child welfare unit to serve First Nation clients. No such directives had been issued to other regions, and at the time the ministry was attempting to transfer responsibilities for Native child welfare to First Nation bands rather than maintaining this function itself. The decision to use these new-found resources for a Native child welfare unit was a regional one, based on the conviction of senior staff in the region that services to First Nation clients "would be more acceptable to native people when delivered in the form of a native unit with culturally sensitive support services and resources" (Milowsky, 1991). This conviction was bolstered by a caseload analysis revealing that almost half of the clients served by Region B were Natives.

Clearly, the concept of convergence of interest is relevant and useful in explaining the development of the Native child welfare unit – the first and still the only such unit in the province. The leadership displayed by senior staff in Region B confirms the position taken by some students of the policy-making process that local-level service delivery units have the potential to assume a much larger role in policy-making than is usually assigned to them. I return to this issue in the concluding section of the chapter.

The report of the working committee contained thirty-five recommendations. It was submitted by the regional manager, Fred Milowsky, through the appropriate structures of the ministry. By October the minister had approved the establishment of the Native child welfare unit. A sample of the recommendations most pertinent to family and child services and the outcomes that have been achieved to date are listed below.

1. That a Native child welfare unit be established in Region B.
   Outcome: The unit was established and staffed in March, 1990.
2. That there be Native participation in the hiring (panelling) process for all staff.
   Outcome: Two First Nation members of the working committee, Gloria Nicolson and Marg White, participated in the selection process.

3. That ideally all staff in the unit would be Native. It is recognized practically that this goal would need to be achieved over time.
   Outcome: The supervisor, the support staff, and half of the social work complement are Native.
4. That a Native liaison position be funded to facilitate the flow of communication between the Native community and the Ministry of Social Services and Housing. One way of doing this would be to organize community meetings at six-month intervals.
   Outcome: The liaison position has been funded on a contract basis, and three community forums have been held.
5. That a Ministry of Social Services and Housing Native resource worker be hired to seek out and encourage the participation of more Native foster parents.
   Outcome: This position was approved, and funds have been allocated for a foster care recruitment video for recruiting Native foster homes.
6. That the Native unit would ideally stand alone and not be housed with other ministry Family and Child Service units.
   Outcome: The Native unit moved to its own building in August, 1991.
7. Dollars should be made available by the Ministry of Social Services and Housing to fund a Native organization to assist, support, and counsel Native parents whose child or children are the subject of an investigation or apprehension under the Family and Child Service Act.
   Outcome: A contract has been awarded to the United Native Nations to provide family support services to these Native families.
8. Training of ministry social workers in the areas of Native culture, heritage, and traditions should be recognized as a primary need, and the ministry should develop ongoing training programs for new and experienced workers.
   Outcome: The ministry, with funds from the Native Education Centre, offered training workshops for over 400 ministry staff in 1990.
9. That the ministry provide funds to hire a day-care developer to assist Native organizations in establishing day-care spaces and new centres.

Outcome: The responsibility for day-care development was assigned to a resource development worker and a First Nation Daycare Society has been formed.

10. That the ministry contract with a Native organization to operate a Native-run job action program to assist aboriginal people in making the transition from welfare dependency to job entry, training, education, or regular full-time employment.

    Outcome: The Job Action Program was established in 1990.

11. That the ministry support the development of a Native Transition House.

    Outcome: A Native Transition House operated by the Helping Spirit Lodge Society was opened in May, 1991.

While it is obviously too early to judge the effectiveness of the unit, several indices augur well for success. First, in a ministry often characterized by low morale and frequent staff turnover, staff of the Native unit are enthusiastic about and committed to their work. In my visit to the unit in October, 1990, both social work and support staff reported that this is the best office they have ever worked in, and several staff members are veterans of the ministry. They went on to talk about the mission – to work with and provide services to a group of people who have rarely received satisfactory services from the ministry. Thus there is an identification with a cause, a sense of being different and distinctive. The distinctiveness is revealed in part by the way clients are treated – as friends, rather than people with problems.

Second, staff see themselves as innovators and creators. Rather than simply and only implementing established policy, the Native unit is helping the ministry to develop policy for Native child welfare. Examples include the need for ministry staff to visit the band when arranging the placement of an Indian child and to spend time with family and band members.

Third, the unit has assumed a responsibility to identify cultural norms and practices of Natives and to transmit this knowledge to other staff in the ministry. For example, Native funerals are lengthy and full of ceremony, not simply brief church-centred events. Ministry staff who work with Native children and family must be aware of such cultural differences in arranging for foster children to attend the funeral of a parent or grandparent.

The unit is thus a unique place to work. The characteristics that make it unique include the commitment to a mission and being allowed by the ministry to take charge of this mission. The unit is not simply one of many child welfare offices in the ministry but has an opportunity to develop policy and practice in Native child welfare and to educate other staff about Native traditions and values.

It should be emphasized that the unit is nested within a supportive region and ministry. Indeed, given the explicit mandate of the unit to focus on children in care, the responsibility of pursuing other recommendations in the report (the development of an Indian day-care centre, a transition house for Native women, a job-training program for Native youth, and family support services for Native families whose children are before the court) has fallen to management staff in the regional office. These staff members have entered into partnership arrangements with a number of Native organizations, which develop the service or program while ministry staff work in the background finding resources and dealing with the bureaucratic requirements of their and other ministries. The partnership has been effective, as can be seen from the list of accomplishments noted above.

Particular attention should be paid to the fact that these services have not only been developed by Native organizations but are owned by them. Thus the Transition House will be owned and operated by the Helping Spirit Lodge Society and the professional development workshops for ministry staff were planned and provided by the Native Indian Friendship Centre. These developments are consistent with and implement the theme of the committee's report as cited earlier. It may well be that at some point in the future, ownership of the unit will be transferred to a Native organization, as has occurred in the Yukon.

THE CHAMPAGNE/AISHIHIK PROJECT

The Champagne/Aishihik band in the Yukon has succeeded in gaining control of child welfare services. There are some similarities and differences between this project and the Native Child Welfare Unit. The essential similarity between the two projects is that both recognized that child welfare policy and programs as developed by white policy-makers and delivered by white social workers are completely inappropriate for First Nation families. The extent of the lack of fit between white policy and programs and the needs of Natives has already been described and does not require repetition here, except to emphasize that the small population of the Champagne/Aishihik band and its location in two towns in the Yukon heightened the awareness of band members of the impact of non-Native child welfare services on the lives of band members. The initiative to gain control of child welfare services in this project came from community leaders with the support of child welfare professionals.

The principal difference between the two projects concerns the clients and the communities in which the projects are located. The Champagne/Aishihik band consists of approximately 700 people; of this relatively small number, 162 reside outside the Yukon. The vast majority of the band members live in only three communities: Whitehorse (279), Haines Junction (152), and Canyon (33). The remainder of the band members who reside in the Yukon are scattered throughout the territory. Thus, all affected by the child welfare project in the Yukon are members of a single band and are governed by an elected chief and band council. The Champagne/ Aishihik child welfare project can be characterized as a classic case of locality development, a project that affected a relatively small group of people who shared common values and traditions, who perceived a common problem, and who took collective action to resolve this problem.

The aboriginal clients of social services in Vancouver come from a large number of bands from across the province and do not have elected representatives to present their needs, though the United Native Nations attempts to represent the interests of aboriginal people living in Vancouver. The contrast between the size and characteristics of the Champagne/Aishihik community and Vancouver is obvious. Vancouver is Canada's third largest city and is home to residents from many different cultures and races. First Nation residents of Vancouver are typically young people attached to the city because of its promise of employment and excitement. Both promises go frequently unmet, and Native residents all too often live in the skid row sections of the city.

The Beginnings of the Project

The first public statement of the position of the Champagne/Aishihik band with respect to child welfare was released in 1973 as part of what was to be a seventeen-year struggle for the settlement of land claims in the Yukon. The statement is one of the first pronouncements by First Nation leaders that gaining control of child welfare services is of crucial importance.

> Many white men say we do not care for our children. They point to welfare, truancy and juvenile delinquency statistics to prove their point. Nothing could be further from the truth. The main concern of Indian parents is what is happening to our children. ... Please tell us what you are doing to our children, because they are breaking our hearts. We are accused of giving up our children for adoption and foster homes. If you gave us back control over our lives no Indian child would be in need of a home. Solutions to Indian problems must be found within the framework of our culture. This is why control and responsibility over social programs for Yukon Indians must be placed in the hands of the Yukon Indian people. (Yukon Native Brotherhood, 1973)

No further action on the child welfare issue occurred until 1980, when, as part of the continuing discussion on land claims, the territorial Department of Health and Human Resources prepared a paper outlining several options for providing child welfare services to First Nation people in the Yukon. The options included hiring more Native staff members, forming Native advisory committees, developing legislation to transfer responsibility to First Nation band councils, and establishing a pilot project. The latter option proposed that all social services for Natives be consolidated and be administered by bands in a manner that would respect Native values and traditions. Although the department favoured this option, the attention of the government was focused on land claims and later on the larger child welfare issue of legislative reform.

The first Yukon Land Claims Health and Social Programs Agreement in Principle was signed in November, 1982. The agreement provided First Nations with the opportunity to participate in planning and delivering health and social services, and Section 6.11 allowed the territorial government to delegate these services to Indian bands or to a central Indian authority.

During this same period the Department of Health and Human Resources was engaged in a review of its child welfare legislation, principally because of the need to include new provisions regarding adoption and regulations concerning the disclosure of adoption information. The first drafts of the new legislation contained no provision for delegation of authority to Native bands, and because of this omission the Council for Yukon Indians objected vigorously to the proposed new legislation. In February of 1984 the Council made a presentation to the cabinet of the territorial government in which the case for Indian control of child welfare services was advanced and defended. The Council emphasized that its support for the new Children's Act was contingent on the Act providing for delegation of authority, and such provision was included when the Act was proclaimed in May, 1984.

It is important to add that the concern about the inappropriateness of the child welfare services provided by the Department of Health and Human Resources was not confined to First Nation leaders and the Council for Yukon Indians. Staff of the department, including the deputy minister and the director of child welfare, were greatly disturbed by the lack of effectiveness of their programs for Native peoples. Caseload analyses revealed a similar picture to those in other jurisdictions, namely, the high number of Native children in care and the almost total lack of Indian foster homes. Thus, in 1985-86 there were 269 children in care in the Yukon, representing 3.6 per cent of the children under eighteen. Not only was this one of the highest percentages of any jurisdiction in the country, but it was accounted for in large part by the fact that between 70 and 80 per cent of the children in care were Natives.

In addition, several key members of the department came to their positions from backgrounds in social development and community work. They were therefore predisposed to consider the community context as being important, and their presence made for a sympathetic departmental environment with respect to the case for First Nation control of child welfare.

Finally, the Champagne/Aishihik band was uniquely positioned to advance its claims for control. The band has a history of economic success and stable government. In contrast to most other bands in the Yukon, the Champagne/Aishihik was not preoccupied with the chronic issues of poverty and unemployment but had the time, energy, and interest to devote to child welfare.

A number of factors thus converged to push the issue of child welfare onto the agenda in the Yukon. Representatives of the First Nations and of the territorial government were in agreement that the existing arrangements for providing services were unsatisfactory, and the extensive discussion over land claims resulted in a climate in which issues such as child welfare could be explored. Key political figures and senior bureaucrats in the Yukon live in close proximity and often know each other on a first-name basis. The closeness of the web of relationships was forcefully illustrated when an NDP government was elected in 1985. A First Nation woman, Margaret Joe, was appointed as Minister of Health and Human Resources. "Ms. Joe's husband and the chief's wife were brother and sister and her brother-in-law the legal advisor to the Band. Ms. Joe was personally committed to the position that natives should deliver child welfare services to their own people" (Hume, 1991). Her appointment signalled to all concerned that progress was to be achieved in transferring responsibility for child welfare to First Nations.

Prior to the passage of the Children's Act, the Champagne/Aishihik band and the Kluane tribal council requested that they be allowed to deliver all social services to their members living in their respective regions. This request mirrored the option favoured by the department in its discussion paper of 1980, but the department rejected it on the grounds that the legislation then in place did not allow for such a broad delegation of responsibilities. Nevertheless, the request served official notice to the department of the serious intent of the Champagne/Aishihik band to take control of social services, particularly child welfare. With the passage of the Children's Act and the provision for delegation, the band redoubled its efforts, but it was not until May, 1986, that a formal agreement for the transfer of responsibility was signed between Margaret Joe, the minister, and Paul Birckel, chief of the Champagne/Aishihik band. The objectives of the agreement were as follows:

a) To reduce the incidence of child neglect and abuse.

b) To support and strengthen families by providing services that promote the welfare of children.

c) To reduce the number of children removed from the custody of parents or persons entitled to the care and custody, pursuant to Part IV of the Act.

d) To facilitate the placement of children who are in need of protection with Indian families, preferably with other members of the child's extended family.

e) To facilitate, where appropriate, the return of children to the community and their extended family. (Champagne/Aishihik Social Services Society and the Yukon Territorial Government, 1986: 3)

The project was administered by the Champagne/Aishihik Social Services Society – a new society formed expressly for this purpose. The board of directors of the Society was comprised of the chief and councillors of the band, and regular reports were made at band council meetings on the progress of the child welfare project. The agreement specified that a number of committees would be established, and one, the Joint Band/Department Committee, met on a regular basis to identify and resolve management and resources problems that affected the project. The support and assistance provided by this committee were invaluable, particularly in the early days of the project.

As in the deinstitutionalization experience in New Brunswick, a set of principles proved to be invaluable in charting directions for the child welfare project. The principles reflected the values of the Champagne/Aishihik band with respect to families and child welfare. They were drafted by John Hoyt, who had been hired on a contract basis by the Department of Health and Human Resources to co-ordinate the delegation of social programs to Yukon First Nations, and by David Joe, legal adviser of the Champagne/Aishihik band. The principles were then reviewed and approved by the director of child welfare, the deputy minister and minister, and by the chief and council of the Champagne/Aishihik band. The advice of band elders was obtained at each stage of the drafting process. The principles are contained in the agreement that launched the project and are of sufficient importance to be included here.

Both parties to this Agreement accept the following principles as the basis of the Champagne/Aishihik Child Welfare Pilot Project.
a) All children need care, affection, nurturing and protection.
b) As a result of culture, geography and past history of Indian/non-Indian relations, Indian people have unique needs.
c) Promotion and support of cultural identity is of critical importance to members of the Society.
d) The family is the first resource for the nurture and protection of children, but some families need support for their parenting role, and children, for a variety of reasons, may need substitute care.
e) Any delegation of the powers of the Director should serve to:
  i) strengthen and unify the community through the provision of supportive services to families and children in need of protection;
  ii) encourage and assist the Society in the planning, designing and controlling of its own child and family support program requirements appropriate to traditional customs, culture and way of life;
  iii) create an environment that will eliminate those circumstances requiring the removal of band children from their homes; and
  iv) provide the mechanisms and related financial arrangements for the provision of child and family welfare services.
  (*Ibid.*: 2)

These principles guided the work of the first child welfare worker hired by the band. Frances Woolsey, a long-time resident of Haines Junction, filled the position of co-ordinator of child welfare services from 1986 to 1990. At the time of writing the band employs two child welfare workers: one resides and works in Whitehorse and the second in Haines Junction. Guided by the principles outlined above, Woolsey and Barbara Hume, supervisor of social services for the band, developed an approach that reframed child welfare from being primarily concerned with the protection of children to a recognition that "the family is the first resource for the nurture and protection of children." This change in focus to support for families has yet to occur in a fully formed fashion in Canada, and hence the practice approach developed by the Champagne/Aishihik band may well be in the forefront of child welfare practice in the country. Some of its distinctive characteristics are noted below.

First, the primacy of family care means that any form of substitute care is by definition secondary and temporary. Where family care breaks down the first response is to provide support in the form of counselling or temporary respite care by relatives or friends. If these responses are inadequate, a placement in a Native child-care home may be required. Thus the Champagne/Aishihik project has recognized that a number of short and temporary care arrangements may be necessary and that a pattern of care from parents to relatives to child-care homes and back to parents is preferable to long-term substitute care. At first glance this flowing pattern of care, involving frequent moves, may be viewed as a fundamental violation of the principle of permanent planning. However, this pattern contains the distinct benefit of ensuring that children remain in their community, can attend the same school, and can keep their friends. For the Champagne/Aishihik and other Native bands, this pattern is infinitely preferable to a permanent placement in a white foster home.

Second, the assistance of family and relatives is sought when parents experience problems. Family meetings are initiated and chaired by the child welfare co-ordinator to plan for the care of the children and to resolve the difficulties facing parents. In turn, this planned involvement of family members and friends transforms the private matter of child welfare to a community concern. The holding of family meetings and the smallness and the self-contained nature of the Champagne/Aishihik community, particularly in Haines Junction, mean that awareness of behaviour becomes an integral part of a community-based approach to child welfare. Since they live in the small communities in which they work, child welfare staff have a comprehensive and detailed knowledge of families and child-care. They extend this knowledge by regular contacts with the principal and counsellor in the local school to review the progress of children.

Third, this approach to practice requires community-based resources. In Haines Junction and Whitehorse, Indian child-care homes have been established.

To summarize, the practice approach in the Champagne/Aishihik band is characterized by:

- establishing trust with the parents and the child;
- identifying the needs and the strengths in the family;
- indicating acceptance of parents, but insisting that they own the problem;
- together with the parents, and with the extended family if necessary, developing a plan of action;
- identifying resources in the community, connecting families to these resources, and providing supportive counselling.

The agreement specified that an evaluation of the project would be carried out at the end of two years. The objective of the evaluation was to provide information on the effectiveness of the project and was seen as one of the crucial components in deciding whether to continue the project on a permanent basis or to disband it. The evaluation was conducted by Andrew Armitage, Frances Ricks, and this writer from the University of Victoria and Elizabeth Lane, a human resources consultant and resident of Whitehorse.

The evaluation concluded that the project had been successful. The team noted that no serious cases of child neglect and abuse had occurred during the two-year period under review. Eighteen children had been taken into temporary care with the agreement of the parents. None of these agreements required the involvement of the family court, and thirteen children were returned to parental care. The evaluation concluded that the overall objective of the project, to support family and to keep children in the Champagne/Aishihik community, had been achieved. In April, 1989, a new three-year agreement was signed between the band and the Yukon government, confirming the continuance of the project as a social service program with core funding.

SOCIAL REFORM AND SOCIAL POLICY

It is clear from the foregoing that the Champagne/Aishihik band council did influence social policy in the Yukon by its insistence that it, as the governing body for its members, was the appropriate authority to provide child welfare services. The tenacity of the council in promoting this vision, coupled with a relatively receptive climate within the Department of Health and Human Resources and a newly elected NDP government, eventually produced a successful, ongoing project. The convergence of interest becomes complete when credible organizations succeed in getting their issues on the policy agenda and then implemented. Similarly, representatives of First Nation peoples and a receptive Ministry of Social Services and Housing combined to establish a Native child welfare unit in Vancouver.

THE CONCEPT OF COMMUNITY AND COMMUNITY CONTROL

The two child welfare projects discussed in this chapter yield some interesting insights about the concept of community. In turn, these insights have implications for practice. Both projects are located in the communities they serve and are accessible, in the language of the Seebohm Commission in England, within "pram-pushing distance of clients" (Committee on Local Authority and Allied Social Services, 1968). Such a location is essential for accessibility, and it also enhances the likelihood that staff members will see, listen to, and address the needs of the community. Certainly this capacity to hear the voice of the community and respond to it is present in the Champagne/Aishihik project. Staff live in the community and the services are governed by the band council. But even in Vancouver, location is one way of promoting identification with community and clients. It is, of course, reasonable to inquire whether decentralized locations always enhance connections with community, and the response here is that it is a necessary but not sufficient condition. Needed, too, are staff members who identify with their clients and their community. In both projects, recruiting and retaining staff who are committed to the cause of working with Natives and who are sensitive to Native values and traditions are crucial for effective services.

The two key ingredients identified thus far are a community base that promotes accessibility for clients and staff who are so committed to the enterprise that they can use their community base as a way of learning about and responding to community needs. A third ingredient, found only in the Champagne/Aishihik example, is community control of services. Some communities can govern child welfare services, and the Champagne/Aishihik example is supported by the experience of a number of band and tribal councils across the country that have assumed control of child welfare services (see, for example, Hudson, 1980; Hudson and MacKenzie, 1984; Tester, 1985).

The Champagne/Aishihik band does not completely control its child welfare services. The band is subject to the authority of the territorial legislation governing child welfare and is funded by the territorial government. The arrangement represents an example of delegated control, which in Arnstein's classification of eight levels of citizen participation constitutes the second most extensive degree of control (Arnstein, 1969: 216). Indeed, it would be neither feasible nor desirable for communities to obtain full control. Local communities, as a rule, cannot raise the necessary funds; also, provincial legislation and standards are required to ensure that minimum standards with respect to the care and safety of children are met.

In a recent issue of *The Northern Review* devoted to the social services, Frank Cassidy outlines several potential benefits of community control:

- People are more sensitive to their own needs.
- Community organizations have more access to local information; they frequently "have the advantage of a long memory and of the collective family histories of those most deeply involved" in various activities.
- Commitment to and the chance of success are greatly strengthened when those who have to live with the outcomes of governmental activities are involved in decisive ways in such activities.

- The need for transactions between external and local parties is reduced, and, as a result, programs and services tend to be more appropriate, efficient, and effective.
- More integration between government strategies, programs, and services takes place, as citizens rather than bureaucracies assert their needs.
- Involved publics are more aware of community problems and the resources that might be available to address them. (Cassidy, 1991)

It can be argued with some conviction that the Champagne/Aishihik project has realized all of these potential benefits. There are, of course, some negative aspects of community control, and some limitations have been noted above. The principal downside is that small, isolated, and relatively self-contained communities can become worlds unto themselves. I have recorded elsewhere the distressing example of Kings County in rural Nova Scotia as an extreme example of "acute localitis" (Montgomery, 1979). This condition takes the form of local standards and conditions unconnected and unrelated to those prevailing outside the community. In one isolated area of Kings County the condition resulted in residents setting their own standards of child care and in frequent incidents of incest and sexual abuse of children. Provincial legislation, standards, and monitoring are required to ensure that the condition of acute localitis does not occur.

CONNECTING POLICY AND PRACTICE

The Vancouver and Champagne/Aishihik projects, in pointing to the significance of values and principles for connecting policy and practice, support the conclusions of Chapter 2. While the principles underlying the Vancouver project were not as carefully elaborated as in the Yukon, the objectives of the two were essentially similar: return control of child welfare services to First Nation people, and in so doing recognize the importance of cultural values in child welfare. As noted earlier in this chapter, the principles enunciated in the agreement between the band and the Yukon territorial government gave clear direction to practitioners. From the experience of deinstitutionalization in New Brunswick and from these two projects, an adaptive approach to policy implementation is clearly preferred in the human services. The characteristics of the adaptive approach are: freedom to change policy and adopt new strategies during implementation; clear statement of policy that enunciates guiding principles for practitioners; delegation of responsibility to local-level delivery units; inclusion of representatives of outside groups and staff in the policy process.

The adaptive approach was used in both projects. In Vancouver the minister and senior staff of the Ministry of Social Services and Housing allowed Region B to take control of the development and the subsequent operation of the Native child welfare unit. However, as noted in the account of this unit, its geographic and service boundaries are quite narrow, and the unit functions within the overall context of the ministry. By contrast, the agreement between the Champagne/Aishihik band and the Yukon government has delegated responsibility for child welfare to the band, although the territorial government retains overall legislative authority.

A second point flowing from the Champagne/Aishihik project reinforces an observation made in Chapter 3 about the integration of policy and practice in the Social Planning Council of Metropolitan Toronto. It was noted in that chapter that integration is easier in small organizations where both policy-makers and practitioners are involved in all phases of the policy process. Certainly this is the case with respect to child welfare in the Champagne/Aishihik band. Both band council and staff members are knowledgeable about the social problems of the community. Staff are expected to provide leadership in suggesting new policies, but their recommendations are made to a concerned and informed group of elected council members. While such closely knit systems of government can result in the problems of acute localitis where new ideas are resisted and old habits die hard, there is no doubt that small-scale organizations enhance the integration of policy and practice.

CONNECTING THEORY AND PRACTICE

In common with the other case studies, the projects reviewed in this chapter were carried out in a highly pragmatic fashion. None of the key child welfare staff could identify a specific set of theories or frameworks that guided their practice. Regional manager Milowsky described his approach to practice as follows: "My instincts told me to be open, to listen and to trust the process and the people I was working with. In fact, when I made a mistake it was usually because I tried to control the process rather than facilitate and trust the process" (Milowsky, 1990). Milowsky's observation applies equally well to the approach to practice in the Champagne/Aishihik project and is reminiscent of practice in the New Brunswick projects described in Chapter 2. Both the New Brunswick and the child welfare projects were anchored in clear values and implemented in an adaptive fashion. Policy and practice were folded together in a way Lindblom would describe as incremental (Lindblom, 1968) and Elmore as backwards mapping (Elmore, 1982). These descriptions of the policy process were outlined in some detail in Chapter 2 and are reviewed again in Chapter 7. One issue for the final chapter is how to connect these explanations of the policy process to the practice of community work.

Despite the acknowledged pragmatic rather than theoretical approach in these two projects, it is apparent that both included all of the approaches identified by Rothman. They sought to enhance, and in large measure succeeded in enhancing, the problem-solving capacity of the community (locality development), and in so doing they solved substantive social problems (social planning), shifted power relationships (social action), and improved social policies and programs (social reform). However, the strategies employed were those of negotiation and co-operation. While Rothman acknowledged the need for mixing both approaches to practice and the strategies usually associated with them, these two projects tend to confirm O'Brien's observation (noted in Chapter 1), which is supported by Chris McNiven: "the realities of practice cut across the Rothman models to the extent of obliterating their boundaries" (McNiven, 1979). Hence, from the experience of these community work projects in child welfare it is suggested here that the Rothman framework is not helpful as a guide to practice. I return to the Rothman framework in the final chapter and examine its utility from the experience of all of the case studies.

However, a number of connections to the literature on community work can be established. As noted throughout the chapter, these projects confirm the utility of the concept of convergence of interest. In both projects, those proposing the change not only possessed the legitimacy of their positions but were committed to the transfer of child welfare to First Nations.

Both projects conform to the themes of enhancing competence and strengthening social provisions identified by Perlman and Gurin. In a very real sense these projects have been all about self-determination and empowerment, which involved not only enhancing the capacity of First Nation people to care for their children but restored a sense of pride in First Nation values and traditions.

CONNECTING SOCIAL WORK AND COMMUNITY WORK PRACTICE

Again, the congruence with the case studies in New Brunswick is striking. The generalist approach to social work practice can comfortably include community work when the latter is devoted to developing resources for individuals and families. Individual service plans did not guide the practice of staff in the child welfare projects, but despite their absence practice proceeded in much the same fashion as in New Brunswick. It seems reasonable to suggest that when community work is concerned with meeting the needs of individuals it is congruent with social work practice. However, when divorced from individuals and concerned with surveys of need, research, and policy analysis, community work moves away from the generalist approach to practice and into the realm of specialized social planning. The connections between social work and community work practice form the content of Chapter 8.

CHAPTER V

Abortion Advocacy in a
Canadian Community:
Organizing to Gain Control of
Abortion Policy and Services

*by Marilyn Callahan and
Carol Matthews*

WHY A CHAPTER ON ABORTION AND COMMUNITY ORGANIZATION

This chapter documents the story of abortion politics and community action in one community in Canada, Nanaimo, British Columbia. Without doubt, similar events have occurred in many other communities in the country and this account certainly has national relevance. It is an important story to record and analyse for several reasons. First, at the national level, the abortion debate has been drawn in the media with very broad strokes: feminist women firmly united on one side; religious fundamentalists, Roman Catholics, and anti-feminist women on the other. However, in a small city of 54,000 people, the situation is not nearly so simple. Women with feminist sympathies may work on both sides of the issue. Their allegiance to one side or another and the results of their efforts are much more visible to themselves and to their neighbours. This case study is an excellent example of community action by women on behalf of women, and augments the scanty literature on women's contributions to community organization (Mayo, 1977; Dominelli, 1990; Wine and Ristock, 1991).

Second, this case study provides an opportunity to examine what happens when communities are asked to address social policies that extend beyond their usual boundaries. Decisions made at the community level usually concern those issues that residents share in common by virtue of the fact that they live in a similar geographical area: land use, commercial development, social amenities, public services. Abortion is different. It is a hotly contested social issue involving legal and human rights and deeply held beliefs about women, children, sexual relations, and reproductivity. Traditionally, such controversial issues of fundamental importance have been decided by the national government.

It was something of an accident that the abortion issue was fought at the local level. In 1988, when the Supreme Court struck down Section 251 of the Criminal Code on the basis that it violated the Charter of Rights and Freedoms, the country was left without criminal legislation dealing with abortion. In the absence of any national consensus, the decision fell to local hospital boards. In fact, each side of the debate (Pro-Choice and Pro-Life) has an argument about where abortion should be decided, and neither favours the community level. The Pro-Choice group believes that women should make their own decisions about abortion and that it is not a matter for legislation. The Pro-Life group believes the decision should be made by the federal government and enshrined in criminal law. However, this "accident of history" and the furore it created across the nation provide the opportunity to sharpen our notions about community decision-making and community control.

Finally, this study is noteworthy for the absence of social workers, in spite of the crucial importance of abortion policy in their work. The lack of social work involvement in this local contest relates at least in part to fears about becoming visibly involved in political processes. By doing so, social workers could alienate clients, on the one hand, and potential or actual employers or funders, on the other. Thus, because of this real or imagined danger, service providers who have a wealth of information about the actual situation facing women have had little voice in the policy debate. For female social workers, this is another example in which women's service to others negates their participation in the larger political process. They are silenced, and their experience is not considered. Historically, their work in the private sphere of the family disqualified them from political leadership; in this case, their caring work in the public sphere similarly prevented participation in the abortion debate.

We began this study determined to concentrate on the process of change that occurred and to put aside the actual question of abortion. In this we were only marginally successful. Through our interviews with ten key informants in the community we soon became aware that each of them had a profound commitment to the issue and we began to explore with them the reasons for their convictions. For these women, beliefs about abortion were deeply connected to personal experiences: because of personal experiences, they were committed to action. In their individual stories, they described these commitments.

Beryl Bennett, a retired nurse and hospital administrator, had been the head nurse on a gynecology ward during the war. She saw the results of disastrous abortion attempts by frightened married women whose husbands were away at war. These usually law-abiding women were willing to break the law and risk their lives to preserve their families. Some died. She also noted the hypocrisy of the law: for influential and well-to-do women, abortions and tubal ligations were performed regularly under the general rubric of "appendectomies," while less advantaged women had to risk illegal abortions. In the face of this evidence, Beryl came to a deep belief that abortion could not and should not be legislated. She has acted forcefully on the issue for more than forty years.

Sile Simpson-McGowan was a young woman in Ireland when she desperately needed an abortion. She had been raised an "illegitimate child" and, knowing the pain of this experience, was not prepared to continue a pregnancy. With great difficulty, she finally found the connections and funds to leave home and have an abortion in England. In the beds beside her were women from South Africa, Scotland, and Portugal, all as desperate and as fortunate as she was. At once she felt that abortion was both a personal and an international issue of social injustice, and she has worked for choice causes since then.

Mary Dunstan was only four years old when her mother cuddled her on her lap and let Mary feel the movement of her unborn sibling. Mary says that she knew then that life began well before birth. She also discovered that we have many resources to deal with unexpected birth; her mother had five children under five years of age and coped with each new child by simply "putting another potato in the pot." Mary is the founder of Birthright in Nanaimo and has been a volunteer there for fourteen years.

Wendy Barta, the youngest of our correspondents, made her commitment to the Pro-Life movement when she realized that the absence of an abortion law meant that second and third trimester abortions could occur regularly. This realization, coupled with the imminent birth of her first child, made a powerful impression on her. She became convinced that life begins at conception, and she began to feel that she had a moral responsibility to defend human life through her Pro-Life work.

Clearly all these women, and the others we interviewed, were unlikely to change their beliefs or to withdraw from the issue, and we were soon aware that the story of their actions could only be understood in the context of these deep convictions. It is a central belief in the women's movement that "the personal is political," and the significance of this connection was evident in the way our informants perceived their personal experience as motivating and empowering them to take political action.

Although we had always supported Pro-Choice causes, our own involvement in the Nanaimo story had been relatively modest. To gain a balanced view of events, we posed the same questions to ten informants, reviewed files and press clippings, interviewed a reporter who covered the issue at the time, and sent a questionnaire to social workers in the area. However, the research process itself was not without impact. Despite our attempts at neutrality, by asking questions we stimulated further activity on both sides of the issue. When we posed the final question to our informants – "What are you doing now?" – members of the Pro-Choice group remarked that they had intended to call a meeting or phone a colleague and must get on with it. Whether because of us or not, the temporarily inactive Pro-Choice group held a meeting shortly after our interviews with them. The Pro-Life members seemed already hard at work, but they did issue a press release shortly after our interviews.

FEMINIST COMMUNITY ORGANIZING

This case study is an example of feminist organizing at the community level and as such differs in some ways from other definitions of community work identified in Chapter 1. Feminist community work is founded on the central belief that power imbalances in society created by patriarchal, capitalist traditions are fundamentally responsible for the oppression of women. The overall aim of community work is to challenge and change these traditions (Dominelli, 1990). Thus the issues of concern to feminist community workers may differ from those defined by other community activists. Feminist community work also aims to change traditional approaches to community organizing. It is based on the assumption that women must have full participation in the institutions and processes that shape their lives so that these can be changed or replaced in ways that are compatible with women's needs. New forms of practice, such as consciousness-raising, collective organizational structures, the development of a social movement, and building connections with other oppressed groups, are a part of feminist community organizing.

Given this overall definition, feminist community organizing takes on many different shades. At least two different continuums describe different dimensions of feminist community organizing. The first of these is based on the degree of change sought for women and the forum for action – from the geographical community, to a local community of interest, to a national political community. At one end of this continuum is the long tradition of women working in women's groups to make communities better places for themselves and their families. These efforts do not rely on any explicit analysis of power imbalances or gender inequities but instead are founded more on a sense of good citizenship. Often the organizations emerging from these efforts are traditional ones, although frequently women occupy leadership positions in them. The efforts of these women resemble the locality development approach identified by Rothman and outlined in Chapter 1. Nonetheless, women working in these groups often take the opportunity to set their own agendas for community improvement based on their own needs. In the middle of this continuum are women's organizations explicitly based on feminist analysis of the problems facing women and the intractability of community structures to deal with these problems. The aim is to create women-centred changes at the community level using feminist methods of organizing. The development of transition houses and sexual assault centres with their service and education components is an example of this kind of organizing. At the other end are women's organizations that aim to create full-scale national change by building blocks of support at the community level across the country. Such organizing has an explicit focus on broad social policies, not on community change as such. One feature of this type of organizing is the importance of developing connections among communities and their action groups so that their experiences can accumulate. The Canadian Association for the Repeal of Abortion Legislation is one such group. With its local chapters and their local efforts, CARAL has established a national voice.

The second continuum delineates differences in feminist community organizing based on different views about the nature of women and desired strategies of change. Vogel (1986), for instance, notes the historical difference between rational and romantic feminists. Rational feminists are those who believe that reason is the fundamental human quality that women, as well as men, possess, and thus women, like men, must have similar rights and freedoms to prosper. Romantic feminists emphasize the integration of reason and feeling, spirituality and sensuality, and emphasize diversity over uniformity, including the differences between men and women. The goal of the romantic feminists is independent femininity.

These different perspectives are not casual differences about the most effective ways of accomplishing women's freedom. They are deeply held views about women's relationship to the world and express woman's ambivalence about autonomy and collaboration, about isolation and integration.

> One way of describing the major differences and cleavages within contemporary feminist thinking is to apply to them the philosophical and historical categories by which we commonly distinguish between the political doctrines of Liberalism, Socialism and Marxism. However, some of the most characteristic and more impassionately argued divisions in the present debate among feminists cut across these familiar ideological boundaries. They can perhaps best be summarized in the contrast between a political and an aesthetic conception of women's liberation. Stated in a simplified form: whereas the former aims at ending women's oppression by political means (through changes in the legal and institutional structure of society), the latter is committed to a strategy of revolutionizing the very basis of personal experiences and intimate relationships, at the expense, so it may seem, of a retreat from politics. . . . the romantic position differs from the rationalist mainly in that it considers the political sphere as altogether marginal to the experiences and endeavours through which individuals (men as well as women) can realize their truly human potential. (Vogel, 1986: 19-20)

Adams (1989) has analysed two approaches to feminist organizing: identity politics and coalition politics, which correspond in part to the feminist orientations noted above. Identity politics arises from the romantic conceptions that women are best able to work on their own oppression from their own experience. The aim of identity politics is to attract more and more women to the feminist cause and to create significant social change through transforming relationships, one by one, woman by woman. Coalition politics, on the other hand, stresses the development of action groups with common ends that can join together and separate as the occasion demands. Adams makes the argument that, in fact, the women's movement has become a coalition over time because of the limitations of identity politics.

Vickers (1989) has traced some of these ongoing tensions between Canadian women and politics and argues for the value of both approaches. She observes that women, historically, have resolved the tensions between coalition and identity approaches in several ways. In earlier years women either remained unmarried and committed themselves wholeheartedly to participation in mainstream political organizations (Charlotte Whitton, for example) or created locally based women's organizations mostly for married women as an alternative political structure (the Women's Institute, the Voice of Women). Second-wave feminists have debated these strategies of separation and integration, have tried both, and have found them wanting. Separate feminist political systems often fail to influence mainstream structures; integrating into mainstream political structures obscures and frequently marginalizes the contributions of the few women involved. Vickers suggests that a third vision, transformation, is proving more useful for individual women and for women's groups. In this approach, feminism is viewed as an overarching agenda and an ongoing process rather than an achieved state. It is also recognized that there is no one best way to tackle that agenda. Thus the debate about whether women should work alone in their own groups or join with coalitions and whether women should work on the outside or on the inside is viewed as fruitless and distracting. Instead, if the aim is to transform institutions and social processes, then women must tackle change on all fronts in different ways.

As we probed women's experiences in community organizing, we uncovered the importance of both these continuums. Women aimed for different goals at different levels of change. They also had profoundly different views on the nature of the women's movement and the preferred approaches for change.

THE CONVERGENCE OF INTERESTS

This case study could be limited to the highly visible events of the recent two-year period in which Pro-Choice and Pro-Life forces battled for control of the Nanaimo hospital board. Indeed, one politician described the recent Nanaimo abortion debate as a partisan political battle between the Socreds and the New Democrats, rather than as a case of women struggling for control over their reproductive rights. But political issues do not emerge on their own accord; social problems become acknowledged as political issues only after becoming the focus of attention of individuals and groups whose work, usually over many years, pushes them into the political sphere.

Abortion is no exception, and it is by no means a new issue in the Nanaimo community. Historian Lynne Bowen (1991) cites early records of an "inquisition" into a case of suspected abortion in 1886. This report tells the story of a woman who died after attempting an abortion by three methods: using a syringe; consuming a variety of powders (quinine, morphine, and potassium bromide); and drinking a concoction of warm beer and ginger. The report of the inquest contains references to a doctor who had a reputation for "helping women" but who didn't want to "go to prison for 65 years," a woman who was ready to walk the five miles from Wellington to Nanaimo to see her doctor and who was "not ashamed" of what she planned to do, as well as an unsympathetic husband and too many children. There were conflicting reports about these events from two women neighbours, and the charge was dropped because of insufficient evidence. In short, this report from over 100 years ago contains the same array of pain, hypocrisy, and conflict that we see in such cases today.

Although Nanaimo is not known as a forum for debate about the moral and legal status of abortion, Nanaimo women have been organizing on both sides of this issue for many years. As early as 1967, Beryl Bennett, the Nanaimo nurse we interviewed for this study, wrote the brief advocating abortion law reform that was presented by the National Council of Women to the House of Commons on December 8, 1967, just prior to the Trudeau abortion bill of 1968. At the same time, the newly formed Nanaimo Family Life Association was developing counselling services related to sexuality and parenting. In the two decades that followed, Nanaimo citizens developed a variety of organizations to grapple with problems of sexuality, reproductivity, and family life. These groups included Nanaimo Family Life, the Steps to Maturity Program, Nanaimo Women's Place, Planned Parenthood, Rape Relief, the Mid-Island Sexual Assault Centre, Nanaimo Women's Resources Society, Pro-Life of Nanaimo and District, Birthright, and Nanaimo Citizens for Choice, among others. A number of these organizations and the individuals who work with them have been involved not only in service provision but also in lobbying and public education for abortion law reform.

Our respondents identified two significant events that intensified the local conflict about access to abortion and increased their own involvement in action at the community level. First, as mentioned above, the Supreme Court struck down Section 251 of the Criminal Code in January, 1988, a judgement known thereafter as the Morgentaler decision as it ended, at least briefly, the long litigation between the courts and Dr. Henry Morgentaler and his abortion clinics. Pro-Choice forces applauded the decision and encouraged the federal government to abandon any further attempts to develop legislation. Second, in March, 1988, the Premier of B.C. and some of his cabinet attempted unsuccessfully to prohibit medicare funding for abortions in direct response to the Supreme Court decision. These actions were supported by Pro-Life forces, which lauded the Premier for his courageous stance.

As a result of these two decisions, the Nanaimo debate intensified. Pro-Choice and Pro-Life groups were quoted regularly in the media and the sharp divisions between the two positions were clearly demarcated. The media also portrayed the two levels of government at loggerheads with one another. At the provincial level, these decisions further politicized the abortion issue as the New Democrats favoured the Supreme Court decision and the ruling Socreds appeared to line up with the Premier and his Pro-Life position. Rejuvenated individuals and groups began further action and focused their energies quite logically at the community level. With no federal abortion legislation, and no capacity for the province to deny funding for abortions under medicare, then the likely target seemed to be community hospital boards, which could decide to maintain or discontinue abortions.

In Nanaimo the two groups soon squared off. Initially our respondents made or renewed individual commitments and undertook some individual action. Jan Pullinger, a Pro-Choice advocate, was elected as a provincial member of the Legislative Assembly in March, 1989. She made the abortion issue a high priority and stated that she felt her activities were consistent with her party's commitment to women's rights. Shirley LeBrasseur, a public health nurse who was previously reluctant to take a strong stand on abortion, reflected on the Supreme Court decision and rekindled her commitment. For her, if the highest court in the country determined that abortion law contravened the Charter of Rights and Freedoms, then she could defend the right to abortion not only from a feminist perspective but also from a legal and human rights position. Beryl Bennett, a long-time Social Credit supporter, and Sile Simpson-McGowan, an NDP member, were both infuriated by the Premier's attempt to tamper with abortion funding. Beryl wrote a letter to the Premier; Sile organized an impromptu but successful protest outside the Social Credit constituency office. Wendy Barta made her first commitment to the cause on the Pro-Life side by organizing Pro-Life forces in small communities north of Nanaimo. She brought her organizing skills and experience to Nanaimo when she moved to that city a short time later.

These individual commitments and actions soon moved to a second stage: group organizing. The Pro-Choice voice first emerged from a fledgling organization begun by Sile, Cathy Holland, Barbara Hourston, and others: the Concerned Citizens of Nanaimo for Choice. This group organized a trek to the Pro-Choice rally in Victoria in the summer of 1988, which among other outcomes identified individual and group support. The work of this coalition was also supported by a more established feminist group, the Nanaimo Women's Resources Society. The Pro-Life organization emerged from several Christian churches in Nanaimo. It was led by a Christian pastor and supported primarily by members of the congregations.

The two groups differed on several dimensions. The Pro-Choice movement was composed of a loosely knit collection of groups and individuals, most of whom were women and most of whom had a deep commitment to feminist issues and organizing approaches, including shared leadership and consensus-style decision-making. Initially there were few resources or structures to co-ordinate their efforts, and the most established group, the Women's Resources Centre, was busy with many other issues and projects. The Pro-Life forces had a more focused agenda and formal structure. They had established a local chapter of Pro-Life, with provincial and national affiliations. Further, their connection with the churches provided ready access to sympathetic supporters and communication systems. Although women constituted the majority of the members, the leadership was vested in a male pastor with an authoritarian style. However, in other ways the groups were similar. Both shared a deep commitment to their cause and contained individuals willing to make outstanding personal contributions to the effort.

The Pro-Life forces won the first round. In June, 1989, when the annual hospital board elections were held, Pro-Life members turned out in full force and captured the majority of positions on the board of directors of the Nanaimo Regional Hospital Society. Wendy Barta observed that the achievement was not really a result of a highly organized campaign on the part of the Pro-Life forces. Instead, she thought it was a victory by default: the Pro-Life group was marginally better organized than Pro-Choice. In any case, the election prompted a continuation of vigorous activity from both sides.

A third period of intensive work followed the victory of the Pro-Life forces. The following year, from June, 1989, to June, 1990, was marked by a shift on the Pro-Choice side from more casual feminist organizing to intensive political campaigning. Pro-Choice was determined to win the next hospital board election. The Pro-Life forces were similarly determined to make this year a time for action. They began an intensive campaign directed at the sympathetic hospital board members that was designed to ensure that they followed through on their commitment to discontinue abortions. These two opposing and seemingly parallel efforts were actually very much intertwined, as action on one side prompted reaction on the other.

As early as September, 1989, the press reported that the hospital board was reviewing abortion policy. At an in-camera meeting, the board decided to establish three committees to examine the question, one of which was to survey medical staff. Although none of the committee reports was ever made public, it was known that the medical staff report did not favour a change in policy. Nonetheless, on December 7, the hospital board voted to rescind abortions effective January 1, 1990. Wendy Barta stated that board members were under intensive pressure from her group. She felt that it would have been wiser for Pro-Life to move slowly to ensure that sufficient support was forthcoming from several quarters. Others in her group favoured swift action and their opinions carried the day.

The hospital board announcement stunned Pro-Choice advocates. However, the swift, direct decision provided an excellent opportunity for organizing, and the Pro-Choice group lost no time in calling a meeting of concerned women from all political stripes and groups and in developing an action plan. From the first meeting of forty or more, the action group became about a dozen regular workers who could call on a larger cadre for specific tasks. After some discussions and minor disagreements, the group decided to adopt a traditional political organizing approach. Under the guidance of members of the Legislative Assembly, Jan Pullinger and Dale Lovick and their staffs, the core group worked backwards from the election day in July, identifying deadlines, tasks, and responsibilities. A great deal of the work involved finding sympathetic supporters and registering them as members of the hospital board society. The group also devoted energy to gaining public sympathy and ongoing publicity to maintain the momentum of their work. Another task was to find suitable and credible candidates to run for office. A final major assignment was to develop a plan for election day, including a scrutineering system, drivers, phone workers, and celebrations.

The vocal and persistent public outcry that followed the board's announcement in December resulted in a reversal of the policy by the hospital board at a meeting in January. The board decided that abortions would continue pending further review and also proposed a public referendum to provide greater public input. Both Jan Pullinger and Dale Lovick had publicly rebuked the board (Pullinger and Lovick, 1990) and the local newspaper had carried an editorial condemning the board's decision, which likely contributed to the reversal. In any event, the change in policy resulted in a much revitalized Pro-Life movement. At its January annual meeting, sixty members attended and action plans were developed soon after. The hospital board's indecisiveness led to a fevered political climate in the community and reinvigorated forces on both sides.

There are some interesting strategies that both groups used in an attempt to maintain public interest and garner public support. Both groups imported "outside" experts. The Pro-Life choice was very effective: Pat Hansard, founder of Abortion Recovery of Canada, carried out a speaking tour of Vancouver Island and was interviewed several times in the press and on radio because of her controversial message. Her group maintained that many women came to Abortion Recovery after an abortion with deep regrets, which she termed "abortion trauma syndrome." Although she provided anecdotal material to support her claims, she had very little other evidence. Nonetheless, her message was compelling and difficult to refute. It put the Pro-Choice group in a difficult position: could they say that women didn't care about having an abortion and that it left them with little concern afterwards? Through this strategy the Pro-Life group switched its focus from a long-standing concern with the fetus to a focus on the mother, the usual domain of Pro-Choice. Similarly, Pro-Choice could have raised the issues of child poverty and neglect, although they did not in fact do this.

In the same vein, Wendy Barta, the leader of the Pro-Life group, is the founder of Feminists for Life of Canada, an organization that proposes "a return to the roots of feminism which is a loving, nurturing response to human suffering, be it the suffering of women, men, the unborn, the aged, the handicapped, the poor, or the downtrodden minorities." Although the goals of the organization focus on providing information and advocacy to oppose abortion, the group also states its opposition to capital punishment, to offensive military action, to discrimination against individuals and minority groups, and to threats to the environment. Clearly such a stance is effective in diluting many Pro-Choice arguments.

In the end, the Pro-Choice forces were able to elect a majority of hospital board members at a crowded, annual general meeting in July. Although the victory brought both great pleasure and despair, the two groups realized the battle was far from won. The doctors immediately announced that they did not like becoming the target of such pressure and later announced that they would not perform abortions under the federal government's proposed new bill, C-43. Both groups were immediately engrossed in new work related to the bill, which won the favour of neither side. And the hospital board fight was far from over, as another election loomed the following year.

LESSONS AND CONNECTIONS

What was learned from this process? All the women we interviewed claimed that they had discovered a great deal from their organizational work on the abortion issue. Although there was, of course, considerable difference of opinion about what the lessons had been and about what they would do differently in future, there was general agreement that involvement in the process had taught participants a great deal. In this section, we will include the lessons identified by our informants, as well as our own observations about women and community organizing as seen in this case study.

1. *Women in this study held deeply ambivalent views about their involvement in social policy issues and political organizing.* Two general attitudes were evident, particularly in feminists in the Pro-Choice group. These correspond to the romantic and rational perspectives outlined at the beginning of this chapter. Women with a more rational stance were unequivocally in favour of placing social policy issues at the top of the feminist agenda and using formal political structures and methods of organizing to elect hospital board members sympathetic to maintaining abortion. Most of the women adopting this stance had worked within traditional institutional structures and hierarchical political organizations. These women did not feel that they were betraying feminist values by adopting political methods. Instead, they emphasized the need for women's groups to recognize how patriarchal political systems work and to be able to use it when necessary. Such action involved developing goals, structure, discipline, and alliances and providing technical training on political organization skills.

These rational feminists were frustrated in having to work with somewhat disorganized consensus models and seemingly naive approaches to political organization in the name of feminist philosophy espoused by more romantic feminists. This latter group believed that a truly egalitarian society will be created through an ongoing process of consciousness-raising, working in collectives, and consensus decision-making. They expressed some concerns that perhaps the "main prize" of women's liberation and empowerment might be lost in the interests of specific policy agendas and short-term political advantage. In this case, the crucial importance of abortion for women's freedom dispelled these concerns. However, in the process of creating change in abortion policy, these women believed that they must remain conscious of building a strong movement. In fact, short-term victories were seen as hollow if they alienated the women in the movement and denigrated their ways of working. For these women, events like marches, demonstrations, coffeehouses, billboards, and other forms of public education and engagement are crucial. The attitude of this group toward political organizing as a strategy for change is ambivalent. Some see it as necessary at times. Others feel that it is diversionary and that women can best win their victories through their unity together and through their joint action in changing relationships and attitudes.

Our informants did not divide neatly into these two perspectives. Most women had sympathy for both but exhibited a stronger identification with one or the other. However, in the process of working together, several women commented that they learned a great deal from each other. One of the women in the Pro-Choice group who had come from a political organizing background said she had never worked so closely with such committed feminists before and found the experience exciting and thought-provoking. Some feminists found political organizing, although foreign to their nature, a smart, swift piece of action for a time-limited endeavour.

The Pro-Life group also faced ambivalence from many members about the use of political organizing. Only a few women were feminists with a strong commitment to coalition politics. The majority were women with traditional beliefs about women's place in the home. They worked behind the scenes but were not fervently involved in policy development and strategic planning. Nonetheless, their strong beliefs about the issue similarly encouraged them to take risks and participate more openly than many had done before.

Although the women involved in this study held widely differing views about political involvement, they were able to put these aside and work together, at least within their separate camps. Undoubtedly this occurred because of the fundamental importance of reproductive issues for women of all political persuasions. Another reason for such co-operation relates to the size of the community. It was evident to all that there were finite resources. In larger communities women might join different groups that share their point of view. In smaller communities, such a division of resources is wasteful if not fatal to the cause. Nonetheless, these differences were not discussed among women in any explicit way in either the Pro-Choice or Pro-Life groups. The ongoing distance between the "radicals" and "mainstreamers" was evident in some of the remarks of our respondents in each group. Although there was clearly new-found admiration, some of the previous prejudices remained.

There were even some attempts to bridge the gaps between the Pro-Choice and Pro-Life groups. A newspaper reporter brought together feminist representatives of Pro-Choice and Pro-Life to seek out areas of "common ground," and while both sides described the meeting as a waste of time in terms of changing any positions, the journalist who organized the event suggested that maybe the act of being together helped to break down some of the fragmentation and to lessen the tendency to dehumanize each other. She wondered if this attempt at reconciliation might help some of these women unite on another front at another time.

2. *Coalition-building was required to ensure electoral victory but contained some longer-term risks.* Because the issue had been framed in terms of an election victory, organization and numbers were essential. Both groups noted the importance of effective coalition-building. The original action groups were often viewed as fringe groups: feminists and religious zealots. The more they could attract credible mainstream individuals and groups, the more their cause would seem a just one to a broader constituency. One aspect of coalition-building was to involve feminists of different perspectives. However, both sides needed to expand their constituencies beyond women. To do so, both sides developed a range of arguments and identified sympathetic constituencies. Pro-Choice supporters used the legal and human rights arguments to

attract a larger group of supporters. Moreover, because a political party, the New Democratic Party, was identified with the Pro-Choice position, the group was able to appeal to political allegiance as well. The Pro-Choice selection of Beryl Bennett as a speaker at their coffeehouse fund-raising event was an excellent strategy. Ms. Bennett was a long-standing and highly respected member of the community, a well-known nurse and medical administrator, and, most importantly, a supporter of the Social Credit Party. Those on the Pro-Life side added a feminist appeal to an ecumenical religious argument. They were also able to mobilize support from those with allegiance to the church, if not to the abortion cause. As noted above, the Pro-Life group also used the strategy of appealing directly to the other side's constituency by confounding arguments about the impact of abortions on women.

One of the clear lessons from this experience is the need for members of the original action group to ensure that their agenda and their perspectives are not irrevocably diluted in the quest for supporters. The Pro-Choice members noted that, in the end, their victory was not necessarily a feminist one. The candidates they recruited and supported were people who they believed would make a knowledgeable contribution to the board and who were "electable." However, they delegated the recruitment of candidates to someone outside their group. While the candidates were sound, several were physicians and nurses, and thus, unintentionally, the Pro-Choice efforts may have resulted in a more professional medical board with less broad community representation. The group did not use this opportunity to advance local feminist candidates and to further the feminist cause in the community.

3. The unintended consequences of organizing for abortion reform were as important as the stated agenda. One of the most significant lessons that many women learned was that, as individuals, they have the power to make a difference. Several women commented on the sheer exhilaration they felt when they realized that they could act and by that action affect the process of change: it was possible to organize a rally, take over an organization, or hold a debate without much help. Some women commented that they did not just gain satisfaction from the results of their actions but also from the sense of belonging they felt in their relationships with others. Despite the intensity of the issue and the feelings it generated, several women commented on the good times they had. Respondents also commented that while community action can have these benefits, it is also important to take care of themselves and others, even in the heat of the action.

One of the most substantial individual efforts in this instance was provided by the MLA, Jan Pullinger. It is often debated in feminist circles whether the few women in political life can make a difference. In this situation, Ms. Pullinger worked for Pro-Choice causes before her election and decided shortly afterwards to make it a priority of her term of office. She was fortunate to have the support of her political party but told us she did not really care whether she gained political kudos or not. She brought resources, expertise, and credibility to the fledgling Pro-Choice movement in the community. She took many risks and received a few menacing letters in the process. When the hospital board decided to discontinue abortions, she refused to meet with them and wrote a public letter to them explaining her strong opposition to their stance. The Pro-Life group stated that they felt greatly disadvantaged because of her tireless work and the credibility of her position, particularly in a small community. Both the Pro-Choice group and Ms. Pullinger noted the importance of forging a strong long-term relationship with one another for support, action, and further political successes. The major purpose of feminist organizing at the community level was the abortion issue. Unintentionally, it provided an opportunity to develop an action system for a feminist politician that could be mobilized on an ongoing basis for further issues and to advance women in political life.

Just as individuals can have an impact on change, members of both Pro-Choice and Pro-Life commented that they were surprised to learn how a small cohesive group can quickly stake out territory and become a force for change, sometimes much to the surprise of its fledgling membership. Long before the Pro-Choice group was anything except a very loose network of interested women, it had been named in the press and supporters had been identified. The group did not really become an organization until much later. As one respondent remarked. "When I read that the Pro-Choice Coalition held a rally, I thought, 'Hey, that's me and two friends. I didn't know we were official.'" Similarly, Wendy Barta stated that when she finally met the Pro-Life group, she found a small and largely inactive group, hardly the smoothly run powerful machine portrayed in the press. For this reason, our respondents commented that it is important not to make assumptions about the opposition until it has been honestly evaluated nor to underestimate the strength of a small single-minded group.

Several women also commented that, just as individual women needed to care for themselves, groups had to pay attention to group organization and to group process. One of the interesting strategies the Nanaimo Women's Resources Society used in this regard was evident at their 1989 annual meeting, held in the heat of the hospital board election planning. The organizers selected the theme of "Choice Care" and asked guest speakers to help the group create a vision about what an excellent community health care system for women might look like. The title was intended to convey a positive association with choice and good health care. The exercise of envisioning a better system greatly invigorated tired workers and, for a short time, they were able to leave their role as resisters and imagine what it might be like to make policy of their own. "Choice Care" buttons were sold and worn for a number of months.

Both the Pro-Life and Pro-Choice workers noted that although it is crucial to attract, engage, and involve a diverse group of individuals and organizations in the long-term process of change, the active working group will be smaller and more homogeneous. The challenge is to maintain space for different people with different degrees of time and commitment. Too often the working group disparages the broader support group, which in turn feels put down and left out by a core group of insiders.

Several respondents commented on the advantages of working in women's groups. Not only could the group set its own directions and develop its own structures, but also there was the possibility for women to take more risks, to ensure that their actions reflected women's perspectives on the issues, and simply to enjoy themselves. This comment is echoed by Dominelli and Jonsdottir (1988) in their examination of the feminist organizing of the Kwenna Frabothid political party in Iceland. They recount several examples of spontaneous, women-designed actions. On one occasion when a politician said that any woman should be able to feed her family on her wages, the women went to a local supermarket (with the press). They presented the cashier with the ingredients for rice pudding and tried to pay only two-thirds of the actual cost, the proportion of their salaries in relation to those of men. When the mayor, presiding at a beauty contest, said that if the women of the KF were as beautiful as these contestants he would not have a chance to win the next election, the women of the KF held a beauty contest of their own. The contestants used a beauty contest format (without swimsuits) to present their credentials for public office. The mayor did not win.

However, at crucial stages in the change process, the action group must choose its strategies carefully so that its coalition is not alienated. After its defeat in the 1990 hospital board elections, the Pro-Life group held a vigil outside the hospital. Members carried white crosses and carnations to symbolize the souls that had been aborted. This strategy was probably appropriate for the time: the election was over and the group was interested in attracting core members to its cause. It would have been inadvisable prior to the election when less fervent supporters would be reminded of the fervently religious aspects of the movement.

4. *Passionate and irresolvable debates can have deleterious as well as positive effects in small communities.* Several negative consequences were reported by some of our respondents. One woman said that she did not want to attend the International Woman's Day rally because she had taken a Pro-Life stance and feared she would be shunned. Other women commented that the long-standing abortion debate continues to take a heavy toll on women: not only are they divided from one another but the energies of their groups are funnelled into the ongoing battle. One woman commented that it was important to identify the enemy correctly: the patriarchal system and indecisive politicians, not local community women. She felt that by making this distinction, women could maintain their solidarity and work on other issues together in the future. While a useful sentiment, the fact remained that women on either side referred to each other derogatorily and had clearly stereotyped each other.

Although these consequences are undoubtedly real, it is also true that the debate on abortion stimulated a kind of activity that seldom takes place in a local community. As mentioned in the introduction, most local debates are about sewers and roads and land use, rarely about social policy issues. This occurs primarily because local governments have little jurisdiction in social policy. Instead, those concerned about social policy issues either fulminate alone or join special interest groups. These latter groups may have local chapters, which are very small, even in large cities, and members may remain relatively isolated from the rest of the community. Instead, their attention is usually directed toward provincial and/or national linkages.

In this case, members of the community had to meet together and debate with one another because there was a local decision-making body to adjudicate the issue. The debate occupied a prominent place in the media and in the work of many groups. Moreover, many women who felt that political life was irrelevant to them became acutely aware of its importance. Participants learned that social policy issues are far from clear, that policy-making is a long-term process, and that individual people matter in the process of change. It is unlikely that they will view social policy-making (and makers) in the same light after this experience. It can be argued that social policy would be invigorated by similar debates on other issues at the local level. Over time, some of the negative consequences apparent in this case study may become less evident as community groups gain sophistication with the issues and the process and as community decision-making bodies obtain a clear mandate for their work. It is also true that the more social policy systems are moved to the local level, the more women can be involved in them.

5. *Social workers were not actively visible, in spite of the clear importance of the abortion issue to their clientele and their work.* We felt their apparent lack of involvement merited further investigation. What did practitioners see as the appropriate role for the individual social worker or for the social work profession in the debate about abortion? Did social workers believe that abortion legislation had significant consequences for social work practice? Were there factors that might have restricted or encouraged their involvement in this forum? To answer these questions, we asked for comments from local social workers employed in college, hospital, health, and public welfare settings.

Almost all who responded believed that abortion legislation has significant consequences for social work practice. A few noted that it was extremely important, particularly in terms of poverty, child welfare, family violence, family breakdown, and mental health. For them, the debate on abortion had important ethical, legal, practice, and resource implications. One respondent suggested that if legal abortions became unavailable, social workers might have to develop an "underground network" to provide client access to safe abortions. A few respondents indicated that the importance of abortion to social workers may depend on their area of practice, and while it was particularly important for women, it was not necessarily a priority for the profession.

Nonetheless, only six of the ten respondents thought that individual social workers or the professional association should take a role in the debate. Those who supported action noted that the social work role might include advocating for the rights of individuals to make informed choices, ensuring that women's reproductive rights are protected, modelling non-judgemental attitudes, working to increase women's options, and supporting the choices they make. Some of these respondents also thought that the profession should speak on behalf of the client groups. One respondent suggested that the profession could advocate a human rather than a political approach to the debate that might be espoused by both sides: this approach could focus on concern for rights of individuals, good care for children, access to information regarding contraception, and support for families.

Social workers were no less personally enmeshed in the issue than were our other interviewees. One respondent stated that the B.C. Association of Social Workers had been "decidedly one-sided" in its position on abortion, although in fact the local branch has been inactive for several years and no statement was made by BCASW on the local issue. Another commented that to take a role in the abortion debate is risky from within the profession as well as outside it. Many noted that they experienced personal and professional constraints that prevented them from freely discussing the abortion question.

Indeed, the two main reasons cited by almost all respondents as influencing (either encouraging or restricting) social work presence in the debate were personal philosophy and the restrictions of employers. It was also suggested that making one's values public on this volatile issue might hinder one's ability to help people who disagree. One respondent commented that it is useful to have a professional association to speak on sensitive issues, and the lack of a local BCASW branch made it difficult for social workers to express themselves. Finally, it was noted that the effects of privatization and the dismantling of social services have separated social workers from one another and disrupted or discouraged support systems through which issues like abortion might have been discussed in the past.

Whatever their views on abortion, many social workers did take out membership and attend the annual meeting of the hospital society and at least a few worked to sell memberships in the society.

From their overall invisibility, their modest response to our questionnaire (only ten of twenty-one responded), and their generally divided views on the importance of professional involvement in the issue, it is clear that these local social workers generally separated their practice concerns from this policy matter. This separation was also evident in the responses of the practitioners we interviewed at Planned Parenthood and Birthright. Both of these women felt that public action was inappropriate for workers and volunteers in their organization. Social work was not the only profession silent on this issue. The professional associations of teachers, nurses, and physicians made no comments.

Although service providers and professionals are united in their view that it is too risky to involve themselves in the abortion debate, their silence poses some clear ethical issues. Social workers and others could provide information about the impact of abortion or the absence of abortion and family planning services in the local community based on significant experience. Should the community not have access to this knowledge? Has the debate become so political precisely because there is an absence of such experience and information provided by professional members of the community? Has "speaking out" become synonymous with political action rather than public education?

It is interesting to speculate what social workers could have said about abortion that would have made a difference yet maintained their need for impartiality. For instance, they could have used the opportunity to raise the issue of the care of children in the Nanaimo community. How many were living in poverty? How many had inadequate or non-existent care arrangements? How many were bearing children themselves? In this way, the narrow issue of abortion could have been transformed to one of profound interest to social work professionals and to one where they have recognized expertise. Similarly, nurses and physicians could have used the opportunity to speak of the health of children and women. Professional education and advocacy can begin with the premise that the issue defined by the public and the media may not be the issue of greatest importance or in fact may obscure much more fundamental problems. Physicians for Social Responsibility is an interesting example of a professional group that entered a highly political debate, nuclear disarmament, and helped change the focus from national defence and military strength to human health and child care.

Given their concerns about speaking out, this situation also provided an excellent opportunity for professional coalition-building. A committee representing members of the various professional associations could have spoken with a strong voice. Professional associations may have been more willing to enter the fray with other, often more prestigious groups at their side.

6. *While women are organizing for change, men are still making the policy.* Historically, the struggle for abortion rights for women has been fought with the strategy most available to powerless groups: civil disobedience. Normally law-abiding women have persistently disobeyed the law. Dr. Morgentaler and the abortion clinics have continued this history of civil disobedience (Antonyshyn, Lee, and Merrill, 1988). In doing so, women have set the agenda and required others to respond. However, in this case study, while women worked valiantly to change policy and likely continued to have abortions in spite of hospital policy to the contrary, they were cast in the position of reacting to policy that men had made at the national, provincial, and even local levels. They were not able to create their own vision or their own policy. Although they carried the burden of the work at the local level, just as in the end they would carry the work of pregnancy and child-rearing, they did not make the decisions. The lack of real female power was evident, as was the enormous amount of time and work it takes to gain small victories.

The frustration that many Pro-Choice women feel about their

powerlessness in this matter is described in a song that Sile Simpson-McGowan likes to sing. "The Song of the Second Serving Maid," by English feminist Frankie Armstrong, has been sung at many Pro-Choice gatherings, yet it expresses the powerlessness of all women, not only those favouring a Pro-Choice position. Regardless of their stance on the abortion issue, women have had little influence on social and health policies that vitally affect them.

Now some people say what I did it was a sin
Should have kept the child not turned to rue and gin
But it's mostly men and ministers that preach to me that way
And I'd like to know what they knew of the anguish I was in

When I think on it now I feel nothing but relief
But what's a woman's feelings gainst a man-made belief
Sure I was young and foolish, I've been more careful since
But should a night time's pleasure bring a lifetime's grief?

And as for the soldier I wonder what's become of him
How many has he killed in the name of kith and kin?
Now he'll be blessed by Bishops, maybe medals broach his chest
And they've the nerve to tell me that they're the ones know best

But we're the ones to bear the pain, our souls will never rest
I ask whose world we live in where we women are but guests
So sometimes we need rue and gin while men get by with jests
We've wound and bleed and maimed ourselves, while men they
    joke and jest
We've hurt, and drown and hung ourselves while men go on
    with jests.

Our chapter could end on this bleak note. Women were not in many positions of decision-making on both sides and much of what they did do to influence legislators and policy-makers did not appear to be effective at first glance. There were marches that were poorly attended and rallies that did not seem well organized. The sophisticated strategies we associate with swift political action were not evident, except when the New Democrats loaned their office to the Pro-Choice cause.

However, if we limit our definition of successful organizing to those activities that clearly result in "beating the other side" at the polls, then we will fail to acknowledge the empowerment that occurs for women who, perhaps for the first time, give voice to their individual experience. For these women, naming their oppression or naming their rights may have more significance than visible gains in partisan political activities. Furthermore, unsophisticated organizing and failed rallies may be useful and even necessary steps to long-term social transformation. Lasting change is slow work, and it may encourage us to remember that every significant social gain occurs on the back of countless courageous failures. We need to value our slow struggles as well as our quick victories; both activities constitute success.

CHAPTER VI

The Healthy Community
Movement in Canada

by Joan Wharf Higgins

Many would be surprised to learn that the greatest contribution to the health of the nation over the past 150 years was made, not by doctors or hospitals, but by local government. Our lack of appreciation of the role of our cities in establishing the health of the nation is largely due to the fact that so little has been written about it. (Parfit, 1986)

This chapter will first review the origins, the conceptual bases, and the key pieces of literature that influenced the evolution of health promotion concepts and principles for cities, and ultimately, the healthy communities model. Second, the chapter will describe the experiences of four selected healthy community projects across the country. Finally, the chapter will examine the healthy community movement, its influence on social policy, and the connections between the movement and social work and community work practice.

"HEALTH FOR ALL" AND HEALTH PROMOTION

Interest in the healthy city or community and health promotion is not new. In 1848, Rudolph Virchow, an epidemiologist and pathologist, observed that all illness has both pathological and political roots. In 1875, when Britain passed the Public Health Act, Sir Benjamin Ward Richardson presented his idea of *Hygeia: A City of Health* (1876) that proposed a clean, safe environment with community-based organizations serving the needs of its inhabitants. The ideal city would be smoke- and alcohol-free, have clean air, adequate public transportation, regional community hospitals, and homes for the elderly and mentally ill. This vision was similar to town planner Ebenezer Howard's "garden city" in Britain as an alternative to its slums. Unfortunately, Ward Richardson's vision soon became overshadowed by Pasteur and Koch's advances against infectious diseases that ultimately led to the development of the medical model of health. Although the World Health Organization's definition of health, originally penned in 1948, encompassed more than the absence of disease and included a complete physical, mental, and social well-being, the medical model of health care remained dominant until the 1970s.

However, in 1971 McKeown's research suggested that death from infectious diseases fell by 80-90 per cent before the availability of vaccines or antibiotics (McKeown, 1971). McKeown argued that the greatest advances in reducing death rates during the last century and a half did not result from medical and surgical techniques but from public health measures such as improved sanitation, nutrition, clean water, and better overall living conditions provided by the local level of government. McKinlay and McKinlay (1977) attribute the alleviation of only five conditions – influenza, pneumonia, diphtheria, whooping cough, and polio – to medical treatment. Ashton (1988) supports this position, listing the most important contributions to better health as planned parenthood, improved quality and quantity of food sources, cleaner and safer environments, and preventive medicine and treatment. Since the victory over infectious diseases at the turn of the century (with the recent exception of the AIDS virus), developed countries have been plagued by chronic, insidious problems like heart disease, cancer, accidents, and violence, which are currently the leading causes of death.

The 1974 Health and Welfare Canada document, *A New Perspective on the Health of Canadians*, often referred to simply as the Lalonde Report, is acknowledged as the first official government document to address the importance of environmental and social issues. The Lalonde Report was heavily influenced by McKeown's work and by several provincial and federal reports over the years 1969-73 that highlighted the need to encourage preventive approaches, health promotion, and decentralized community care.

The Lalonde Report began with a review of the traditional health care system and its inadequacies. It concluded that "future improvements in the level of health of Canadians lie mainly in improving the environment, moderating self-imposed risks and adding to our knowledge of human biology" (Lalonde, 1974: 18). This led to the creation of the health field concept: four elements contribute to health – environment, human biology, lifestyle, and health care. The report emphasized the necessity of looking at the origins of disease rather than the symptoms, that health issues extend beyond the provincial responsibility for health care services, and advocated an extended role for the federal government.

The report was responsible for the establishment of the Health Promotion Directorate in 1976.

The Lalonde Report identified approaches for action and emphasized the importance of health promotion, but it did not outline an implementation strategy. Attempts to operationalize the health field concept resulted largely in wellness and fitness campaigns. As Labonte (1988) has noted, the emphasis on lifestyles did improve the health, or at least health behaviour, of the country's middle- and upper-class citizens. Fitness became big business and an employment opportunity for university-trained educators; smoking rates dropped; and health claims for food reached competitive and creative new heights. However, this focus on individual responsibility had little effect on the health of poor Canadians, whose morbidity and mortality rates far exceed those of the advantaged. A lifespan difference of 6.0 years for males and 2.0 for females still exists between the poor and wealthy (Adams, 1990) and lower-income persons experience fourteen fewer years of disability-free living (Wilkins, 1986). In addition, the reduction in infant mortality overall has not been accompanied by a reduction of the difference between high-income and low-income families. A poor baby is more likely to die in Canada than a baby born into a high-income family (Thompson, 1990). While it is well documented that the poor have higher rates of smoking, drinking, and physical inactivity and poorer nutrition, all of which contribute to ill health and premature death, such personal lifestyle choices cannot be viewed in isolation from the environmental and social contexts in which they occur (Buck, 1985). The Lalonde Report has been criticized for its victim-blaming and its failure to address the social environmental impact on health. The notion of "self-imposed risks" generated a number of thoughtful arguments refuting the idea that "people actually *choose* poor health" (Labonte and Penfold, 1981: 5). In the last analysis, despite its distinct contributions, the Lalonde Report did not truly confront all the root causes of disease.

Internationally, the concern for the health of Third World populations during the seventies prompted the World Health Organization (WHO) to commission research on health care in Third World countries. The reports of this research concluded that effective health care required: the equitable distribution of resources necessary for good health; integration of the health field within a comprehensive program of social and economic development; and community involvement in health planning and delivery. These tenets constituted the crux of the 1978 Alma Ata Declaration on Primary Health Care that outlined the rights of communities to plan and implement their health care, and of WHO's 1981 global strategy for *Health for All by the Year 2000*. This statement advocated "that all people in all countries should have at least such a level of health that they are capable of working productively and of participating actively in the social life of the community in which they live" (WHO, 1981). A listing of the thirty-eight "targets for health" is in Appendix A to this chapter.

The primary health care approach ratified at Alma Ata in 1978 did not spark any interest in the developed nations. In these countries "primary care" means first-contact care dispensed by family physicians, nurses, and health caregivers. Unfortunately, the concepts of intersectoral action and community involvement intrinsic to primary health care were virtually ignored, overlooked, or misunderstood by the developed nations. In an attempt to address these neglected issues, the WHO regional office for Europe established a "Health Promotion" program as its Seventh General Program. In 1984, this office released a discussion paper proposing the concepts and principles for policy and program development in health promotion (WHO, 1984).

The next two years saw a plethora of publications and conferences that sought to explain health status as a product of personal choices, environmental influences, and social conditions. In 1986, Ottawa hosted the first international conference on health promotion. The final day of the conference produced the delegate-written "Ottawa Charter for Health Promotion." The Charter, as it is commonly known, is a four-page action plan for a new "public health," listing the prerequisites for health as "peace, shelter, education, food, income, a stable eco-system, sustainable resources, social justice and equity." It defined a health promotion strategy that is detailed in Appendix B.

At this conference, Health and Welfare Canada released its second influential document, *Achieving Health for All*, which spoke out strongly in favour of reorienting the health system to reduce inequities, increase prevention, and enhance coping. The implementation strategies for accomplishing these challenges were to foster public participation, strengthen community health services, and co-ordinate healthy public policy.

The concept of healthy public policy introduced into the literature by Hancock gained a measure of acceptance at the Beyond Health Care Conference held in Toronto in 1984. A one-day workshop on Healthy Toronto 2000 was held following the conference, in which participants examined the changes required to make Toronto a healthier place to live by the year 2000. In turn, this led to the notion of healthy cities. Dr. Ilona Kickbush, regional officer for health education at the Europe WHO office, was so intrigued with the notion that she subsequently developed a proposal for a European Healthy Cities Project.

Two years later the Healthy Cities Project formed the focus of a symposium organized and hosted by the city of Lisbon. Delegates from twenty-one European cities participated and contributed to the development of the European Healthy Cities model,which was accepted by WHO as the strategy for achieving the goal of health for all by the year 2000. This project was launched in 1986 in eleven cities at the University of Liverpool, which provides consultation and research support to the participating cities. By 1990, the WHO Europe project had grown to include thirty cities (to be expanded to forty in 1991), and more than 400 communities all over Europe, Australia, and North America were officially participating in various national or regional projects.

In his book *Health Planning and Social Change*, Duhl likens a city to a complex organism similar to the human body, with an infrastructure of many organs and functioning parts. "There is no action that takes place that doesn't affect the whole human. So it is with the city" (Duhl, 1986: 284). From this analogy the term "healthy city" was derived, and this forms the basis from which Duhl defends the concept that a city can indeed be deemed healthy.

To summarize the last two decades of "consciousness raising," the beginnings clearly lie with the work of McKeown and his documentation of significant public health measures responsible for drastic reductions in mortality rates. Despite the emphasis on personal responsibility, the Lalonde Report received international acclaim for its recognition of the importance of public and preventive health measures. Its emphasis on personal responsibility was quickly condemned, the outcome being a renewed interest in environmental and social contexts in which lifestyle choices are made. The WHO research conducted during this same time produced the theoretical infrastructure and ultimately contributed to the components of the Ottawa Charter, Health and Welfare Canada's *Achieving Health for All* (Epp, 1986), and the healthy city model. Combined with the increasing costs of health care services and an aging population that would inevitably depend on the system for long-term care, this research and these policy statements set the stage for the preventive agenda and for a renewed interest in the environment and social contexts in which lifestyle choices are made.

THE CONVERGENCE OF INTEREST: THE CANADIAN HEALTHY COMMUNITIES PROJECT

A broadened understanding of health, its determinants, and those responsible for it demanded the development of strategic concepts. If the new conception of health required a participatory approach to health planning, then government action would have to be augmented by local action. (Boothroyd and Eberle, 1990: 4)

The Lalonde Report's insight that improvement of the environment and lifestyles was integral to the betterment of health was first picked up by Toronto and its Department of Public Health. In 1976 the Board of Health formed a Health Planning Steering Committee. Its 1978 report, *Public Health in the 1980's*, represented two years of work and radically changed the future of public health in Toronto. The report outlined a new direction for the department based on the principles of health promotion, health education, disease prevention, community development, health advocacy, and data-based planning (MacDougall, 1990). The report led to the establishment of a health advocacy unit, and in 1982 the department established its mission "to make Toronto the healthiest city in North America." The realization that the department could not accomplish this goal on its own provided the inspiration for the city's 1984 "Beyond Health Care Conference."

Although the idea of healthy cities was discussed at this 1984 conference, little action occurred because of the absence of an organization to act as a central base. Events in Europe prompted Health and Welfare Canada to commission Trevor Hancock to develop a proposal for a national co-ordinating office in 1987. Hancock solicited the help of agencies outside the traditional health arena – the Canadian Institute of Planners, the Federation of Canadian Municipalities, and the Canadian Public Health Association – to co-sponsor an office. The Healthy Cities Project (HCP) office, funded by Health and Welfare Canada, opened in September, 1988, and was located at the Canadian Institute of Planners in Ottawa. A national steering committee reflected the multidisciplinary commitment to the HCP, with representatives from the three national associations, plus delegates from local municipal projects across Canada. This steering committee directed the work of the HCP office.

The project was renamed Healthy Communities, primarily on the recommendation of the Federation of Canadian Municipalities, so that all municipalities, regardless of size and structure, would be able to participate. Also, a change from "cities" to "communities" acknowledged the participatory nature of health and social planning at the local level (for the people, by the people), and the positive connotations associated with the term "community" made it an attractive concept.

The Canadian Healthy Communities Project is designed to encourage local municipal action around health problems broadly defined as: the state of the environment, the aging of our population, the future of work, family and societal violence, all of which will best respond to public policy interventions rather than to traditional health system activities. The healthy community process starts with the development of an interdepartmental and intersectoral committee that identifies local conditions impacting on the health of neighbourhoods (not health conditions) and "doable" projects that will address the identified issues. These projects are then delegated to intersectoral subcommittees responsible for recruiting members and generating funds. A healthy community has representation and support from the municipal council and departments but is not merely an appendage to the municipal structure. The healthy community concept is a means of influencing local government representatives and community members to implement innovative approaches to issues that affect health. While the municipality has to relinquish some of its power in this sharing process, tangible results accrue and the public image is improved.

There are no formal entrance requirements to the project – all interested communities are invited to join. However, the Healthy Communities Project does recommend the following generic model for addressing healthy public policy at the local level (Berlin, 1991):

1. As evidence of municipal will and support towards an intersectoral approach, have city council acknowledge and endorse the local project;
2. ensure every municipal department is aware of the health implications of its day-to-day activities;
3. establish an intersectoral Healthy Communities committee comprised of representatives from municipal departments, community members, and business leaders;
4. have the committee assess the health needs of the community and focus on the realistically achievable ones;
5. using the resources of the member groups and departments, develop, implement, and evaluate programs to address those needs in a co-ordinated and effective effort;
6. share experiences, swap stories, exchange information with other healthy communities.

The Canadian Healthy Communities Project offered community development workshops emphasizing skill training for both professionals and lay people on consensus development, conflict resolution, and team coalition-building by local consultants. Martin (1991) warns of the dangers involved with this service: local community projects can become dependent on keynote speakers offering expert counsel. She is quick to acknowledge the work that communities do intuitively and the importance of recognizing this contribution. Traditionally, the community may have focused on the exclusive needs of one or two groups, but the project encourages communities to open the lines of communication and consider the collective needs. To date, in excess of 100 municipalities have joined the project and have set out to meet its challenges: What does a healthy community mean for you and your community? How do you go about getting a healthy community?

The project puts goals of health for all into action at the community level. The assumption is that these requisites for health may best be satisfied at the municipal level, where the local government is responsible for the basic needs of its constituents – clean water, garbage collection, safe transport and roads, leisure, cultural and recreational opportunities, etc. The project assumes that placing issues that affect health on the local public agenda will be the most effective means of improving the health status of the community since smaller bureaucracies are more sensitive to local needs, and close links exist between the policy-makers and those affected. Indeed, policy-makers make the policies for their own community (Hancock, 1990a). Gray (1985) notes that intersectoral collaboration may be easier to initiate at the local level due to the proximity of those with a stake in the decisions taken and the competition for scarce resources.

However, Hancock (1990a) also notes the difficulties of implementing healthy public policy at the local level. Federal and provincial governments largely control resources, power, and expertise. Some have argued that federal initiatives are required to alter significantly the plight of the poor, where needs are the greatest and the skills to organize and facilitate political support the weakest (Witty, 1991; Wharf, 1989b). Marmot and Smith (1989) compared the life expectancy statistics of the British with those for the Japanese over the past three decades and found that economic progress, especially equal distribution of income, has been crucial for improving life expectancy in Japan. This has been termed the health-without-wealth phenomenon. Countries with a low per capita GNP but high income equality have achieved a high level of health in comparison with countries with the same GNP and a less equitable distribution of income. Similarly, Canada, with a high GNP but low income equality, ranks behind those nations with a lower GNP but a more equitable distribution of wealth (see City of Toronto, 1991).

Competing interests between the private and public sectors may also be a barrier to the process, especially so "in societies in which the pursuit of profit is dominant" (Pedersen *et al.*, 1988: 52). Witty (1991) notes that community action may actually reflect the interests of the financially or politically powerful, rather than the broad issues of the community. Concerns of territoriality or "turf" protection by professionals may also militate against the best interest of communities, a condition that requires the "disabling of professionals" (B.C. Healthy Communities Network, 1989). As Martin (1991) has commented, there will always be people striving for power and control; the very process of community development can get co-opted, a process Farrant (1989) described as community manipulation.

SOME HEALTHY COMMUNITIES ACROSS CANADA

The following section examines the experiences and different approaches of several Healthy Communities projects across Canada. These stories have been selected because of the availability of pertinent information.

Dartmouth, Nova Scotia

In September of 1987, the city of Dartmouth officially joined the Healthy Communities Project by resolution of city council. Both Dartmouth's mayor, John Savage, and city administrator, John Burke, were staunch supporters of the HCP. Rather than ask the community for initial input, the municipality decided first to consider the health impacts of all its policies and planning for a two-year period.

Accordingly, health was continually on the agenda at the senior staff level and a number of significant accomplishments resulted: Dartmouth legislated a non-smoking policy; a Health and Safety policy, complete with an Employee Assistant Program, was established; and, a new AIDS policy encouraged city employees with HIV to remain at work. As well, the city participated in, supported, and set an example in recycling and environmental issues, including the mayor and "Michael Recycle" (a walking tree) visiting elementary and junior high schools throughout Dartmouth to encourage paper recycling and awareness of environmental issues. A Hazardous Spray By-Law was passed to encourage use of non-toxic spray, stipulating that companies must forewarn local areas of impending work. The city also supported arts and culture activities and established a steering committee to assess and upgrade all municipal programs and facilities for accessibility.

At the end of this two-year period, the city advertised for and accepted thirty applications from the citizens of Dartmouth to join a Healthy Communities Committee. Fifteen persons were eventually selected to form the core committee, and two initiatives were immediately ratified: (1) Environment Day, June 2, 1990, an event organized by provincial, federal, and volunteer agencies that underlined the importance of environment and health; (2) establishing the year 2000 as a target goal for the Healthy Communities Project. This ties in nicely with the WHO target, and is also the 250th anniversary for Dartmouth.

The work of the committee has recently been assisted by the appointment of a full-time project co-ordinator, funded by Nova Scotia's Department of Health and Fitness. The committee has undertaken a community needs assessment to determine visions of a healthy community, to compare Dartmouth to that vision, and to establish priorities for the city. It is hoped that by the milestone year 2000, the success of the project will inspire the provincial government to implement it in other communities.

Sherbrooke

In Quebec, where a network of district health centres and community service centres has been established, public health is a regional rather than municipal responsibility, and the Healthy Communities Project provides a convenient link between local and regional influences on health. This structural arrangement motivated the Quebec Public Health Association to set up its own provincially funded project, "Villes et Villages en Santé," with its own office and staff. The following is a brief history of its development in Sherbrooke.

Sherbrooke was one of the first Canadian cities to be declared "a healthy city" and to generate a model for development. After receiving the proceedings from the 1986 Lisbon Healthy Cities Symposium, Dr. Robert Pronovost of the Community Health Department at Sherbrooke University Hospital Centre became intrigued with the concept and proposed in the fall of 1986 that a Healthy Cities project be introduced. The Health and Social Services Regional Council (Estrian region) provided $20,000 to promote the concept to municipal council and local organizations. The project received additional funding of $30,000 to subsidize a co-ordinator salary and costs for office space, telephone, office supplies, and secretarial support; by July, 1987, the project was officially launched with the hiring of the co-ordinator, Louise Gosselin.

Authorization to develop the project and form the committee was granted in November of 1988. The initial Healthy City Committee consisted of representatives from municipal, social, and health organizations, the city manager, the head urban planner, the chief of police, the director of the Community Health Department at University Hospital, and the directors from the local community services centres.

Since Sherbrooke is a large municipality, the committee felt it needed to familiarize itself with the structure, roles, and responsibilities of the municipality before "knocking on doors." Hence, committee members began by reading annual reports from various departments and emergency service staff. This helped to clarify the city's strengths and weaknesses, the range of problems handled by the city, and their potential relationship with the HCP. This invaluable information allowed the committee to assess Sherbrooke's quality of life, common interests, and the depth and variety of expertise within the city.

The committee then prioritized projects on the basis of the following criteria: common motives, impact, and the involvement of a large percentage of the population. Out of an initial list of thirty-six, eight issues were retained: identification and prevention of high-risk situations; urban forest development; smoke-free environments; use of pesticides and collection of toxic products; pedestrian and cycling paths; housing for the elderly; downtown and shopping mall projects; and prevention of vandalism. In addition, two other major projects were approved – the promotion of the healthy city concept and consultation with the citizens of Sherbrooke. A list of individuals and organizations capable of meeting these goals was identified.

On May 16, 1988, the municipal council declared Sherbrooke a "Healthy City," approved the ten-action project, and allocated a shared budget of $15,000 from the city, $10,000 from the Community Health Department at University Hospital, and $5,000 from the local centre of community services. A new Healthy City Committee was formed, with the additions of two municipal counsellors, the director of the Eastern Township School Board, a representative from the Chamber of Commerce, and a citizen representative.

January, 1989, saw the official launch of the project to the public. "Sherbrooke, more than a city, a Healthy City – a shared responsibility" became the city's slogan for 1989. This notion of a shared responsibility was used to sensitize the population to the importance of environmental, physical, and social health and to develop an attitude toward more co-operation and mutual support.

For any project in Sherbrooke to be considered part of the larger Healthy City project, a work group must be multisectoral, include citizen participation, and be approved by the Healthy City Committee and municipal council. Each action project has a work group consisting of, on average, six members who are responsible for developing the project and its budget, obtaining resources, and monitoring results. For example, the urban forest project submitted a preliminary plan to the heads of the organizations represented by work group members to confirm and approve the participation of those organizations. The plan was then forwarded to the Healthy City Committee and municipal council for final approval. This work group then selected an area to plant trees, garnered funds of $5,000, and established a citizen committee to educate the residents of that area and to organize the actual planting. Such participation requires that roles and duties be clearly defined – the plan must be flexible but well organized. This is a concrete example of the application of the healthy city concept: it was a realistic undertaking by the city, both a community and multisectoral project with citizen participation. "It's a method of placing responsibility of a healthy activity on the citizens while providing reasonable and essential support" (Delorme and Gosselin, 1989: 22).

Toronto

As outlined earlier, the entire HCP concept emanated from a one-day Toronto conference held in 1984. While the workshop itself was considered a great success and contributed to a spin-off of several flourishing projects, it was not until 1986 that the Board of Health established a Healthy Toronto 2000 committee. The committee held a number of vision workshops for board members, department employees, and the community to determine their image of a healthy city and catalogue the obstacles to this ideal. The committee also conducted an environmental scan, distributed an issues paper, and held public reviews and hearings. The committee's final report, released two years later, recommended Charter-like ambitions: to reduce inequities in health opportunities, to generate both physical and social conditions supportive of health, and to support community-based health care services.

The report acknowledged that the Department of Public Health could not by itself realize these goals. It suggested that an overall Healthy City Strategy be developed and that the health department have a sub-set of goals, specific to its role within the city. Hence, the department's health goals included: increasing the health expectancy of Torontonians; creating healthful environments and protecting citizens from health hazards; using a community development approach to assist neighbourhoods to tackle environmental and health issues; and compiling health data. The department has developed a number of projects that bring Toronto closer to health:

- establishment of an environmental protection office in 1986–87;
- development of by-laws regulating smoking in public places and workplaces (where every workplace must have a smoking policy that is tolerable to the non-smokers);
- prenatal education of high-risk parents that is socially and culturally appropriate for different groups;
- establishment of an energy efficiency office to assist in attaining a 20 per cent decline in CO_2 production;
- CFC reduction by-law;
- CityPlan '91 – a master plan for downtown Toronto that incorporates social equity and sustainable urban environments as twin themes and includes emphasis on public transit, auto reduction, and population concentrations;
- adoption of auto minimization, air quality maintenance,

energy conservation, and water conservation as prerequisites for development approval;

- a Toronto declaration of environmental principles to guide all city actions;
- a workplace program to raise consciousness and address the issues of violence against women;
- the hiring of a corporate director for the Healthy City Office;
- the establishment of community accessible grants (totalling $3.5 million) for action on drug prevention, AIDS prevention, and community health promotion and disease prevention.

Concurrent to the Healthy Toronto 2000 Committee's activities, some informal interdepartmental dialogue had commenced, recognizing the value of the healthy cities concept as a municipal-wide theme for strategic planning. Interdepartmental vision workshops that solidified the shared dream of Toronto as a healthy city ultimately led to the establishment of a Healthy City Office in 1989.

Presently, the Healthy City Office has labelled three strategic directions for making Toronto the healthiest city possible: social equity, environmental sustainability, and community empowerment. A healthy city work group, comprised of the health department's management representatives, oversees the work of the Healthy City Office. The office has established three subcommittees to work on the following themes:

1. communication (to city staff and the community);
2. outreach and advocacy (support and promotion of social equity initiatives and co-ordination of community development for neighbourhood projects);
3. research and policy analysis of health environment and social data to produce a "State of the City" report every three years and to develop a system (healthy city equity and environmental indicators) to monitor the healthy community process.

A second focus of the Healthy City Office is community development. Recently, two community health officers have been hired to implement an outreach strategy, broadening the project to include interest groups and neighbourhood associations. Toronto has been invited to be an honorary member of the European Healthy Cities Project, in recognition of the role the city has played in the birth of the movement.

As Berlin (1991) and Hancock (1990a) have noted, Toronto's healthy city structure is dominated by interdepartmental representation. There are no community (private- or public-sector) members. This also may reflect their decision to use the term "city" rather than "community." However, Kendall (1991) points to the considerable community participation and consultation integral to the Healthy Toronto initiatives through work groups, task forces, and subcommittees; citizens partake in setting terms of reference, drafting recommendations, awarding grants, and determining resource allocation. Kendall defends this lack of official public representation on the Healthy City Committee by citing the wish of those involved not to create "yet another committee, [because] it is more important to forge links and address the public policy priorities adopted by the 100 existing committees, all of which have a part to play in developing a healthy Toronto."

Saanich, British Columbia

In British Columbia the healthy communities philosophy has been evolving over the last five years and has led to one of the most sophisticated and well-organized networks in the country. The provincial scene and one community, Saanich, are discussed.

In 1987, the B.C. Public Health Association president, Sharon Martin, was asked to organize a provincial workshop to respond to the federal government document, *Achieving Health for All*. Forty people from various professions, organizations, and associations attended the workshop. The organizers asked the participants, what do you think about achieving health for all, what is your community perspective, what is your definition of health? A consensus was reached regarding a lack of co-ordination in community services and a lack of political will and finances to promote health *per se* as opposed to health care. As well, the participants agreed that the community "forum/town meeting" format was useful for eliciting the views of the community.

The B.C. Healthy Communities Network was formed in 1988 to assist communities in implementing their vision of healthy communities. The Network serves as a liaison between B.C. municipalities, sharing successes, linking the experienced with the naive, and building an information base. It is chaired by Sharon Martin, with a steering committee consisting of representatives from the Health Promotion Directorate of Health and Welfare Canada, the B.C. Public Health Association, the B.C. Health Association, the provincial Ministry of Health, the Planners Institute of B.C., and the Department of Health Care and Epidemiology at the University of British Columbia. The Network and these associations have sponsored several province-wide community workshops, bringing together local health agencies, politicians, health professionals, and volunteers that have spawned small regional task forces. The Network's steering committee also produces a newsletter, acts as an information resource base, and serves as a consultant for ideas on healthy community issues and funding sources.

Some municipalities in B.C. have formally joined the Healthy Communities Project – Saanich, Vancouver, Victoria, Gold River – by resolution of city council. Others have used the healthy community model to guide developments in their communities. Thus, the HCP framework has been used for some time as an "organizational ideal" in North and West Vancouver, and the city of Vancouver uses it as its "corporate plan."

The provincial Ministry of Health recently established a Healthy Communities Initiative Fund that provided $810,000 to selected municipalities (preference was given to populations less than 30,000). The thirty-eight communities that received funding submitted proposals that were classified in accordance with these four goals: (1) to increase the number of years in good health by decreasing premature death, illness, and disability; (2) to improve equity in health; (3) to create conditions that support health; and (4) to increase skills that foster health.

For a community to be considered, the local government was required to pass a resolution that would stipulate interdepartmental analysis and revision of public policy on the health of the community, and ensure community participation in municipal decisions that affect health. In this way, the provincial government assisted communities to follow the official HCP model.

Healthy Saanich 2000 began in early 1988, prior to the development of the B.C. Network and before the availability of provincial funding, and provides a classic example of a national healthy community project that has flourished in a supportive province. The Saanich story reads like a textbook for healthy communities. Two Saanich councillors, Carol Pickup and Murray Coell, formed a Healthy Communities Committee by appointment from municipal council. They then took responsibility for informing local community organizations about the project, recruiting their involvement and participation in the development of a program and the formation of an advisory committee. These same two councillors, plus two more trustees, formed a steering committee that asked department heads to review existing policies and to incorporate the HCP concept into future considerations. A community workshop was then held to elicit a broader base of volunteers and to establish working *ad hoc* committees for the specific projects approved by the advisory council. These subcommittees currently are using six themes to guide the project: creating a strong community role in planning and assessment; developing and preserving the quality of the local environment; reducing inequities in health, housing, education, and employment; fulfilling the local need for human services; emphasizing innovative delivery methods of programs; and maintaining a data base for planning and evaluation. Meanwhile, a contest was under way among the secondary schools in the municipality that resulted in an official logo for the project.

Saanich has implemented some concrete initiatives over the last three years, both on its own and in conjunction with the Capital Regional District and other agencies. These include by-laws banning the disposal of hazardous household wastes and prohibiting smoking in municipal facilities; a telephone book recycling system and curbside recycling program; improved wheelchair accessibility; development of an environmental checklist for municipal departments; an employment project for the disabled; and a comprehensive Wellness Seniors Program. In the fall of 1990, the advisory committee recommended to council that it receive an additional two-year mandate so that the committee may work with the planning department on the Official Community Plan for 1991-92.

INFLUENCING SOCIAL POLICY

... the best health promotion policy is a good social policy. (WHO Vienna Dialogue, 1987: 1)

Interests have converged to place the healthy community movement on the agenda of over 400 municipal governments in a number of countries. From the admittedly incomplete inventory of healthy community projects contained in the preceding pages it appears that at least two requirements are necessary to place the concept on the agenda of municipal governments. First, "the initiators must have the socially defined right to initiate action in the community" (Sower et al., 1957: 66). Thus, in Dartmouth the mayor and the city administrator and in Saanich two elected councillors clearly possessed this right and were able to convince their respective councils to approve and commit resources to the healthy community projects. In Toronto, Trevor Hancock, who along with Leonard Duhl conceived the notion of healthy communities, had the strong support of councillor Jack Layton, chair of the board, a number of city councillors, and members of the Board of Health in pushing for approval of a project. In addition to political sponsorship, the concept must have some measure of support from community organizations and citizens. Without a base of community support, approval from municipal government can become an empty gesture. Perhaps the best examples of wide-ranging community support come from the provinces of B.C. and Quebec with their extensive networks and use of community forums.

In partnership with its companion movement of health promotion and supported by a renewed interest in a socio-environmental approach in departments of public health, the concept of healthy communities has redefined the health field from a preoccupation with sickness to include the social and economic determinants of health. The redefinition is based on a lengthy record of research that has established the connections between social conditions and health. The record dates back to Virchow's calculation in 1948 that disease has two causes: one pathological, the other political (Pinchuk and Clark, 1984). The results have been so consistent that even the Conservative federal government has acknowledged the impact of poverty on health. Thus *Achieving Health for All* contains the following statement:

> There is disturbing evidence which shows that despite Canada's superior health services system, people's health remains directly related to their economic status. . . . Within the low income

bracket certain groups have a higher chance of experiencing poor health than others. Older people, the unemployed, welfare recipients, single mothers supporting children, and minorities such as natives and immigrants fall into this category. More than one million children in Canada are poor. Poverty affects over half of single parent families, the overwhelming majority of whom are headed by women. (Epp, 1986: 4)

A striking example of the recent research on the connections between socio-economic conditions and health is the report on health inequities produced by the Department of Public Health in Toronto. The report examined the effects of risk conditions (poverty, low education and employment status, linguistic, cultural, and ethnic barriers to health, poor housing, and discrimination) in the city.

While a great deal more work needs to be done in this area we know enough already to be clear about some of the implications for public policy. When our results are set along side other Canadian and international studies, there is compelling evidence of the existence of inequalities in health. We do not need more health care spending to create more health, we do not need more economic growth to create more health, but we do need more economic equity to create more health. (City of Toronto, 1991: 4)

As concepts the healthy community movement and health promotion have indeed arrived, and the redefinition of health on which they are based has been accepted by governments at all levels. The challenge facing these movements now is whether they can generate sufficient momentum and commitment at the local level to change social policies at the provincial and national level. To have even a modicum of success local governments will require a greater share in social policy than is presently the case. As noted above, *Achieving Health for All* identified the impact of poverty on health but did not contain any national strategies, such as improving the social security system and reforming the tax system. Rather, *Achieving Health for All*, by focusing on local-level strategies such as self-help and mutual aid, suggested implicitly that poverty could be addressed and resolved by community organizations. In fact, many communities have been forced to turn to churches and voluntary organizations to create food banks. Such responses, while necessary, are a stopgap measure rather than a solution. One review commented on the lack of congruence between national problems and local solutions in the following vein.

It simply does not make sense for the Minister in his capacity as Minister of Health to acknowledge the impact of poverty on health and then in his role of Minister of Welfare to take no action. It should be noted that the Lalonde report published in 1974 was hailed as a breakthrough in its identification of the health field concept and the importance of the environment in determining health conditions. Yet, the intervening years have seen few if any improvements in environmental conditions. If *Achieving Health for All* is to avoid the same fate as the Lalonde report, the Minister might well begin by heeding the advice of his advisory body, the National Council of Welfare, on the dire need for an improved social security system and tax reform. (Wharf, 1989b: 48)

More recently, the federal government has reduced its commitment to social programs. It has successfully put a ceiling on expenditures of the provinces of Alberta, B.C., and Ontario in the Canada Assistance Plan and it is progressively reducing its contributions to zero cash transfers under the Established Programs Financing Act, through which it has traditionally supported health and education programs in all provinces. The federal government has also introduced a new Goods and Services Tax that affects the poor and low-income groups most severely, and, significantly for the future of health promotion and the healthy community movement, withdrew its financial support of the Canadian Healthy Communities Project office in 1991.

The federal government's record with respect to health promotion and healthy communities can best be described as schizophrenic. It has provided leadership through Health and Welfare Canada in producing innovative statements such as the Lalonde Report and *Achieving Health for All*. Yet despite the conclusions of these reports, the federal government remains unconvinced by its own evidence. Poverty is acknowledged to be largely responsible for poor health, but by some perverse logic this condition brought about by national fiscal and employment policies is to be addressed by the indigenous efforts of local communities.

In addition, the healthy community movement faces at least two other difficulties: measurement and the structural arrangements in place at all levels of government. The issue of measurement is addressed in a perceptive article on "Healthy Community Indicators: The Perils of the Search and the Paucity of the Find" (Hayes and Manson Willms, 1990). Essentially, these authors present the dilemma posed by trying to evaluate healthy communities and to arrive at some global measure of effectiveness, when the objectives of healthy communities vary from community to community. Given the variety of objectives and approaches, how can a common set of indicators be developed? The authors go on to argue that communities "may be better advised to evaluate their particular projects relative to the goals they have set and the circumstances they face, and . . . forget the common yardstick" (Hayes and Manson Willms, 1990: 165), an attitude now shared by most Canadian Healthy Communities Project supporters (Hancock, 1991).

Building on this suggestion, it might be appropriate to follow the model developed for accreditation by the Canadian Association of Schools of Social Work. This approach requires that local communities establish their own objectives within the broad set of goals set by the Canadian Healthy Communities Project, and demonstrate both the fit between these two sets of goals and the outcomes of the local-level projects.

The second difficulty concerns the organizational structures now in place at all levels of government. Healthy community projects are based on a vision that embraces all aspects of the community and the entire range of work performed by municipal governments and a variety of other organizations. However, municipal governments are structured along departmental lines: parks and recreation; public works, including roads and sewers; health; planning; land use; and, in some jurisdictions, social services. It is apparent that each of these departments has some impact on and control over the health of the community, and yet the community health projects are typically small units with no power to affect the work of the traditional, larger, and more powerful departments.

Hence, healthy community offices are dependent on the co-operation and good will of these departments. The most successful healthy communities have been those whose municipal governments' strategic/operational plans have embraced the concept and whose initiatives have crossed not only departmental lines but private and public sectors as well.

As noted in the discussion of the Healthy City Office in Toronto, some success has been achieved by creating interdepartmental task forces to tackle such problems as traffic and homelessness. Thus the office acts as a catalyst in identifying problems and taking the initial responsibility for developing a strategy to deal with them. And, as Hancock points out, the issue is by no means restricted to the structural arrangements within city halls.

> The 21st century challenges that cities face are holistic and complex in nature. No one group or discipline has the answer and indeed in working alone they run the danger of making matters worse. The approach needed now and in the future is for a multi disciplinary and multi sectoral approach that combines government, public and private sector. (Hancock, 1990b: 21)

However, leaving these difficulties aside, there is evidence that the movement has already tackled some serious community issues. Thus the Healthy City Office in Toronto has recently released reports and provoked action on homelessness in the city and on traffic and vehicle emission problems. Many community projects have gained approval for no-smoking by-laws in their jurisdictions, have initiated action on literally scores of environmental issues, and have developed programs to address affordable housing and nutrition for the elderly and adequate access for the disabled.

CONNECTING THEORY AND PRACTICE

In many ways, the healthy community movement is similar to the other case studies in the book. Like deinstitutionalization in New Brunswick, child welfare in the Yukon and Vancouver, and even the reform of income security in Ontario, the movement is rooted in a vision of change. In turn, the vision relies on an ecological or socio-environmental framework for health. This comprehensive framework is well known in biology, psychology, and sociology, but first gained currency in health with the publication of the Lalonde Report. As noted in Chapter 1, the attraction of the ecological approach is that it insists on viewing individuals within their surrounding context. But the essential limitation of the framework is the lack of attention to power and its distribution in society and in organizations. Hence, despite increasing our understanding, the ecological framework does little to enhance our ability to alter even the ordinary problems, let alone the grand issues of social policy (Wharf, 1990).

In addition, changing the environment and societal institutions is very difficult. Thus, just as direct service practitioners find it easier to engage an individual or a family in treatment than to alter the societal conditions of housing and poverty, so have healthy community workers turned to developing specific projects such as anti-smoking and recycling campaigns.

The movement has relied heavily on the locality development approach to community work to involve community associations, interest groups, departments in municipal governments, and citizens in its work. Perhaps the chief distinction between the community development work of the healthy community movement and the traditional approach first outlined by Murray Ross (1967) is that staff have taken an almost missionary stance to their work. Thus, rather than being employed in the classical Ross tradition of assisting residents of a particular area to identify their needs and solutions, healthy community workers bring a definite value stance to their assignments. Their task is to involve others in joining the healthy community movement. To be sure, this mission permits neighbourhoods to identify particular needs or projects, but there is no doubt that all must fit under the banner of healthy communities.

It is important to add that community development in original and pure form was based on the assumption that societal power structures and institutions are essentially benign. In this view, policy-makers respond positively to needs identified through the community development process. But as residents of neighbourhoods have learned, the reception to their needs and problems depends to a very large extent on the nature of the need, on the availability of resources to meet the need, and on the views and priorities of policy-makers. Thus, efforts to preserve neighbour-hood parks, to establish child-care centres, or to alter the pattern of industrial growth have not always been greeted with enthusiasm.

Again, the question is raised as to the extent to which an essentially locally derived process can affect conditions that are provincial or national in scope. Can a cross-country network of healthy communities demand changes in the priorities of senior levels of government? The infancy of the movement prohibits any definitive statements on the connections between theory and practice. From this review it appears that the movement is strong in vision, but light on theory and power.

CONNECTING SOCIAL WORK AND COMMUNITY WORK PRACTICE IN THE HEALTHY COMMUNITY MOVEMENT

It is clear that the healthy community movement has relied to a large extent on the locality development approach. Despite the fact that this approach to community work was developed by a social worker, taught in schools of social work, and practised by social workers, there are no evident connections between the healthy community movement and the profession of social work. In effect, healthy community staff, drawn largely from backgrounds in public health, have "discovered" community development. Given the newness of the discovery it is not surprising that the limitations of this development approach, anchored as it is in local efforts and resources, have yet to be experienced in the healthy community movement.

Social workers have a long history of employment in the health field. They have worked in hospitals, in institutions for the disabled, and in the deinstitutionalization experience. As Manson Willms et al. (1991: 20) note, "Social workers can play a catalytic role in bringing together key stakeholders and in providing information about the needs of individuals and families and the consequences of such conditions as housing and homelessness." Yet, despite their involvement in health and in community development, social workers have not played a prominent part in the healthy community movement. Their absence should not be attributed to the healthy community movement or to public health. Perhaps the chief explanation can be found in the social work profession and schools of social work, which have watched this major innovation on the community scene emerge without clamouring to be involved. However, the emerging case for intersectoral and interprofessional collaboration identified by Hancock may remedy the lack of connection in the future.

APPENDIX A: TARGETS FOR HEALTH FOR ALL BY THE YEAR 2000 (WHO, 1981)

Health for All

1. Equity in health
2. Adding years to life
3. Better opportunities for the disabled
4. Reducing disease and disability
5. Eliminating measles, polio, neonatal tetanus, congenital rubella, diphtheria, congenital syphilis, and indigenous malaria
6. Increased life expectation at birth
7. Reduced infant mortality
8. Reduced maternal mortality
9. Combating diseases of the circulation
10. Combating cancer
11. Reducing accidents
12. Stopping the increase in suicide

Lifestyles Conducive to Health for All

13. Developing healthy public policies
14. Developing social support systems
15. Improving knowledge and motivation for healthy behaviour
16. Promoting positive health behaviour
17. Decreasing health-damaging behaviour

Producing Healthy Environments

18. Policies for healthy environments
19. Monitoring, assessments, and control of environmental risks

20. Controlling water pollution
21. Protecting against air pollution
22. Improving food safety
23. Protecting against hazardous wastes
24. Improving housing conditions
25. Protecting against work-related risks

Providing Appropriate Care

26. A health care system based on primary health care
27. Distribution of resources according to need
28. Reorienting primary medical care
29. Developing teamwork
30. Co-ordinating services
31. Ensuring quality of services

Support for Health Development

32. Developing a research base for health for all
33. Implementing policies for health for all
34. Management and delivery of resources
35. Health information systems
36. Training and deployment of staff
37. Education of people in the non-health sector
38. Assessment of health technologies

APPENDIX B: THE OTTAWA CHARTER FOR HEALTH PROMOTION

The following material is an abridged version of the Ottawa Charter.

I. Build Healthy Public Policy

Health promotion goes beyond health care. It puts health on the agenda of policy-makers in all sectors and at all levels, directing them to be aware of the health consequences of their decisions and to accept their responsibilities for health. Health promotion policy requires the identification of obstacles to the adoption of healthy public policies in non-health sectors and ways of removing them. The aim must be to make the healthier choice the easier choice for policy-makers as well.

2. Create Supportive Environments

Our societies are complex and interrelated. Health cannot be separated from other goals. The inextricable links between people and their environment constitute the basis for a socio-ecological approach to health. The overall guiding principle for the world, nations, regions, and communities alike is the need to encourage reciprocal maintenance – to take care of each other, our communities, and our natural environment. The conservation of natural resources throughout the world should be emphasized as a global responsibility.

Health promotion generates living and working conditions that are safe, stimulating, satisfying, and enjoyable. The protection of the natural and built environments and the conservation of natural resources must be addressed in any health promotion strategy.

3. Strengthen Community Action

Health promotion works through concrete and effective community action in setting priorities, making decisions, planning strategies, and implementing them to achieve better health. At the heart of this process is the empowerment of communities, their ownership and control of their own endeavours and destinies. Community development draws on existing human and material resources in the community to enhance self-help and social support, and to develop flexible systems for strengthening public participation and direction of health matters.

4. Develop Personal Skills

Health promotion supports personal and social development through providing information and education for health and by enhancing life skills. By doing so, it increases the options available to people to exercise more control over their own health and over their environments, and to make choices conducive to health. Action is required through educational, professional, commercial, and voluntary bodies and within the institutions themselves.

5. Reorient Health Services

The responsibility for health promotion in health services is shared among individuals, community groups, health professionals, health service institutions and governments. They must work together toward a health care system that contributes to the pursuit of health. Reorienting health services also requires stronger attention to health research as well as changes in professional education and training. This must lead to a change of attitude and organization of health services, which refocuses on the total needs of the individual as a whole person.

CHAPTER VII

Community Organizations
and Social Policy

This chapter deals with the first of the two objectives of the book –
to determine if community-based organizations can influence the
shape and direction of provincial and national social policies.
Chapter 1 developed the argument that the responsibility for social policy has been concentrated at senior levels of government
but that the consequences of these policies are played out at the
local level: on city streets, neighbourhood playgrounds, First Nation reserves, and a host of other local arenas. One objective of the
case studies was to determine if the social reform activities of
community organizations could influence social policies. The second objective, examining the connections and compatibility between social work and community work, forms the subject matter
of Chapter 8.

The case studies represent examples of social reform activities
that changed social policies. The purpose of this chapter is to
identify insights from these experiences and to examine the potential of these insights for guiding social reform activities in the
future. The discussion is organized by three questions. First, do
organizational auspices matter when engaging in social reform?
Second, how can community organizations get their proposals for
change onto the policy agenda? Third, how can community organizations ensure that their proposals are implemented? The chapter concludes with a discussion of current issues in governing and
delivering social services.

DO ORGANIZATIONAL AUSPICES MATTER?

As noted in Chapter 1, many writers on community organization
have argued that auspices influence, if they don't in fact control,
the kind of community work organizations can engage in. "There
is widespread recognition among practitioners that the organizational situation sets both the opportunities and constraints that
govern the practitioner's operations" (Perlman and Gurin, 1972: 76).

Auspices also are an integral component of the Rothman framework that identifies typical agency auspices for three approaches
to community work: formal public- and private-sector organizations for social planning; neighbourhood-based associations for
locality development; and social movements for social action.
However, Rothman gives only cursory attention to social reform
and does not identify appropriate organizational auspices for this

approach. He describes social reform as organizing "a coalition of concerned interests to apply pressure on appropriate decision making bodies" (Rothman, 1974: 36). This description suggests that social reform is all about persuading decision-making bodies to change their policies or to rearrange their priorities. Organizations that pursue social reform are

> pressure groups whose members act together to influence public policy in order to promote their common interest. The chief characteristic of the pressure group is the fact that it tries to persuade governments to pursue the policies it advocates. (Pross, 1975: 2)

According to these views social reform is the exclusive property of pressure groups and social movements: almost by definition, public-sector organizations cannot engage in social reform.

This conception of social reform is consistent with the position of many writers, including the authors of *Community Organization and the Canadian State* (Ng et al., 1990), who contend that the state, its organizations, and staff oppress the poor and members of minority groups. Indeed, the state bureaucracy is frequently seen as an enemy to be overthrown rather than an ally in bringing about change. Thus a prominent position in community work is that public-sector organizations are the target and not the agent of social reform. To bolster their position, proponents point to the rigidity and remoteness of public-sector agencies and the residual policies and determination of many governments in Western democracies to reduce, if not eliminate, existing health and social service programs.

However, the case studies in this book raise questions about the validity of this view. For example, the chapter on healthy communities reveals that departments of public health have a long and distinguished record in social reform. Given their location in municipal governments, the tradition of reform in departments of public health is instructive for this discussion. From a social policy perspective, municipal governments have been regarded as the most conservative level of government in the country. How then to account for social reform in public health?

In a recent book on the history of the Department of Public

Health in Toronto, Heather MacDougall points out that the emergence of Toronto as a city brought in its wake:

> ... the burgeoning urban health problems of slums, polluted water supplies and waste disposal. The first medical officers of health in Toronto were prominent participants in the progressive reform movements which flourished from 1880 to 1920.... They worked through lay and medical organizations to publicize the benefits of the reforms that they proposed and acquired a high public profile as a result of their activism. Such personal involvement in reform crusades demonstrated the extent of their commitment to social change.... (MacDougall, 1990: 10)

Dr. Gordon Jackson, who became medical officer of health in 1929, questioned the value of early reforms:

> However, with the discovery of the germ origin of disease came a change in the status of organized public health. The revelations of Pasteur and the many famous workers who have followed have raised public health administration from the position of glorified broom squads to that of intensive scientific investigators. (*Ibid.*: 33)

It is clear from the above quotation from Dr. Gordon Jackson that the reform activities of his predecessors, which characterized the department for its first forty-seven years, had by the time of his appointment become something of an embarrassment. Social reform activities lacked a scientific explanation and hence were deemed to be inappropriate for the newly emerging profession of public health. In a virtually identical fashion to social work, also emerging as a profession at this time, public health officers deserted social reform in favour of interventions focused on individuals and based on scientific explanations.

It was not until the late 1970s, when pressure from environmental groups and in particular from members of these groups who had been elected to city council and to the boards of health and education, that the Toronto Department of Public Health began to reclaim its tradition of social reform. And as the chapter on healthy communities makes clear, the reclaiming process was greatly aided by the publication of the Lalonde Report and the subsequent interest in health promotion and in healthy communities.

The reclamation can be regarded as complete with the department's investigation into health inequalities in 1991. The investigation represents a scientific and professional approach to social reform. It is scientific because it uses social science research methodology in determining mortality rates in the city. It is professional partly because of its scientific base, but also because the current medical officer of health, Dr. Perry Kendall, believes that investigating and reporting on health conditions is an integral part of the role of a public health worker.

> As a public health professional I would be remiss if I did not point out the evidence that appears to demonstrate fairly consistently that countries with economic policies aimed deliberately at achieving more equitable after tax distribution of wealth as well as wealth production, produce more in the way of health for their population than do those countries which rely on aggressive free market principles to both produce and distribute their wealth.
>
> Despite having a large foreign born population whose mortality rates tend to be relatively low, the City of Toronto has a higher mortality rate, overall, than either Ontario or Canada. The most effective way to close this gap may be to reduce poverty in the City of Toronto. (Kendall, 1991: 4)

The similarity between Kendall's *Health Inequalities in the City of Toronto* and *Living on the Margin* (1986) and many other reports on poverty in Toronto produced by the Social Planning Council of Metropolitan Toronto is striking. While the beginning points of examination differ – *Health Inequalities* on mortality rates and *Living on the Margin* on the incidence of poverty – both conclude that poverty is a condition that cannot be tolerated and can be resolved only by redistribution of wealth. Both the Department of Public Health and the Social Planning Council defend their involvement in social reform by pointing to their respective mandates and the credibility of their research.

There are also some differences. The Department of Public

Health reports to a Board of Health, and through the Board to city council. Once having presented its reports and recommendations the department has to rely on the Board and on city council for further advocacy activities. By contrast, the Social Planning Council does not have direct and immediate access to elected officials and hence lacks the clout of a public-sector department. The Council can, however, present its work in a variety of community arenas, can co-operate with other community groups in organizing workshops, forums, and other educational events, and, when deemed necessary, can engage in demonstrations.

The crucial point for the discussion on auspices is that *Health Inequalities* is the product of a department of local government, an arena that traditionally has been viewed as inimical to social reform. Is this commitment to social reform an anomaly on the part of one Department of Public Health?

A beginning response derived from the case studies is that there are two fundamental requirements for engaging in social reform: a vision for change and a commitment to achieve this vision. (A detailed elaboration of these requirements is contained in the section on the convergence of interest.) As the case studies suggest, social movements, grassroots associations, and voluntary organizations have been in the forefront of recent reforms dedicated to improving the lot of the poor and the powerless.

Nevertheless, these organizations do not possess sole and exclusive rights to social reform. The history of social policy in Canada provides contrasting examples of the involvement of government in social reform. Some governments have agreed to assume responsibility for social programs only very reluctantly and only as a last-ditch measure to save the capitalist state. Thus the federal government of R.B. Bennett introduced unemployment insurance in 1935 not only to counter the ravages of the depression but also to preserve the capitalist system. "A good deal of pruning is sometimes necessary to save a tree and it would be well for us in Canada to remember that there is considerable pruning to be done if we are to preserve the fabric of the capitalist system" (Bennett, quoted in Finkel, 1977: 350).

An example of a government committed to social reform is afforded by the CCF government in Saskatchewan in 1947 when it introduced the first compulsory health insurance plan in North

America. In 1962 the same province initiated an even more radical program, which ensured that the costs of out-patient physician services would be covered. The Medical Service Plan led to a province-wide strike by the physicians and to such controversy that the government was defeated in the next election.

While many other examples on both sides of the argument could be cited, one important aspect of the discussion deserving special mention is that the more reforms challenge the status quo and the closer they approach the grand policy issues, the more intense will be the opposition. Thus the tax reforms proposed by the Royal Commission on Taxation in 1967 were greeted by a veritable storm of opposition from industry and business. David Lewis noted that "68% of the presentations made to the House of Commons Committee on Trade, Finance and Economic Affairs were by individual corporations or by corporate interest groups such as the Canadian Manufacturing Association" (Lewis, 1972: 101). The consequence of the opposition was, of course, that the reforms proposed by the Royal Commission were not implemented and Canada's tax structure remains inequitable and unjust.

The argument being developed here is that the crucial requirements for social reform, a vision for change and commitment to this vision, can be found in a wide variety of organizations. However, the nature and direction of the vision are determined by the ideology of the key actors in the organization rather than by the auspices of the organization: public, voluntary, or a social movement. Thus, governments led by politicians who have embraced a universal or social development ideology will, as in the case of Saskatchewan under the leadership of Tommy Douglas, institute changes to improve social well-being. By contrast, federal and provincial cabinets committed to the cause of residualism will seek to dismantle social programs. Given the definition of social reform outlined in Chapter 1, these efforts for change, while constituting radical shifts, cannot be classified as social reform. They are more appropriately described as changes dedicated to downsizing if not eliminating social programs.

A vision for change is expressed in the form of a mandate or statement of the overall purpose of an organization. Public-sector organizations are awarded a mandate through legislation, while the mandate of a voluntary agency is established by a board of directors. The mandates of the Social Planning Council of Metropolitan Toronto, the Association for Community Living, the Champagne/Aishihik band council, the healthy community projects, and the Pro-Life and Pro-Choice groups clearly commit these organizations to social reform. The auspices of these organizations vary considerably from local and informal associations to voluntary agencies, to a First Nation band council, and to a department of municipal government. Missing from the list are ministries of provincial governments, which provide most of the social services in Canada and which are attacked most severely for their rigidity and remoteness. Could these public agencies be awarded a mandate for social reform?

Consider the case of child welfare. As noted in Chapter 4, only a few provinces have given their child welfare departments or agencies a mandate that allows them to evaluate the impact of environmental factors such as poverty and poor housing on family life, and none have provided the resources necessary to ameliorate these factors. Indeed, a monumental irony is that all provincial social assistance programs provide such low benefits that recipients live well below the poverty line established by Statistics Canada. Provinces are then virtually united in the residualist position that child neglect and abuse are a private trouble. The mandate awarded by provincial governments to child welfare departments is limited to dealing with issues of neglect and abuse on an individual, case-by-case basis despite clear and compelling evidence that the majority of the families coming to the attention of child welfare agencies are poor and lack adequate housing. "A major metropolitan child welfare agency reports that 83% of the families which it served in 1988 had incomes below the Statistics Canada low income cut offs and that an additional 11% of its clientele was economically vulnerable" (Novick and Volpe, 1989: 81). Similar conclusions have been reached by the National Council of Welfare (1979), by the Canadian Child Welfare Association et al. (1988), and by the Child Poverty Action Group and the Social Planning Council of Metropolitan Toronto (1991).

In summary, the federal and provincial governments have maintained social assistance benefits below the poverty line even though a federal Minister of Health and Welfare acknowledged the crippling effects of poverty on health (Epp, 1986). In addition, provincial governments have shrunk from the challenge of assigning to child welfare agencies the task of investigating, monitoring, and reporting on the effects of poverty on family life.

By contrast, the environment is an integral component of the mandate of public health departments. These departments have the authorization not only to inspect water, sanitation, and housing conditions but to ensure that standards are maintained. Some public health departments and the healthy community movement have extended their mandates to include poverty and other social environmental factors.

It is intriguing to inquire why the environment has been considered an appropriate responsibility in public health and not for social service agencies. Clearly the physical environment – matters such as clean air and water – affect everyone and over time have been accepted as public issues that should be dealt with by public authorities. On the other hand, the social services are concerned with family life – matters currently defined as private troubles and hence inappropriate for public agencies. The question is raised whether some aspects of family life, such as income and housing, should be redefined as public rather than private matters. Indeed, definitions are of crucial importance in social policy, and a discussion of their significance in shaping social policies occupies a central place in this and the following chapter.

Although auspices are important, the mandate awarded to an organization by its governing body is the crucial factor in determining whether the organization will engage in social reform. In turn, mandates are established by the visions and the ideologies of the key actors within organizations, be they public or voluntary.

THE CONVERGENCE OF INTEREST

The case studies confirm the relevance of the concept of convergence of interest, and the following discussion is intended to assist community workers to craft convergence – to shape the forces that bring interests and people together. The concept is particularly suited to situations where those proposing the change do not have the power to ensure that their proposal will even be considered by policy-makers, let alone implemented. While municipal governments have jurisdiction over recreation programs and some aspects of health, they have virtually no capacity to make or change social policy. Hence the following discussion applies to municipal governments as well as voluntary agencies. It should be noted, too, that since the social reforms discussed here attempt to promote the cause of disadvantaged groups, they will encounter resistance. In large measure the task confronting reform groups is overcoming resistance.

A review of the case studies suggests that the following set of conditions is required for interests to converge and for the change to be placed on the policy-making agenda. A later section of the chapter considers the difficulties typically encountered at the implementation stage.

1. A community organization is in place or can be put into place.
2. The organization possesses detailed knowledge of the problem or issue being addressed.
3. The organization is dedicated to the task of overcoming the problem.
4. The organization has developed a vision for change and can communicate this vision to policy-makers and the public.
5. The organization can establish connections with policy-makers, and through these connections influence the policy process.
6. Lacking connections, the organization has the capacity to bring pressure to bear on policy-makers.

A detailed discussion of these requirements follows.

1. *A community organization is in place or can be put into place.* It will be recalled from Chapter 1 that a community was defined in a pragmatic fashion as a network of individuals with common needs. The advantage of this simple formulation is that it focuses attention on two crucial aspects of community – the pattern of relationships between individuals and needs or issues that require attention. In order to address these matters the concerned individuals must either belong to an organization or develop a new organization. Individuals on their own can proffer ideas and become crusaders for reform. However, social reformers most often face daunting obstacles and overcoming these obstacles requires

an array of resources that individuals do not possess. At some point social reform requires the resources and the sponsorship of a community organization.

In addition, as Sower *et al.* (1957) have pointed out and the case studies confirm, the organization must be led by individuals who are respected and have earned the right to speak out. Thus the Association for Community Living in New Brunswick was represented by Lorraine Silliphant and Gordon Porter, who had earned their legitimacy through years of hard work on behalf of children with special needs in that province. Similarly Paul Birckel, chief of the Champagne/Aishihik band council, was a respected First Nation leader in the Yukon.

2. *The organization possesses detailed knowledge of the problem or issue being addressed.* A common denominator emerging from the case studies reviewed here is that the organizations possessed detailed information about the problem or issue being addressed. This information can be obtained in two ways, and in some instances by a combination of these two methods. The Social Planning Council of Metropolitan Toronto gathered its information through research and the analysis of existing programs. In contrast, members of the Pro-Choice and Pro-Life groups in Nanaimo and of the band council of the Champagne/Aishihik gained their knowledge of the problems of abortion and child neglect and abuse from direct personal experience. The Association for Community Living in New Brunswick represents an example of an organization that obtained information both from research and from the personal experience of members of the Association whose children were developmentally delayed.

Regardless of the source, a necessary condition for initiating action is the possession of accurate information. If the target of change can dispute or reject the information base, the entire proposal can be discredited. Hence, organizations like the Social Planning Council of Metropolitan Toronto are extremely careful in collecting information and in analysing policies and programs.

It is important to add that the information possessed by organizations with a commitment to a mission is likely to be rich in its description of the issue or problem. It supplements the factual data compiled and released by government bodies with the knowledge gained from direct personal awareness of the suffering of individuals and families. It is suffused with intimate details of the circumstances of individuals and families and communicates a sense of pain and urgency. Because of its authenticity it compels policymakers and the public at large to pay attention.

3. *The organization is dedicated to the task of overcoming the problem.* As emphasized in the introductory section of this chapter, commitment to a cause is a vital ingredient in social reform. Like information, commitment can arise from a number of sources. Perhaps the easiest source to identify is personal experience. Thus the Association for Community Living from its inception has been largely composed of parents whose children are developmentally delayed. These parents and the Association have adopted the cause of developing appropriate and effective social policies for their children as a virtual lifelong mission. Similarly, members of the Champagne/Aishihik band have witnessed the disastrous outcomes of child welfare policies developed and delivered by government departments with no attachment to the traditions and values of First Nation communities. Commitment to a cause is vividly illustrated by the groups involved in the struggle around abortion. The authors of the case study on abortion write:

> Clearly all these women ... were unlikely to change their beliefs or to withdraw from the issue, and we were soon aware that the story of their actions could only be understood in the context of these deep convictions. It is a central belief in the women's movement that "the personal is political," and the significance of this connection was evident in the way our informants perceived their personal experience as motivating and empowering them to take political action.

Whether rooted in personal experience, religious values, cultural mores and traditions, or in the mission of an organization, commitment to a cause results in a determination to struggle against often intransigent bureaucracies, a disinterested public, and the chronic shortage of funds. In short, a fundamental requirement for change is the establishment of a constituency dedicated to reform and prepared to wage campaigns for as long as necessary. The latter component of tenacity is often overlooked in analyses of the change process. "An idea whose time has come" does not simply appear on the policy agenda. All of the successful outcomes of the case studies reviewed here were based on long and extensive campaigns. For example, the Association for Community Living campaigned for some ten years for the closure of the William F. Roberts School before its argument was accepted by the provincial government.

4. *The organization has developed a vision for change and can communicate this vision to policy-makers and the public.* The policy process can be viewed as a continuing series of negotiations. In turn, these negotiations are shaped in large part by defining and redefining the roles of individuals and the mandate of public agencies.

The concept of redefining or reframing problems is based on the work of a number of scholars. Schon argues that "the problems of public policy are not given. They are constructed by human beings in their attempts to make sense of complex and troubling situations, often in the context of the disaster produced by the last solution" (Schon, 1980: 36). The essence of the argument is that policies are set by ideas that have currency at a particular time. Schon labels ways of viewing problems as "frames." Some frames are in fundamental conflict, as occurred in the case study on abortion, but others can be reshaped and altered in such a way as to provide a new direction. Let Schon sum up his argument.

> I think it must be admitted then, that in the context of social policy dilemmas, frame restructuring does sometimes occur. We are sometimes able to coordinate two competing descriptions of social reality, restructuring conflicting frames in such a way as to yield an integrating image that includes, redescribed and coordinated, the purposes and values that seemed before to be incompatible. (*ibid.*: 63)

The work of three other scholars provides support for the concept of reframing. In his discussion of the contribution of research to social policy, Roy Parker develops a remarkably similar version of reframing:

> After all re-search is, as the word implies, a process of looking again; of being curious; of being interested in surprising pat-

terns; of being able to reflect upon what happens in a systematic fashion and, above all, of having the confidence to adopt a critical attitude towards conventional wisdom, accepted practice or current fashion. (Parker, 1989: 5)

For sociologist Richard LaPiere, reframing constitutes an innovation:

a departure from the established ways of thinking and acting – an idea for accomplishing some recognized social end in a new way or for a means of accomplishing some new social end.... Whatever the manifestation, the innovating consists of the creation of a unique and significant mental construct. (LaPiere, 1965: 128)

An innovator is one who "is sceptical of conventional thinking in general" (*ibid*.: 130).

To depart for a moment from the discussion of reframing, it is pertinent to point to examples of innovators in the case studies. Wolf Wolfensberger, who developed the notion of normalization, Trevor Hancock and Leonard Duhl, who initiated the concept of healthy communities, and First Nation leaders such as Chief Wayne Christian of the Spalumcheen band in B.C. and Chief Paul Birckel of the Champagne/Aishihik band, who rejected the traditional approach to child welfare, fit the image of the innovators who are sceptical of conventional thinking. And, importantly so for this discussion, these individuals worked in organizations that supported the need for innovative thinking and social reform.

It is necessary to add that innovators are seldom solely responsible for the adoption of their ideas. Implementation requires advocates, and in these case studies advocacy was supplied both by voluntary organizations and by the public sector. Thus Gordon Porter, among many other members of the Association for Community Living, was a tenacious advocate for normalization, and the cause was subsequently embraced by the minister, deputy minister, and other senior staff of the Department of Health and Community Services.

Perhaps the clearest description of reframing comes from the feminist writer Doris Lessing.

What one can observe happening over and over again is that some minority view which is regarded as totally crazy, ten years later is a mainstream view. The question that interests me is why do these ideas have to be outlawed to begin with? Why do we always have to reject something new? I'm always interested in looking around and seeing what totally screwball ideas are out on the edge and which of them are likely to be in the centre quite soon. The forces that support them are the fact that they are needed, that they correspond in some way to reality, otherwise they wouldn't succeed. The ones that just die and are forgotten, they don't have any kind of reality behind them. (Lessing, 1991)

Not only is this a succinct statement of reframing, but it suggests some criteria, albeit very broad and general ones, for differentiating between the screwball ideas – those that come into the centre are needed and those that die "don't have any kind of reality behind them."

The case studies provide examples of the power of the reframing concept and illustrate Lessing's criteria of need and reality. The first example comes from the study of deinstitutionalization in New Brunswick. Over a period of some ten years the Association for Community Living advocated a philosophy of normalization, individualization, and integration that redefined the social role of developmentally delayed children. Whereas these children were formerly seen as helpless and as requiring institutional care, this redefinition changed their status to children with special needs but entirely capable of living with families and in communities. The "reality" of this reframing effort was aided by the work of similar associations in other jurisdictions, but in essence it resulted from the commitment of the Association to wage a decade-long campaign to secure the approval of provincial officials to close the William F. Roberts Hospital School.

A second example comes from the case study on child welfare, where the Champagne/Aishihik band succeeded in redefining the capacity of Native people to provide care for their children. Again over a long period of time, band members argued that the notion that First Nation parents did not care for their children and were incapable of looking after them was inaccurate and insulting. This assertion of reframing, repeated over and over again, was coupled with requests to take control of child welfare and other social programs. These efforts and the barrenness of the existing approach to child welfare in First Nation communities finally persuaded policy-makers in the Yukon territorial government that transferring responsibility for child welfare from the territory to the Champagne/Aishihik band was indeed an idea whose time had come – which in Lessing's words "corresponded to reality."

A third but unsuccessful example of changing the definitions of individuals comes from the case study on the Social Planning Council of Metropolitan Toronto and the reform of income security in Ontario. The Council has attempted to change the image of the recipient of social assistance from the able-bodied male malingerer to the female-headed family with children. The Council's efforts were based on the actual profiles of the provincial caseload. Certainly these efforts influenced the work of the Social Assistance Review Committee and may have altered the perceptions of some influential members of the business community and provincial politicians, but the public notions of welfare recipients remain largely unchanged.

A fourth and as yet incomplete example is provided by the healthy community movement, which is attempting to redefine the mandate for health. The redefinition asserts that poverty, the quality of work life, and the environment should be included as integral components of health and of the healthy community movement. Chapter 5 notes that while the redefinition has been asserted, it has yet to be implemented in full and committed fashion.

The final example is not derived from the case studies, but is included here because it represents an attempt to redefine both the role of women and the mandate of child welfare agencies. This reframing effort represents the latest in a series of redefinitions that have occurred in Canadian child welfare with respect to the appropriate division of responsibility between the state and parents to care for children. Each of these redefinitions has been shaped by changes in the structure of the family and of society. They have been influenced, too, by the changes in attitudes and perceptions around the rights of women and children, and the example noted below continues the effort to realign responsibilities between parent and state in a way that recognizes current realities.

From her research in child welfare, Marilyn Callahan (1992) argues that the child welfare system is predicated on the outdated conception of a family structure where fathers work outside the home and mothers stay home to care for children. This conception further holds that most if not all families possess the resources to care for their children and that looking after children can be considered as work, and hence as requiring a wage, only if it takes place outside the home. However, the reality in Canadian society in the 1990s is that one-third of marriages end in divorce, and the usual consequence of divorce is that the mother becomes the sole parent and she and her children live in poverty. The crux of the argument is that mothers care about their children, but they do not have the resources to care for them.

Redefining the mandate of child welfare requires that priority be given to an adequate income or wage for the parent who stays at home to provide child care; that child welfare agencies refocus services to provide support for mothers in the form of day care, protection from violence, and support; that neglect be removed from legislation; and, finally, that physical and sexual abuse be defined as criminal acts to be investigated like any other criminal activity. The redefinition is above all concerned with improving the status of women in Canadian society and is an example of the "confidence to adopt a critical attitude towards conventional wisdom, accepted practice and current fashion" (Parker, 1989: 5).

In summary, the case studies confirm the conceptual work of Schon, Parker, LaPiere, and Lessing that ordinary policies can be changed by redefining the roles of individuals and the mandates of public agencies. Such a strategy focuses attention on the analysis of roles and responsibilities in society. It requires the ability to think beyond the conventional wisdom, to suggest new ways of understanding how public issues and private troubles connect and influence each other, and to mobilize support for these new understandings so that they are seen as corresponding to reality rather than as "totally screwball ideas."

While the focus here is on the ordinary issues of policy, it is instructive to note that other writers have employed the reframing concept with regard to the grand issues. For example, Pateman

(1988: 237) has argued that "paid employment has become the key to citizenship and the recognition of an individual as a citizen of social worth to other citizens is lacking when a worker is unemployed." In contemporary Western societies, where unemployment is maintained at a consistently high level, there exists a "permanent underclass of social exiles" (ibid.: 235). A second group who also lack full citizenship are women whose work has always been undervalued and underpaid. Thus for Pateman, Western societies have developed grand policies that exclude two groups from full citizenship.

Redefining the roles of these two groups is no easy matter. Both confront grand issues of policy in a direct fashion: the unemployed because a high level of unemployment is required in a capitalist society; women because an adequate wage for mothers appears to stretch role definitions beyond all reasonable limits. Stretching the limits will require both innovators who can argue the case and advocates who can champion the cause. Pateman suggests that "one necessary condition for the creation of a genuine democracy in which the welfare of all citizens is served is an alliance between a labour movement that acknowledges the problem of patriarchal power and an autonomous women's movement that recognizes the problem of class power. Whether such an alliance can be forged is an open question" (ibid.: 256).

From different beginning points, Callahan in child welfare and Patemen in citizenship, both scholars call for redefining the role of women. Indeed, reframing the role of women affords an opportunity to connect the ordinary and grand issues of policy in a direct way. The connection is explored in the concluding section of the chapter.

5. *The organization can establish connections with policymakers, and through these connections influence the policy process.* As noted in the case study on reforming income security in Ontario, the agendas of governments at all levels are crowded with issues, all deemed urgent and all clamouring for attention. Partly because of the crowded nature of the policy agenda and partly because there are no easy access routes or mechanisms for social reform groups to register their concerns, simply getting items onto the agenda is extremely difficult.

The Canadian political system presents great impediments to those who want to raise new issues and who lack either the knowledge or the power to command access.... If public authorities are unreceptive to an issue it may be years before it is discussed at all. Conversely if the public authority is receptive to an issue it can act with dispatch. The Canadian political system tends to favour elite groups making functional, accommodative, consensus-seeking techniques of political communication. (Pross, 1975: 19)

By no stretch of the imagination can social reform groups be considered as elite, and neither can their reforms be characterized as accommodative and consensus-oriented. As noted throughout the book, social reform groups seek to alter the status quo, and their proposals to aid the poor and powerless are regarded as presumptuous, unnecessary, and costly. As noted earlier, the closer reforms approach the grand issues of redistributing power and income, the greater the resistance. Thus the proposals of the Social Planning Council of Toronto and of the *Transitions* report, while gaining initial support, encountered formidable difficulties when the full impact of the provincial deficit and the recession was felt. Other reforms, which cut across class and income lines, encounter less resistance. The call to close institutions for children with special needs was supported by parents regardless of their class and income level, and as will be recalled from Chapter 2, representatives of the Association for Community Living were included in the deliberations that resulted in the closure of the William F. Roberts School and the establishment of a community support system.

Connections between policy-makers and representatives of social reform organizations are relatively easy to establish in small communities and sparsely populated political jurisdictions such as New Brunswick and the Yukon. The close network of relationships between members of the Champagne/Aishihik band and the Yukon territorial government were described in Chapter 4. However, in Ontario representatives of the Social Planning Council of Metropolitan Toronto had few connections with key politicians in the provincial government. It was, therefore, forced to rely on the pathway of rational persuasion and the resource of professional expertise. Yet the magnitude of the change and the resources required to implement it were such that even the best of connections might have been to no effect.

6. *Lacking connections, the organization has the capacity to bring pressure to bear on policy-makers.* Even with connections in place the Association for Community Living and the Champagne/Aishihik band council pressed their respective cases to their governments with vigour. In these two instances the governments were allies – reluctant allies at first but then active and willing collaborators.

The variety of tactics required to bring pressure to bear on policy-makers is described in the case studies on abortion and on reforming social assistance. In Nanaimo both the Pro-Life and Pro-Choice groups organized public meetings, held rallies, and lobbied members of the hospital board. Both sought to augment their influence by recruiting new members and building coalitions with other groups. Bringing new members into the fold expanded the range of connections and served to ameliorate the image of the Pro-Choice group as radical feminists and that of the Pro-Life association as religious zealots.

As Chapter 5 makes clear, engaging in such activities was far from easy for women who had not been involved in any form of public action. They were, however,

> surprised to learn how a small cohesive group can quickly stake out territory and become a force for change, sometimes much to the surprise of its membership. . . . As one respondent remarked, "when I read that the Pro-Choice Coalition held a rally, I thought 'Hey, that's me and two friends. I didn't know we were official.' "

The efforts launched in Ontario to convince the provincial government of the need to implement the *Transitions* report were described in Chapter 3. The campaign, including as it did public forums, coalition-building, the recruitment of prominent media and business leaders, and coverage through the media, represented one of the most extensive efforts to bring pressure to bear on policy-makers ever developed by social reform organizations in Canada. While the immediate impact of this large-scale campaign may have been disappointing to its organizers, its long-term public education effects are only now being realized as the NDP government in Ontario tackles the implementation of *Transitions*.

THE IMPLEMENTATION PHASE OF THE POLICY PROCESS

I turn now to a discussion of the second issue posed at the beginning of this chapter – the implementation of social reforms. The discussion is based on the position articulated in the preceding chapters that implementation is the most difficult phase of the policy process. The case studies suggest that there are three central aspects of implementation that confound community organizations in their attempts to ensure that their proposals will be carried out. These troublesome issues and some tentative strategies for resolving them are outlined below.

The Short-Term and Crisis-Ridden Nature of the Policy Process

Despite the contention that policy-making and practice are essentially discrete activities carried out by two groups of people with little in common, there are some similarities. For example, both are "front-end driven" in the sense that crises continually cry for attention. Often, both policy-makers and practitioners find their time and energy consumed by dealing with crises, and at the point an assessment of a client has been made and a report completed on a policy issue, new demands are clamouring for attention.

The discussion in Chapter 3 suggested that social reform organizations must recognize that policy-makers have a short-term horizon. Politicians frequently focus on a particular issue of interest to them, one that can be accomplished within their term of office and will be a significant achievement. Ministers of departments are interested in "making their mark." Thus the former federal Minister of Health and Welfare, Jake Epp, is remembered for his work in the health field and for the important documents *Achieving Health for All* and *Breaking the Barriers*. An alternative strategy for ministers operating in an environment characterized by scarce resources and by a lack of priority for their portfolio is to do as little as possible, avoid mistakes, and hope for a more important assignment.

The task facing social reform organizations is, therefore, fraught with difficulties. Reforms that involve a redefinition of social roles and fields of service require a long-term horizon. Yet these organizations are faced with a context in which only short-term reforms that fit the particular interests of the minister will be considered. The dilemma reflects the reality of the public policy process, which will not be changed in any fundamental fashion. Since social reform organizations have to adapt to this agenda, they might adopt a very deliberate and analytic approach to implementation of reforms.

It was suggested in Chapter 3 that social reform organizations might employ a conceptual framework such as the one developed by Morris and Binstock in order to assess the feasibility of the reforms being proposed. Is the reform an "idea whose time has come"? If not, can a campaign be developed to gain support for the reform? Can existing definitions of people and problems be changed? Is there support for the reform from other organizations and from within the bureaucracy? Alternatively, will the reform provoke resistance, and if so how much? Is the timing of the request appropriate or should it be delayed? In some instances, the analysis may suggest that it is necessary to hold back a proposal for a major change until more supportive policy-makers are in power.

The following anecdote illustrates a strategy for combining short- and long-term goals and accomplishing the first in an environment that was indifferent if not hostile to the long-term agenda. Dr. J. Willard, one of Canada's leading social policy figures, served as the deputy minister of Health and Welfare Canada under a number of Liberal and Conservative governments. Willard developed long-term objectives for the department, such as the establishment of comprehensive health and income security programs. However, he recognized that the Progressive Conservative government of Prime Minister Diefenbaker attached little priority to these areas. During this administration, Willard advanced suggestions for research and education – suggestions within his long-term agenda but of a sufficiently ideologically neutral nature that they would not offend an administration with little interest in advancing income security and health programs. This strategy enabled Willard to gain approval for the Welfare Grants program within the department – a program that has supported research and education for some thirty years! The potential of this strategy, nicely captured by Trevor Hancock as "goal directed muddling through," is discussed in the final chapter (Hancock, 1989: 28).

The Royal Commission Syndrome

Another common denominator between policy and practice is that it is always easier to plan than to implement. Practitioners find that it is relatively easy to assess the problems facing their clients but often difficult to translate the plan into action. Clients then have to be engaged in carrying out the plan, the resources necessary to the plan may not be appropriate or available, and the required co-operation of other professionals may not be forthcoming. Indeed, practitioners have commented on the irony that the status differences in the helping professions often mean that the best-trained professionals, usually male psychiatrists and psychologists, claim the assessment function for themselves, leaving the much more difficult task of treatment to the female social workers and nurses.

A similar pattern unfolds at the policy level. Faced with an intractable policy issue, governments take refuge by appointing task forces, royal commissions, and other forms of review bodies to study the problem and bring forth recommendations for change. This strategy assigns planning to one group and action to a second in a similar fashion to the breakdown between the assessment and treatment functions. The similarity continues in the sense that those appointed to royal commissions are experts in their field, and they devote countless hours to hearing and reading submissions and to reviewing the findings of researchers appointed to assist the commissioners. Their expertise is greatly enhanced by their involvement in the process of review, and a typical consequence is that they produce a blueprint for change characterized by the most innovative recommendations that can devised. The assessment is then delivered to a group of harried policy-makers who have not had the opportunity to immerse themselves in research and contemplation. A not unusual response of policy-makers is amazement at the audacity of the report.

The essential point arising from the above discussion is that, in the world of social services practice, assessment must take into account the realities of practice, and in policy, research and planning must be connected to implementation.

One way of overcoming the royal commission syndrome was noted in Chapter 3 and is worth repeating here. The strategy is based on a recent investigation by the Office of the Ombudsman in B.C. into services for children and youth. The investigation concluded that services were scattered among a number of ministries and private agencies and that a central authority responsible for legislation, policy, and services was required. However, rather than delivering a scathing report on the inadequacies of current services to the legislature, the ministries, and the public, the Ombudsman worked with the ministries to develop an action plan to address the identified problems. Only at that point was the report, including the approved action plan, published and released. Thus, provision for implementation was included as an integral part of the investigation, rather than treated as a separate matter.

The Closed Nature of the Policy Process

The royal commission syndrome illustrates a frequent problem in implementing social reforms. A second and equally difficult aspect of implementation is that all too frequently the resources and commitments required to put plans into place have evaporated by the time the implementation stage is reached. An example of this difficulty is provided by the case study on reforming income security in Ontario.

Strategies for overcoming this problem are suggested by the New Brunswick and Yukon case studies. To set the context for these strategies it is necessary to refer to the discussion in Chapter 2 on programmed and adaptive approaches to the policy process. Both are useful and valid approaches, but they must fit the policy environment. The criteria for selecting one approach over the other are: the scope of the change, the certainty of the theory or technology underlying the change, the extent of agreement around the objective of the change, the degree of control that can be exercised by the organization, and the stability of the environment (Berman, 1980: 205). Most social policies affect a large number of people, the theory is uncertain, agreement around objectives is usually limited, and the environment is turbulent. Thus the adaptive approach, which acknowledges the need for changes and alterations during the course of implementation, is the preferred approach in the social services. By contrast, the programmed approach assumes that policies can be implemented in a mechanical fashion by issuing detailed sets of instructions and regulations and then monitoring the behaviour of staff to ensure that the instructions have been followed.

The adaptive approach allows for and indeed encourages extensive participation in the policy process. The participation of representatives of voluntary organizations, consumer groups, and line staff brings a range of views and opinions to the early stages of the policy process and ensures the support of these groups at the implementation stage. Thus involving representatives of the Association for Community Living in developing a policy on deinstitutionalization in New Brunswick not only enhanced the policy process but guaranteed their support during implementation. Similarly, including members of the Champagne/Aishihik band in discussions on the transfer of child welfare services virtually precluded opposition at the implementation stage. Even though the Association and the band council had set the stage for their involvement by initiating the reforms, it would have been possible, though highly undesirable and unproductive, for the New Brunswick and Yukon governments to exclude them during the policy process. Opening up the policy process to outside groups is a promising strategy for overcoming the evaporation problem and, indeed, for improving the product of the process.

CURRENT ISSUES IN GOVERNING AND DELIVERING THE SOCIAL SERVICES

Given that social policies are initiated and developed at national and provincial levels but implemented in local communities, are the existing linkages and connections between levels of government sufficient to ensure that policies meet the needs of individuals and families? Should the role of local government be strengthened? Is the community a viable base for governing the social services?

The following discussion is based in part on insights from the case studies but also builds on previous studies on the governance of the social services. The anchor point of the argument is that a

new partnership among federal, provincial, and municipal governments and the voluntary sector is necessary. The partnership envisaged here has much in common with the notion of welfare
pluralism whereby the state surrenders the responsibility for the
direct provision of services but retains overall responsibility for
legislation, financing, and ensuring that standards of service are
maintained. The notion of welfare pluralism has gained ascen-
dancy in the U.K., where the inappropriateness and inefficiencies
of state monopolies have become apparent. The advantages of the
welfare pluralist model are described by one advocate as including:

> elements of decentralization (more local involvement in deci-
> sion making), de-standardization (more support for innovative
> and experimental programs) and de-professionalization (more
> emphasis on informal caring and self help) together with a shift
> to prevention and the horizontal integration of services. In such
> a scenario the role of government becomes the upholding of
> equity in resource allocation, the enforcement of minimum
> standards, the fostering of more pluralistic legislation and the
> use of fiscal and regulatory law for income maintenance and to
> reinforce a preventive approach. (Gladstone, 1979: 101)

The partnership model favoured here departs from the above
formulation by rejecting the call for deprofessionalization and an
emphasis on informal caring on the grounds that such recommendations inevitably result in more unpaid work being assigned to
women. In addition, the above depiction of welfare pluralism, like
many other models developed in the U.K., focuses on the relationship between the state and the voluntary sector while neglecting
to differentiate between levels of government. The partnership
model envisaged in this book has more in common with Australian frameworks that see local government at the core of a reorgan-
ized system of social services.

My approach to partnership begins with the federal government
and its responsibility to develop framework legislation that would
ensure equality of benefits and services for all Canadians. Thus
the federal government would maintain responsibility for health
and social security programs, and indeed would expand its pres-

ent commitment by eliminating poverty in Canada through a combination of tax reform, improvement of existing programs, and development of new programs such as a wage for mothers.

The argument for a national presence in social policy is forcefully presented in the case study on abortion. The policy vacuum at the federal level meant that community groups concerned about the abortion issue had no option but to convince local hospital boards to accept their particular position. In a very real sense policy on abortion was decided community by community with the consequence that there was no equality of treatment for women across the country. The abortion case study illustrates the absurdity of abrogating a national responsibility to communities.

Given, then, a case for a federal presence in social policy, the discussion now turns to the provincial level. Provincial governments would retain responsibility for establishing legislation, policy, budgets, and standards for the personal social services – services such as child welfare, day care, and counselling. However, the responsibility for delivering these services would be delegated to the municipal level. In turn, municipal governments could provide services through their own departments, establish boards of social services, as has occurred in the fields of health and education, or delegate responsibilities to voluntary agencies.

To make the partnership work municipal governments must develop social planning capabilities; indeed, provincial legislation will be needed to require all municipalities to develop community health and social service plans. These plans would specify the range of services and the administrative structures required in all municipalities. A plan would, for example, decide whether the social services should be combined with health, with education, with recreation, with all or none? Communities might well develop different governing structures and different patterns of integration.

As noted above in the discussion on the closed nature of the policy process, this partnership would open up the process. Planning departments and other community organizations would be charged with the responsibility of monitoring the outcomes of existing policies and, on the basis of these reviews, of suggesting change. Their reviews would determine whether policies had been implemented as intended and would evaluate their effectiveness. The intent would be to avoid the current discontinuities so vividly illustrated by child welfare policies and their impact on First Nation children. Communities would in effect become the primary contributors to the beginning and end phases of the policy process.

This partnership retains primary responsibility for the social services within the public sector but distributes particular responsibilities among the various levels of government and, where appropriate, to the voluntary sector. The position taken here is that the social services are essential and should be available to the public in the same way as health and education. Hence, elected officials must be held responsible for these services.

The call for a partnership arrangement among levels of government, with each taking clear responsibility for certain functions, is consistent with the recommendations of a number of reviews in this and other countries. Given the degree of similarity in governmental arrangements between Canada and Australia, the conclusions of a recent Australian study on *Better Services for Local Communities* are pertinent (Australian Local Government Association, 1990). In Australia the responsibility for health and social services has been delegated to local governments, particularly in the state of Victoria, on a much more extensive basis than has occurred in Canada.

> The New Cooperative Federalism is a major attempt to reverse the top down, centralist approach to planning for local services and to place the emphasis where it rightfully belongs. Local government, because of its role in municipal management is the appropriate sphere of government to ensure that local planning occurs and is integrated with State and National planning strategies. Community services are more efficient and effective when they are locally planned, delivered and coordinated with other local services. (Australian Local Government Association, 1990)

A recent inquiry in Ontario identified eight principles "intended to lead to a better managed, more effective and more responsive social service system and to support and reinforce a good working relationship between the two levels of government" (Report of the Provincial-Municipal Social Services Review, 1990: 14). While some of the principles selected provide little direction for awarding social services to the appropriate level of government, there is nevertheless a clear emphasis on the balance between equity and provincial standards on the one hand and community priorities on the other hand. The Provincial-Municipal Social Services Review assigns the responsibility for legislation, policy, establishing budgets, and standards to the province, leaving direct services to be provided by municipalities and voluntary agencies. The Review also clearly recognizes the case for a strong social planning capacity at the local level.

While the overall position of the Review that responsibilities should be clearly divided between different levels of government is eminently sensible, there are two serious flaws in the recommendations. First, the Review awards responsibility for income security programs to the municipal level. In my view the need for equity across the province clearly outweighs the case for discretion at the local level with respect to income assistance programs. Indeed, as noted earlier, my clear preference is that income security become the sole responsibility of the federal government and be integrated with the tax system. The second weakness is that the Review did not include affinity as one of its guiding principles. Affinity has been described as assisting

> potential users to assess their state of personal identity with the provider as a condition for using their service. Areas where affinity judgements are made often involve the more intimate areas of personal need. Affinity is the perception that a provider possesses a unique set of characteristics which are important to the consumer. (Social Planning Council of Metropolitan Toronto, 1976: 106)

The principle of affinity suggests that services such as counselling, day care, and other support and self-help programs should be organized in such a way as to permit a close identification with the consumer. Evidence from such disparate sources as the best-selling text on business firms, *In Search of Excellence*, and from studies of participation in the human services reveals that consumers and other citizens affected by and interested in a particular agency will commit endless hours of dedicated work to ensure that its programs are effective. The argument is supported here by the Champagne/Aishihik child welfare project in which the band council governs the services on behalf of band members and by the Association for Community Living in the case study on New Brunswick. Other examples of the concept of constituency governance include services for women being managed by women and agencies providing programs for workers being run by trade unions. (For an extended discussion of this notion, see Wharf, 1990.)

The concept of affinity clearly supports the case for community or constituency control within the overall context of the partnership model. The case studies of child welfare in the Yukon and Vancouver argue that at least in this important and complex field of service, community and constituency control are promising strategies for reforming the governance of the social services. (For a review of the concept of community control see, among other sources, Clague et al., 1984.)

Implementing this strategy will require that provincial governments relinquish their present monopolistic hold on the social services, that the partnership arrangements described above be put into place, and that planned and conscious diversity characterize community social services. The argument is supported by Shragge's conclusions in his study of alternative service organizations in Montreal.

> The community based option has shown itself to be responsible and innovative, creating new approaches and service delivery at a level that can respond directly to a range of community needs and problems. One critique of the post war welfare state centres on its bureaucratic structure, over reliance on professionals and the fact that planning and control of services is remote from the local community. Clearly, the Alternative Service Organizations are able to address these problems even with their chronic underfunding. (Shragge, 1990: 152)

While the attributes of community ownership, small size, and a low level of bureaucratization may not be sufficient to offset completely the negative features of remoteness, rigidity, and regulation that characterize many provincial departments of social service, they are a promising start. To complete the discussion it is necessary to reaffirm that the extent of community or constituency control advocated here is within the context of partnership with senior levels of government. The problem of "acute localitis" (Montgomery, 1979) referred to in Chapter 4 is not likely to obtain in a partnership arrangement whereby legislation and budgets are established by the provincial or, in some rare instances, the federal government.

The concept of community and constituency governance has been discussed for many years and even implemented on a modest scale in some jurisdictions. A new strategy for reforming the governance of the social services is the notion of individualized funding mentioned in Chapter 2. Because of its significance as a social reform the concept is reviewed below in some detail. Individualized funding builds on and extends the notion of individual service plans by allocating funds directly to individuals rather than through a department of government or a private agency. The concept is based on the principles of self-determination, dignity, and autonomy, and in the view of the Association for Community Living this is a logical and desirable extension of individual service plans.

> Individualized funding is based on the following principle: persons with disabilities require money for basic living needs such as food, clothing, shelter, and utilities. Second they require money for their special disability related needs (e.g. medications, equipment) and for services (e.g. homemaker assistance, life skills training or attendant care). (G. Allan Roeher Institute 1991: 132)

The Association recognizes that some disabled individuals may experience difficulties in locating appropriate services, and further that the assistance of family and friends may not be sufficient to overcome this problem. Hence as a companion notion the Association has developed the concept of service brokerage. Brokers are employed by independent agencies to assist the disabled in finding services. In effect, this new service pattern transforms the New Brunswick plan by providing funds directly to individuals rather than to case managers, and it changes the latter role from manager to broker.

The individualized funding approach appears at first glance to be a promising strategy for reforming the governance and delivery of the social services. It is based on sound principles, it is supported by a well-respected association, and it represents an attempt to meet both the basic income and the special needs of the disabled. However, this approach has the potential to meet only the basic income needs, not the special needs, of the client-consumer.

The disabled should receive an adequate income as an entitlement for two reasons. First, most disabled individuals in Canada are poor and many are unable to find suitable employment (see G. Allan Roeher Institute, 1988). The condition of poverty should be recognized and separated from employment. Second, disability is a universal phenomenon that will affect most people either because of an accident or as a result of aging. Like other universal needs, the condition of poverty among the disabled should be addressed in a way that does not single out the disabled as deviant or different. This requires that the disabled receive an income in the form of a demogrant, delivered through the mail and taxed as income. I should add that I have no difficulty extending the argument for a guaranteed adequate income to all Canadians. Hence, considered as a strategy to end poverty among the disabled and as a pilot strategy to test issues of administration and cost, individualized funding makes sense and should be supported.

However, the same arguments do not apply with respect to the special needs of the disabled. In the first place individualized funding would result in the proliferation of service providers, ostensibly accountable to the consumer but in the last analysis accountable to no one. If we have learned anything from our experience in health care it is that physicians who control admissions to hospitals and prescribe care for patients are accountable only to their professional association and their patients, but not for the costs of health care. Individualized funding in health has, therefore, created a system where those who create the demand, patients and physicians, are not held accountable for the consequences of these demands.

In the second place the individualized funding approach to the social services would encounter difficulty with respect to professional competence. At least in health it is relatively clear which professionals are licensed to practice. In areas such as homemaker services, attendant care, and counselling such clarity does not obtain. One can only guess at the complexities created by having a conglomeration of certified rolfers, massage therapists, naturopathic healers, and others providing services and being paid from the public purse. It simply is not good enough to argue, as advocates of individualized funding will contend, that incompetent providers will be identified and receive no requests for service. Over time this may occur, but at what cost to consumers? And unless the supply of competent professionals increases dramatically, this faith in the natural law of the marketplace may not occur at all.

In the third place individualized funding would in all likelihood result in the phenomenon of "creaming," whereby those most able to take advantage of services do so at the expense of others. Thus the articulate and well-educated would be the first to take advantage of individualized funding and unless funds were unlimited, budgets would be exhausted by the time less forceful consumers presented their case.

Finally, individualized funding would isolate consumers from one another and weaken their ability to join together in collective action. Rather than empowering consumers, individualized funding will have the opposite effect. It cannot be emphasized too strongly that individualized funding is the very antithesis of the community and constituency approach to governing the social services.

The parallel with privatization in the social services is instructive. Contracting out services has resulted in fragmenting the voluntary sector and pitting agencies against each other in a competition for scarce funds. The individualized funding plan applies to individuals rather than agencies, and hence its potential for promoting fragmentation, competition, and lack of coherence is considerable.

While the rules and regulations of both public- and private-sector agencies are often complicated and cumbersome, they do provide some safeguards by attending to quality and to accountability. Ironically, attempts to ensure that all consumers receive the same benefits and are treated equally have resulted in the establishment of rules and regulations that severely limit the ability of staff to respond in a prompt and individualized fashion. But it may well be that the cause of consumers is better served in the long run by community-controlled social service agencies that are visible and responsive than by implementing individualized funding.

FROM THE ORDINARY TO THE GRAND ISSUES OF POLICY

While the case studies cannot be used as a final and complete argument, they do suggest that community organizations should assume a larger role in social policy than has been the case in the past. The point that social policies are played out in community arenas has been emphasized repeatedly in the preceding chapters, and because of their intimate awareness of the match between problems and policies, community organizations, including municipal governments, should have a more significant part in the initiation and implementation phases of the policy process. The cattlemen in the Chilcotins, the Champagne/Aishihik band in the Yukon, the Association for Community Living in New Brunswick, and the emerging healthy community projects across the country have demonstrated a capacity to assert their definitions of social policies in a way that is appropriate for their communities. These examples of local-level capacity illustrate the viability of John McKnight's vision for communities.

> There is a mistaken notion that our society has a problem in terms of effective human services. Our essential problem is weak communities. While we have reached the limits of institutional problem solving we are only at the beginnings of exploring the possibility of a new vision for community. It is a vision of regeneration. It is a vision of reassociating the exiled. It is a vision of centering our lives in community. (McKnight, 1987: 58)

The vision, however, needs to include the idea not only of strengthening communities but also of seeing communities contributing to the development of national social policies. I disagree with McKnight that we have reached the limits of institutional problem-solving. One characteristic that has always distinguished Canada from the U.S. has been our ability to establish universal social programs. How might communities contribute to the development of national and provincial policies that unite rather than fracture communities? How might the capacity of community organizations to change the ordinary issues of policy influence the grand issues? Some threads have emerged in the preceding pages.

Clearly one issue that connects community and national policy agendas and the ordinary and grand issues of policy is that of poverty. It is an issue presented in stark reality in community arenas that affects health and family life, that community organizations and consumer groups have tried to address, and that by confronting the grand issue of income redistribution provokes resistance and opposition from those who prowl the corridors of power. It is an issue currently being addressed by the healthy community movement and by an emerging social movement dedicated to the eradication of child poverty. It is of fundamental concern in the Callahan call to redefine the role of women by recognizing that caring for children in the home is a crucially important responsibility not only for children and their families but for community and society (Callahan, 1992). Child care should be paid work either in the form of a parental wage or in a children's benefit.

Equally clearly, the issue of poverty or of child poverty cannot be resolved on a community-by-community basis. But in a very important way the movement to end child poverty can begin in local communities. The abortion case study points to the gains that can be realized by having social policy issues debated within communities:

> . . . many women who felt that political life was irrelevant to them became acutely aware of its importance. Participants learned that social policy issues are far from clear, that policy-making is a long-term process, and that individual people matter in the process of change. It is unlikely that they will view social policy-making (and makers) in the same light after this experience. It can be argued that social policy would be invigorated by similar debates on other issues at the local level. . . . It is also true that the more social policy debates are moved to the local level, the more women can be involved in them.

If citizens in community forums could debate the poverty issue they might come to appreciate the connections between the grand issues of income distribution and poverty. In turn such debates might set the stage for a grassroots revolt dedicated to changing the distribution of income and wealth. Yet, as noted in Chapter 6, local campaigns will not suffice. Perhaps the crucial requirement is for the national women's and labour organizations to declare child poverty as a pressing priority and to lead a national campaign on the platform that by altering the definition of work, by recognizing that child care is work and should be paid for both in and out of the home, women will at last gain full citizenship.

Novick puts the case for a national policy to end child poverty in the following terms:

> European countries with the lowest levels of child poverty have not succeeded because they introduced early intervention programs or cobbled together a children's benefit only for the poor. These countries have succeeded because they assumed that a national system of family policies was essential both to maintaining a decent standard of living for the largest number of families and to the well being of the nation. In these countries, national family policies are based on the recognition that there is a shared responsibility between the larger community and parents for the care and well being of children. Every family with children is endowed with public benefits as part of the intergenerational legacy by which these societies recognize the essential social value of family work for both the present and future of their nations. (Novick, 1991: 19)

The challenge is then not only whether community organizations can govern and deliver social and health services. They must cross traditionally closed boundaries between the health and social service sectors and between formal organizations and social movements in order to address the grand issues of social policy. Only in this way can they propose national policies for reforming the present inequities in the distribution of wealth and power and expect to have those proposals heard.

CHAPTER VIII

Connecting Social Work and
Community Work Practice

A useful introduction to a discussion of the connections between social work and community work practice concerns the utility of theory and research for community work practice. While theory and research were not selected as major objectives of the book, they are of crucial importance for practice and some insights on their contributions can be discerned from the case studies.

Both policy-makers and practitioners reported that they practised their craft with little reference to theory. Their work was anchored in commitment to a cause or mission. Policy and practice proceeded from this base in a rather common-sense, problem-solving fashion. Thus the principle of normalization served as a beacon of change for policy in New Brunswick and its derivative, individual service plans, shaped the role of the case manager. Similarly, the work of the child welfare staff was based on a conviction that First Nation values and traditions must provide the context for both policy and practice. The campaigns conducted by the Pro-Life and Pro-Choice groups were firmly grounded in a commitment to the rights of the unborn versus the rights of women to control their bodies. The healthy community movement is based on the conviction that fundamental and large-scale improvements in health will be achieved only by a comprehensive approach that includes the socio-economic and physical environment as well as individual lifestyles.

Commitment to a cause emerges from the case studies as an important foundation of community work practice. In issues such as abortion, commitment is based on values and ideologies and is only dimly influenced by facts and evidence. Thus Pro-Life advocates can identify examples of individuals tormented by having an abortion, while the Pro-Choice group can mount an equally persuasive case by pointing to women who by virtue of poverty, immaturity, or other circumstances were obliged to bear children they could not care for. Neither set of arguments can be defended as objective, nor are they influential in changing opposing opinions. In other instances commitment flows both from values and evidence, as illustrated by the work of the Social Planning Council in Toronto.

It is, of course, a slippery task to determine the respective contributions of values and evidence in the construction of commitment. However, where values dominate, the struggle is likely to be eschewed by professionals. By contrast, where commitment is grounded in a mandate to investigate social conditions and is buttressed by evidence emanating from careful research studies, a solid case for professional leadership in social reform can be mounted. Thus staff of the Department of Public Health and of the Social Planning Council in Toronto were on relatively safe ground in advocating change. Their findings were grounded in well-designed research studies even though recommendations for change can always be debated.

In contrast, only a few professionals took part in the abortion debate in Nanaimo, and even these tended to leave their professional roles on the shelf and to participate as private citizens. It is important to add that some professionals became involved in the struggle because of experiences they had encountered as professionals. Nevertheless, once into the debate they contributed as citizens, not as professionals.

While it is not difficult to identify with this stance, it is based on a view that holds that professionals should not participate in essentially political debates, and when they do their involvement should rely on findings of research studies. Such a view excludes the information and professional wisdom gained from practice. Callahan and Matthews, in Chapter 5, make the telling point that professionals have valuable information to contribute to the debate on abortion. Professional social workers and nurses are intimately aware of the crucial need for information, education, and counselling services to allow women and men to avoid pregnancy. Professionals are also knowledgeable about the impact of poverty on children and the likelihood of poverty in female-headed households. Callahan and Matthews argue that practical wisdom can contribute to social policy debates and should not be excluded simply because of its origin in practice rather then research.

The same point can be made with equal cogency about information that agencies might collect but rarely do, so that it never does become part of the public debate on social policy. For example, an analysis of clients coming to the attention of the Ministry of Social Services and Housing in B.C. as a consequence of complaints of child neglect revealed that while two-parent and lone-parent families were equally represented in the client population, there were marked differences between them. Lone parents were much more likely to be characterized by poverty, by low education, and by difficulties in caring for young children. Two-parent families were not as poor and came into contact with child welfare workers primarily as a result of difficulties with teenagers (Campbell, 1991).

It is significant to add for the purposes of this discussion that the analysis was undertaken by a student for his Master in Social Work thesis. The fact that the student is an employee of the ministry and that the ministry readily made records available does not take away from the central point of the argument – that the ministry should itself conduct such analyses, should make the information public, and should use it in developing policy not only for child welfare but for education and income security. In short, such information should be an intrinsic part of the social policy process of the provincial government.

The discussion poses the ticklish question of whether commitment to a cause can be combined with dispassionate inquiry. Would the commitment interfere with and influence both the search and the presentation of findings? Can a researcher or a research organization combine objectivity in research with advocacy for the findings? Many social scientists and professionals maintain that there must be a clean separation between research and advocacy. The position is apt to be expressed as "it is our job to do research, we have the competence and credibility for this task, but we have neither attribute when it comes to advocating for our findings. In fact, advocacy would undermine our credibility for research."

However, the case studies suggest that commitment to and advocacy on behalf of a cause and dispassionate inquiry are not incompatible. Agencies such as the Social Planning Council of Metropolitan Toronto conduct research studies of exemplary quality, but within a value-based context that clearly places the Council on the side of the poor and oppressed. Similarly, the Association for Community Living has been guided by an explicit commitment to the principle of normalization and has supported this commitment by careful inquiries into institutional and community care.

To return to theory, the case studies point to its absence in guiding practice in community work. The case managers in the New Brunswick study and the child welfare workers in Vancouver and the Yukon practised their craft as general social work practitioners. They incorporated into their roles the theory and skills central to that approach. Indeed, these workers functioned and saw themselves as general practitioners rather than as community workers. The staff of the Social Planning Council of Metropolitan Toronto relied heavily on their research skills as the basis for practice, and as noted previously, social workers were conspicuous by their absence in the case studies on abortion and healthy communities.

The demands of practice are such that, like their social work colleagues, community workers are hard pressed to find time to read and keep up with the literature. Unless one received a thorough grounding in a very explicit theoretical framework while at university and used this framework on a continuing basis as a practitioner, theory simply takes a back seat. To be used, theory has to useful, and the case studies suggest that practitioners have not found this to be the case. From the experience of the case studies some suggestions for community work practice can be made. I hesitate to dignify these with the label of theory. Rather, they refer to some discrete pieces of knowledge, to frameworks and to insights derived from the literature on power and its distribution at the community and societal levels.

THE HISTORY OF SOCIAL POLICY

Given the importance of the concepts of the convergence of interest and of redefinitions, it is suggested that community workers would benefit from knowledge of the development of social policy in Canada and other countries. In turn, this knowledge might assist community workers to appreciate the importance of the context of social policy and how it is shaped by the definitions in place at particular times. It would provide a sense of policy as a process of "negotiation involving elusive and continually changing definitions" (Fox and Willis, 1989: 1). In particular, historical accounts of the development of social policy would afford an opportunity to discern the factors leading to the convergence of interest and to significant redefinitions. Over time the accumulation of such factors might permit the beginnings of a theory of social reform.

There are few historical accounts of the development of social policy in Canada and still fewer that search for connections between social reform and social policy. Nevertheless, a beginning could be made by examining the development of social welfare in Ontario (Splane, 1965) and in B.C. (Clague et al., 1984), the emergence of social security (Guest, 1980), and old age pensions in Canada (Bryden, 1974). An analytical and critical account of the origins of the welfare state in Canada is provided by Finkel (1977). In child welfare the Jones and Rutman book (1981) tells the story of the crusade of J.J. Kelso to establish a children's aid society in Toronto and hence makes a direct connection between social reform and social policy. And an important literature is developing on the contributions of feminists to social policy (Rooke and Schnell, 1988; Baines, Evans, and Neysmith, 1991).

KNOWLEDGE OF THE POLICY PROCESS

Both social workers and community workers tend to be disinterested in policy. A typical view is that policy is concerned with regulating practice and controlling workers and clients, and it is made by politicians and bureaucrats who have lost touch with the realities facing practitioners and clients. Hence practitioners frequently greet new policies with scepticism if not downright hostility. And given the dominance of the programmed approach to policy-making the views of practitioners are not without substance.

In addition, practitioners have only a vague understanding of the policy-making process. It is seen as highly esoteric, replete with complex techniques and far beyond the comprehension of line workers. However, as noted in the case studies, one blunt explanation of the process is provided by Lindblom's theory of muddling through. To be sure, Lindblom's work is unnecessarily plagued with awkward phrases such as "disjointed incrementalism," "mutual partisan adjustment," and "proximate policy-makers," but stripped of the jargon the theory describes how policy is made in a straightforward manner – as a series of small steps, each building on and complementing the last and modifying the original statement of policy. While not denying the need for information and analysis, Lindblom contends that the contributions to policy-making of synoptic approaches such as cost-benefit analysis and the program, planning, and budgeting systems analysis have been overstated. Policy-making in the public sector is all about choosing in situations where values and preferences conflict, where time and resources are in short supply, and where, despite the occasional search for comprehensive information, decisions have to be made on the basis of incomplete and perhaps conflicting information.

While drastic and comprehensive policy changes do occur on rare occasions, muddling through accurately describes the usual process and outcomes. In a similar fashion and despite the availability of elegant frameworks in family therapy and other modes of therapy, most practitioners muddle through. Their approach to practice is best captured by approaches such as reality therapy and brief therapy. Reality therapy acknowledges the importance of values and standards of behaviour, argues that detailed assessments concentrating on the past are unnecessary and unhelpful, and suggests that practice consists of assisting clients to face reality and improve their competence in dealing with day-to-day problems.

The notion of "goal-directed muddling through" nicely captures the style of policy-makers and practitioners in New Brunswick, the Yukon, and Vancouver (Hancock, 1990a). In these case studies policy-makers established clear objectives anchored in a philosophical position and a vision for change. The work of both policy-makers and practitioners was chararacterized by adherence to the vision and by pragmatic, step-by-step problem-solving. Indeed, despite the difference between policy-makers and practitioners in terms of status and responsibilities, both follow an essentially similar process. "Both confront knotty and contentious problems, both follow similar stages of development and participants in both processes are faced with similar value dilemmas and technological gaps in attempting to implement change" (Wharf and Callahan, 1984: 37). Goal-directed muddling through allows for flexibility and discretion in pursuing objectives and for the continuous incorporation of wisdom from experience and practice. Indeed, it amounts to the adaptive approach to policy-making.

THE USE OF ANALYTIC FRAMEWORKS

As emphasized repeatedly in the preceding chapters, social reform organizations do not have the power to put into place the reforms they see as desirable. Neither do they have the funds to devote to expensive public relations campaigns or to hire equally expensive lobbyists to act on their behalf. To add to their woes, social reform organizations are not usually well connected to policy-makers, and their reforms represent causes that, if not downright unpopular, are at best of marginal interest to policy-makers. Overcoming this litany of limitations is extremely difficult.

One message from the case studies is that social reform organizations must become extremely adroit in deploying their slender resources. One way to achieve this is to become expert in analysing the policy process. A number of frameworks or, more modestly, checklists have been identified in this and the preceding chapters. Table 1 provides a checklist for three stages of the process. For the sake of simplicity two stages, execution and evaluation, are omitted.

Table 1
Identifying the Requirements To Influence Policy

Stage	Objective	Framework/Checklist
Initiation	Converging interest	1. Is a community organization in place or can one be quickly put into place?
		2. Does the organization possess detailed knowledge of the problem or issue?
		3. Is the organization dedicated to overcoming the problem?
		4. Has the organization developed a vision of change?
		5. Can the organization establish connections with policy-makers?
		6. Lacking connections, can the organization bring pressure to bear on policy-makers?

Table 1 (continued)

Stage	Objective	Framework/Checklist
Formulation	Reframing the policy	1. Can the problem be redefined? 2. Can the roles of individuals be redefined? 3. Can the field of service be redefined?
Implementation	Overcoming the Achilles' heel	1. Can the reform be fitted to the short-term, crisis-ridden agenda? 2. Are sufficient resources, including staff and funds, available? 3. Can the domain issues be overcome? 4. Can the process take an adaptive approach? Can implementation take the form of goal-directed muddling through? 5. Will the redefinitions be accepted by policy-makers? If not, can a long-term strategy be put into place?

In addition to this checklist, the Morris and Binstock (1966) framework can be used to analyse the policy process at all stages. As will be recalled from Chapter 3, this framework requires that social reform organizations identify their resources and the ways in which the targets of change are open to influence. The crucial part of the analysis is to determine if resources match the open pathways of influence. While the resources available to organizations might vary from time to time and indeed vary in relation to the particular reform being sought, a relatively constant inventory of resources can be assembled. With an inventory of resources in place, organizations can begin each reform with an intimate awareness of their strengths and limitations.

In short, two strategies for organizations lacking connections, clout, and money can be identified. The first is to concentrate on analysis, to become expert in crafting the convergence of interest and equally adept in anticipating and considering ways in which the difficulties that will inevitably occur in the implementation stage can be overcome. The second is to develop a capacity not only for research in the conventional sense but re-search in the sense of reframing roles, problems, and fields of service.

THEORIES OF POWER

In addition to engaging in seemingly endless debates about the meaning of power and the differences between power, influence, and authority, social scientists have pursued the issue of power through research studies of who governs in local communities and at the national level. Studies of and debates about power structures represented one of the most popular forms of research for sociologists and political scientists in the 1950s and 1960s.

The conclusions of the studies of local-level decision-making varied considerably, largely as a consequence of the methodology employed. Sociologists tended to approach their studies through the reputational approach. They asked, in effect, "who has the most clout in this community?" Not surprisingly, the results of this approach revealed that a relatively small group exercised a disproportionate share of influence. More surprising was the discovery that this small group typically excluded elected officials and consisted of business and professional men. On the other hand, political scientists analysed who had been involved in making decisions about specific issues such as education, land use, and health. On finding that different individuals participated in these issue-specific decisions, they concluded that pluralism prevailed at the local level. However, with respect to the studies of power structures at the national level in Canada there has been general agreement that the elite exercise more than their share of power and influence (Porter, 1965; Clement, 1975, 1983; Calvert, 1984; McQuaig, 1988).

The subject of power and its distribution has been of enduring interest in the social sciences and in community work. There is a voluminous amount of material for both policy-makers and practitioners who wish to become knowledgeable about power and how it affects the policy-making process. There is neither space nor necessity here to enter into a detailed review of this material. Rather, the attempt is made to extract some insights from the studies of power structures, to tie these threads together, and to determine if they support the lessons that have emerged from the case studies.

The first thread is taken from studies of power at the national level, which, as noted above, have concluded that elites exercise a disproportionate amount of influence and control an equally disproportionate share of the wealth of the nation. The second thread consists of the Lindblom distinction between grand and ordinary policies. The connection between these threads is that grand policies are dealt with at the national level and hence come under the purview of the elite.

A third thread concerns the notion developed by Bachrach and Baratz (1970) of the two faces of power. The first and most readily apparent face is the power to ensure that changes are approved and implemented. The second is to ensure that changes do not reach the policy agenda. In the terminology used throughout this book, the second face of power can be used to block the convergence of interest. This notion is particularly relevant to issues at the national level where the captains of industry ensure that reforms such as those proposed by the Royal Commission on Taxation do not get on the agenda of the federal government. In sharp contrast the expenditures of social programs, and consideration of ways to curtail these expenditures, remain as a constant agenda item.

Yet a fourth thread is provided by space or slack in the system. The notion was originally developed by Robert Dahl in his study of the power structure in the city of New Haven, Connecticut. Dahl concluded that "the existence of a great deal of political slack seems to be a characteristic of pluralistic political systems and the liberal societies in which these systems operate" (Dahl, 1961: 305). Since the concept originated as a consequence of a community study and since the available evidence suggests that if pluralism exists at any level it is in local communities, a reasonable conclusion is that slack is to be found in the ordinary policy issues that are dealt with by municipal and provincial governments.

Tied together, these threads offer useful insights for community work practitioners and support the experience of the projects reported in the case studies. The case studies provide examples of community-based organizations that did take advantage of slack in the policy-making system and brought about changes in social policy. Knowledge of the theory of power structures would provide some comfort and insight for community work practitioners. Indeed, it would be highly desirable if they, as well as researchers and academics, wrote about the process of change in communities and thereby contributed to theory and knowledge.

KNOWLEDGE OF THE COMMUNITY

One of the distinct contributions of the Rothman framework is that it clearly establishes that community work is concerned with many different types of communities. As noted in Chapter 1, locality development is concerned with enhancing the capacity of neighbourhoods to resolve the problems affecting them, whereas social action focuses on disadvantaged groups regardless of their location. For social planners the community is delineated by the boundaries of their agency, be it municipal, regional, or provincial. These approaches are distinguished by differing assumptions about the distribution of power in society and by the strategies required to redress social problems.

Rothman's work in pointing to the differences in communities and community work is supported by other writers. Thus Donald Warren has identified six different kinds of neighbourhoods on the basis of three criteria: identity, interaction, and linkages (Warren, 1981). Warren argues that these neighbourhoods have different problems and varying levels of capacity to address the problems. Starting from a class analysis Marjaleena Repo attacks the concept of "the neighborhood as community" by pointing out that it

assumes a classless society at the local level in a mysterious "people of all classes" work toward a common goal. . . . This geographic definition contains the serious fallacy of assuming that any neighborhood is or can become a community of equals. (Repo, 1971: 61)

Until recently writers in community work have ignored the contributions that women have made in communities by building networks of support and by campaigning to change oppressive conditions. Feminist scholars such as Lena Dominelli and Eileen McLeod are making important additions to the community work literature by analysing "the ways in which a group or groups of women organize collectively around issues aimed specifically at tackling gender oppression" (Dominelli and McLeod, 1989: 46).

The above discussion touches only a fraction of the research and analysis that has sought to understand community life and community change. Such information would materially assist provincial governments in their attempts to deinstitutionalize, privatize, devolve services to communities, and develop programs for women (as yet, efforts here are only beginning). However, provincial governments have yet to establish community work divisions or units that would provide consultation to departments of health and social services in order to inform the process of transferring responsibilities to communities. Indeed, the process is often characterized by a perception of community as a homogeneous entity with common interests and agreement on the issues to be addressed and the strategies to be used. Partnerships with community associations and band councils, as exemplified in the New Brunswick and the Champagne/Aishihik case studies, are all too rare but they provide models of sound community work practice.

It is also noteworthy that the social work profession, which has a rich legacy of experience in community work, has been largely absent in health promotion and healthy communities. In part, the absence can be attributed to the neglect of community work in schools of social work, and the following discussion deals with this issue.

SOCIAL WORK AND COMMUNITY WORK

In the case studies concerned with children, both the practitioners and many of the senior bureaucrats were social workers. However, no evidence of leadership from the social work profession was found in the other case studies. Certainly the professional association of social workers in Ontario and many individual social workers supported the work of the Social Planning Council of Metropolitan Toronto and participated in the campaign to convince the provincial government to implement the recommendations of the Social Assistance Review Committee. The Council, in its hiring practices, does not express a preference for any one profession but seeks to engage staff with a solid background in community work and research and, most importantly, a commitment to reform. Since this organization and many social movements are dedicated to the cause of social reform, the view that social work education does not provide appropriate preparation is a serious indictment of the profession. I return to this later.

Functions in Community Work

The case studies suggest that three community work functions can be identified: resource/locality development, policy planning, and social reform. The salient characteristics of the functions are set out in Table 2 and discussed in relation to the compatibility between community work and social work practice.

Table 2
Community Work Functions

Function	Roles	Auspices	Strategies	Case Study
Resource/ locality development	Generalist Social worker	Prov. min. Child welfare agency	Assisting individuals and groups to identify and meet needs	N.B. Yukon Healthy Comm.
	Community worker	Settlement house		
Policy planning	Planner Policy analyst in head office	Prov. min. Voluntary agency	Research Policy analysis	N.B. SPC

Table 2 (continued)

Function	Roles	Auspices	Strategies	Case Study
Social reform	Researcher Visionary Innovator Advocate	Social movement, voluntary	Research plus organizing and campaign tactics Reflection and imagination	N.B. Yukon Nanaimo Healthy Comm.

Other functions and roles not identified in the case studies are nevertheless evident in the current community work scene in Canada. For example, muncipal governments are increasingly recognizing the need for social planners to analyse and estimate the impact of industrial and housing development on the lives of residents. In addition, the ubiquitous and perplexing function of co-ordinating services continues to be a major if largely unfulfilled expectation of both public and voluntary community agencies.

The case studies on deinstitutionalization and child welfare identify the community work function of resource development for and with a particular group of clients, and a cornerstone of the healthy community movement is the process of community development. Resource development shifts the focus from developing resources for and with a community or neighbourhood to individuals and families with common needs, regardless of their place of residence. The knowledge and skills required are virtually identical.

As noted in Chapter 2, the case managers charged with the responsibility of developing community support systems were relatively recent graduates of Bachelor of Social Work programs. They reported that these generalist programs had provided excellent preparation for both community work and direct service to individuals and families. The same point can be made with respect to the resource and community development roles in the Champagne/Aishihik and Vancouver projects, even though for very legitimate reasons the Champagne/Aishihik project engaged indigenous personnel rather than professional social workers.

There is little doubt, as well, that the organizing and facilitating tasks required in healthy communities are eminently appropriate for BSW graduates.

The policy planning function occurs primarily in the head offices of provincial ministries and large voluntary agencies. At first glance its inclusion as a community work role may seem inappropriate. However, despite its location away from the local action, policy planning is concerned with the well-being of individuals; in the New Brunswick case study, planning provides the support and resources necessary for resource and community development work. In many ways this role resembles the Rothman formulation of social planning, but it departs from this previous notion in its emphasis on a particular group of clients rather than on comprehensive social planning and in particular in its intimate connection to resource and community development work.

Policy planning also appears to be an appropriate role for social workers. The senior staff in the ministries of social services in B.C., New Brunswick, and the Yukon were, in the main, professional social workers. They combined policy analysis skills with knowledge of the policy process, especially in regard to how to push issues onto the policy agenda of government. As with the role of the resource and community developer, these are not by any means exclusive to the profession of social work, but they are congruent with the knowledge base and skills of this profession.

Policy planners typically work in provincial ministries, in municipal departments of public health, or in large voluntary agencies. Their activities include reviewing the effectiveness of existing programs and, on the basis of information gathered for a variety of sources, altering these programs to enhance effectiveness. Conversely, in times of recession they have been required to develop plans to reduce services and benefits. In all their activities policy planners are concerned with political and organizational feasibility, in particular with the availability of funds and staff and the impact of change on the structural arrangements within the organization.

The function of social reform requires staff who have some combination of research, re-search, and community development skills and can put these skills to work in an organization committed to social reform. Indeed, the role of social reformer may be the most problematic for social work given the profession's uncomfortableness with causes and values, its preoccupation with professional status, and its conviction that commitment to a cause and professional status are inimical to one another. What, if anything, can be done to change this situation?

The following comments are meant to provoke debate and stir up interest in the issues and are not by any means intended as definitive responses. Perhaps a beginning might be made by schools of social work. Schools might, for example, take a value position and, like the Social Planning Council of Metropolitan Toronto, declare that they are on the side of the poor and the oppressed. Such a stance has been taken by schools of social work in Australia and neither conservative state governments nor equally conservative universities have questioned these declarations. The adoption of an ideological position does not mean that a school is committed to a particular set of theories and strategies to the exclusion of all others. It does, however, require that schools develop clear statements of mission, and in turn these statements shape curricula.

Schools dedicated to a mission of social reform would want to centre the curriculum around the subject of power and its distribution at all levels in society. They would need to give a prominent place to the theories of oppression now being developed by feminists and by members of First Nations. They would seek to develop courses and practica to allow students to become competent in research, analysis, and the strategies appropriate for social reform. They would insist that students learn about values and value conflict and become comfortable in wearing a value orientation of their own choosing.

Schools of social work, and particularly students, may be concerned about the prospects for employment from programs that declare a commitment to social reform. Will graduation from such schools hinder the chances of employment? Some comfort can be found from two sources. First, and perhaps as a consequence of the residual stance of most provincial and federal departments at the present time, the voluntary sector appears to be in the midst of a renaissance with respect to research and advocacy organizations. There has been a noticeable increase in the number of such organizations, especially in the field of child welfare: the Canadian Council on Children and Youth, the Canadian Child Welfare Association, the National Youth in Care Network, and the Child Poverty Action Group. The emergence of these organizations at both the national and local levels augurs well for social reform in the future. They represent a growing commitment to children and to ensuring that issues such as child poverty and child abuse and neglect assume a more prominent place on the policy agenda than has been the case in the past.

A second source of comfort comes from the experience of the Carleton School of Social Work, which has declared a commitment to social reform. The 1988-89 calendar of the school contained the following statement.

> The Master of Social Work program is based on an analytical and critical approach to social work practice and to knowledge related to practice. The program examines the structural context of personal and social problems and of social work practice. The structural context refers to the interaction between the personal and the social and the social, political and economic aspects of such problems. (Lecomte, 1990: 34)

Despite its critical and structural orientation, graduates of the school have not found difficulty in obtaining employment. Indeed, they tend to be sought by employers because of their capacity for analysis and their critical thinking skills.

I conclude by returning to the central question addressed in the book: Can community organizations, including the healthy community movement and departments of municipal government, influence social policy? The case studies indicate that involvement in the ordinary issues of social policy results in developing the confidence of individuals and groups to such an extent that they can make a difference. The Association for Community Living has drastically altered services for developmentally delayed children in New Brunswick and in other provinces. The Champagne/Aishihik band has demonstrated that it can govern child welfare services, and the struggles around abortion in Nanaimo, although inconclusive in one sense, proved to the women in both camps that they could develop community organizations and express their views.

The case studies also reveal that while ordinary issues of policy are important and can be dealt with as distinct and unique issues, they are also embedded within the grand issues of policy. The case studies are concerned with the poor, First Nation citizens, and women and children – with the groups in Canadian society who are second-class citizens. As Callahan and Matthews argue, the more social policy issues are dealt with in local communities, the more women, in terms of both numbers and level of participation, will become involved in these issues. The same comment could be applied to First Nation communities; in fact, a notable contribution of First Nation control of child welfare has been to enhance the competence and confidence of First Nation peoples. Dealing with social policy issues at the ordinary level serves to demystify these issues. No longer are they seen as such complex matters that they can be dealt with only by politicians, senior bureaucrats, and professionals at provincial and federal levels. We should continually remind ourselves that the key policy-makers at the senior levels of government were in most cases ordinary citizens without any special policy-making expertise until they stood for election and were elected.

Changing the grand issues of policy requires the same components identified through the case studies for changing the ordinary issues: the capacity to redefine problems and solutions and to bring about a convergence of interests so that issues are placed on the policy agenda, then approved and implemented. In a very real sense this book has argued that social policy is all about definitions and redefinitions – whoever defines the problem has in large measure defined the solution! However, attempts to change the grand issues of social policy will encounter resistance on a far larger scale than is the case with ordinary policies. Hence, social reform organizations will require substantial resources if they are to mount campaigns on a nation-wide basis. They will require national and provincial associations with active and large memberships. While there are many national associations in health and social welfare, they are typically concerned with a specific issue such as cancer, heart disease, or mental health. There are no associations with a national office and provincial and local branches dedicated to the eradication of poverty and unemployment. Both national associations and local organizations are concerned with these issues, but they are essentially separate enterprises with sometimes distinct agendas and priorities.

If social reform organizations are to tackle the grand issues of policy, they cannot do so on a community-by-community basis. The case for connecting the efforts of social movements, such as the women's, labour, and First Nation movements, through a set of unifying agendas seems indisputable. The agendas might include defining in-home care as work, thereby simultaneously addressing the labour agenda of employment and enhancing the status of women. Both of these reforms seem eminently suitable for uniting these social movements in national campaigns to alter the definitions of the grand issues of social policy.

To become part of the struggle to redefine both the ordinary and the grand issues of social policy requires that the profession of social work declare its commitment to social reform. In turn, this will require the rejection of the position that the distinguishing characteristics of a profession are those of aloofness and distance from clients and a calm, objective approach to practice. Only in very recent times have we begun to realize that sacrificing the commitment to social reform for professional status requires denying our heritage and the unique contribution we have and can still make to society – the contribution of advocating with the oppressed for social reforms. The irony is that deserting the public issues aspect of our heritage has not resulted in achieving professional status. Many professions attend to private troubles and in this crowded territory it is difficult to assert uniqueness. However, attending to private troubles within the context of public issues has been part and parcel of the heritage of social work. Reclaiming this function would empower and reinvigorate the profession.

ACKNOWLEDGEMENTS

I would like to thank the following individuals, who not only provided information for the case studies but also reviewed drafts of the chapters and gave helpful comments.

Chapter 2: Anne Caverhill, Donna Gordon, Georgio Gaudet, Gordon Porter, Lorraine Silliphant, and Ken Ross.

Chapter 3: Patrick Johnston and Jodi Orr.

Chapter 4: Paul Birckel, John Hoyt, and Sharon Hume for the Champagne/Aishihik study and Ken Clement, Brian Collins, Fred Milowsky, and Gloria Nicholson for the Vancouver Native child welfare unit.

Chapter 5: Jan Pullinger.

Chapter 6: Susan Berlin, Trevor Hancock, Perry Kendall, and Sharon Mason Willms.

I am particularly grateful to Marilyn Callahan, John Cossom, and Michael Wheeler, who reviewed the complete manuscript and made constructive comments, to Richard Tallman, who improved the book by his careful editing, and to Carol Gamey, who did yet another yeoman piece of work in constructing the index and bibliography and in proofreading.

On a personal note, it has been immensely satisfying to work with and have a chapter written by my daughter. Joan and her twin sister, Sandy, have been a constant source of pleasure and pride to their parents for the past thirty years. Joan is now a Ph.D. student in the Institute of Health Promotion Research at the University of British Columbia and is destined to be a leader in health promotion.

BIBLIOGRAPHY

Adams, Mary Louise (1989). "There's no place like home: On the place of identity in feminist politics," *Feminist Review*, 31: 22–31.

Adams, O. (1990). "Life expectancy in Canada – an overview," *Health Reports*, 2: 361–78.

Adamson, Nancy, Linda Briskin, and Margaret McPhail (1988). *Feminist organizing for change; The contemporary women's movement in Canada*. Toronto: Oxford University Press.

Advisory Group of New Social Assistance Legislation (1991). *Back on Track*. Toronto: Queen's Printer.

Antonyshyn, Patricia, B. Lee, and Alex Merrill (1988). "Marching for Women's Lives: The campaign for free-standing abortion clinics in Ontario," in F. Cunningham *et al.*, eds., *Social Movement/Social Change: The Politics and Practice of Organizing*. Toronto: Between the Lines.

Applied Research Consulting House (1983). *Services for Children with Significant Developmental Disabilities or Behaviour Disorders in New Brunswick*. Mississauga, Ont.

Arnstein, Sherry R. (1969). "A Ladder of Citizen Participation," *Journal of the American Institute of Planners*, 4: 216–24.

Ashton, John (1988). *Healthy cities – concepts and visions*. University of Liverpool, Department of Community Health.

Australian Local Government Association (1990). *Better Services for Local Communities*. Canberra, Australia.

Bachrach, Peter, and Morton S. Baratz (1970). *Power and Poverty: Theory and Practice*. New York: Oxford University Press.

Baines, Carol, Patricia Evans, and Sheila Neysmith, eds. (1991). *Women's Caring: Feminist Perspectives on Social Welfare*. Toronto: McClelland & Stewart.

B.C. Healthy Communities Network (1989). *Strengthening Healthy Communities Workshop Report*. Vancouver.

B.C. Office of the Ombudsman (1990). *Public Services to Children, Youth and their Families: The Need for Intergration*. Public Report #22. Victoria.

Berer, Marge (1988). "Whatever happened to a woman's right to choose?" *Feminist Review*, 29: 24–37.

Berlin, Susan (1991). Personal communication.

Berman, Paul (1980). "Thinking about Programmed and Adaptive Implementation: Matching Strategies to Situations," in Helen M. Ingram and Dean E. Mann, eds., *Why Policies Succeed or Fail*. Beverly Hills: Sage Publications.

Boothroyd, Peter, and Margaret Eberle (1990). *Healthy Communities: What They Are, How They're Made*. Vancouver: UBC Centre for Human Settlements.

Bowen, Lynn (1991). Personal communication.

Brager, George, Harry Specht, and James Torczyner (1987). *Community Organizing*. New York: Columbia University Press.

Bryden, Kenneth (1974). *Old Age Pensions and Policy Making in Canada*. Montreal: McGill-Queen's University Press.

Buck, Carol (1985). "Beyond Lalonde – Creating Health," *Canadian Journal of Public Health*, 76, 1: 19–24.

Bullock, Anne (1990). "Community Care: Ideology and Lived Experience," in Roxanna Ng, Gillian Walker, and Jacob Muller, eds., *Community Organization and the Canadian State*. Toronto: Garamond Press.

Burt, Sandra (1990). "Canadian women's groups in the 1980's: Organizational development and policy influence," *Canadian Public Policy*, XVI, 1: 17–28.

Callahan, Marilyn (1992). *A Feminist Critique of Child Welfare Policy and Practice*. Toronto: Child, Youth, and Family Policy Research Centre.

Callahan, Marilyn, and Brian Wharf (1982). *Demystifying the Policy Process: A Case Study of the Development of Child Welfare in B.C.* Victoria: The Sedgewick Society.

Callwood, June (1989). "Child of Adversity Now Champion of the Poor," *Globe and Mail*, October 18.

Calvert, John (1984). *Government Limited: The Corporate Takeover of the Public Sector in Canada*. Ottawa: Canadian Centre for Policy Alternatives.

Campbell, James (1991). "An Analysis of Variables in Child Protection Apprehension Dispositions in B.C. Child Welfare Practice," M.A. thesis, University of British Columbia.

Canadian Association for the Mentally Retarded, New Brunswick

Division (1983). *Institutions and Community Living for People Who Are Mentally Retarded in the Province of New Brunswick*.

Canadian Child Welfare Association et al. (1988). *A Choice of Futures: Canada's Commitment to its Children*. Ottawa.

Canadian Council on Social Development (1978, 1983). *Canadian Fact Book on Poverty*. Ottawa.

Carniol, Ben (1991). *Case Critical*, 2nd edition. Toronto: Garamond Press.

Cassidy, Frank (1991). "Community Control," *The Northern Review*. 7 (Summer).

Cawthorpe, Joe (1983). *Children and Family Services: Toward a Regional System*. A report to Mr. Peter Alderman, Regional Director, Department of Social Services. Fredericton and Toronto: National Institute on Mental Retardation.

Centracare Community Placement Project (1985). *Program Design for Project*. Fredericton.

Champagne/Aishihik Social Services Society and the Yukon Territorial Government (1986). *Child Welfare Pilot Project Agreement*. Whitehorse.

Child Poverty Action Group and the Social Planning Council of Metropolitan Toronto (1991). *Unequal Futures*. Toronto.

City of Toronto (1991). *Health Inequalities in the City of Toronto*. Toronto: Department of Public Health, Community Health Information Section.

Clague, Michael, Robert Dill, Roop Seebaran, and Brian Wharf (1984). *Reforming Human Services*. Vancouver: UBC Press.

Clement, Wallace (1975). *The Canadian Corporate Elite: An Analysis of Economic Power*. Toronto: McClelland and Stewart.

Clement, Wallace (1983). *Class, Power and Poverty*. Agincourt, Ont.: Methuen.

Coleman, Karen (1988). "The politics of abortion in Australia: Freedom, church and state," *Feminist Review*, 29: 75–97.

Collins, Anne (1985). *The big evasion: abortion, the issue that won't go away*. Toronto: Lester and Orpen Dennys.

Collins, Larry D. (1982). "The politics of abortion: Trends in Canadian fertility policy," *Atlantis*, 7, 2: 2–20.

Committee on Local Authority and Allied Social Services (1968). *Report* (Seebohm Report). London: Her Majesty's Stationery Office.

Cossom, John (1988). "Generalist Social Work Practice, Views from BSW graduates," *Canadian Social Work Review*, 5 (Summer): 297–314.

Cowen, Emery (1977). "Baby Steps Toward Prevention," *American Journal of Community Psychology*, 5, 1: 1–22.

Cunningham, F., S. Findlay, M. Kadar, A. Lennon, and E. Silva, eds. (1988). *Social Movement/Social Change: The Politics and Practice of Organizing*. Toronto: Between the Lines.

Dahl, Robert (1961). *Who Governs?* New Haven: Yale University Press.

Davies, Linda, and Eric Shragge, eds. (1990). *Bureaucracy and Community*. Montreal: Black Rose Books.

Delorme, Jean-Claude, and Louise Gosselin (1989). *Conseil Regional de la Santé et des Services Sociaux*. Sherbrooke: Ville de Sherbrooke.

Dominelli, Lena (1990). *Women and community action*. Birmingham: Venture Press.

Dominelli, Lena, and Gundren Jonsdottir (1988). "Feminist Political Organization in Iceland: Some Reflections on the Experience of Kwenna Frambothid," *Feminist Review*, 30: 30–60.

Dominelli, Lena, and Eileen McLeod (1989). *Feminist Social Work*. Houndmills, Basingstoke: Macmillan Education.

Doucet, Gerard (n.d.). *Community Based Services in New Brunswick; A Glance Back and a Look Forward*. Fredericton: Department of Health and Community Services.

Duhl, L.J. (1986). *Health Planning and Social Change*. New York: Human Sciences Press.

Elmore, Richard (1982). "Backward Mapping: Implementation Research and Policy Decisions," in Walter Williams, ed., *Studying Implementation: Methodological and Administrative Issues*. Chatham, N.J.: Chatham House.

Epp, Jake (1986). *Achieving Health for All. A Framework for Health Promotion*. Ottawa: Health and Welfare Canada.

Fanshel, David, and Eugene Shinn (1978). *Children in Foster Care: A Longitudinal Investigation*. New York: Columbia University Press.

Farrant, Wendy (1989). "Health Promotion and the Community Health Movement: Experiences from the U.K.," International Symposium on Community Participation and Empowerment

Strategies in Health Promotion. Bielfeld, Federal Republic of Germany.

Federation of Canadian Municipalities (1986). *Policy Development, Task Force Reports and Resolutions.* 49th Annual Conference, Hamilton, Ont.

Findlay, Sue (1987). "Facing the State: The Politics of the Women's Movement Reconsidered," in H.J. Maroney and M. Luxton, eds., *Feminism and Political Economy: Women's Work, Women's Struggles.* Toronto: Methuen.

Finkel, Alvin (1977). "Origins of the Welfare State in Canada," in Leo Panitch, ed., *The Canadian State, Political Economy and Political Power.* Toronto: University of Toronto Press.

Fox, D.M., and D.P. Willis (1989). "Introduction to Disability Policy, Restoring Socioeconomic Independence," *Milbank Quarterly,* 67, 1–2.

Freire, Paulo (1985). *Pedagogy of the Oppressed.* New York: Continuum Publishing.

G. Allan Roeher Institute (1988). *Income Insecurity: The Disability Income System in Canada.* Downsview, Ont.

G. Allan Roeher Institute (1991). *The Power to Choose.* Downsview, Ont.

Garbarino, James, and Deborah Sherman (1981). "Identifying High Risk Neighborhoods," in James Garbarino *et al.,* eds., *Protecting Children from Abuse and Neglect.* San Francisco: Jossey Bass.

Gavigan, Shelley (1987). "Women and Abortion in Canada: What's law got to do with it?" in H.J. Maroney and M. Luxton, eds., *Feminism and Political Economy: Women's Work, Women's Struggles.* Toronto: Methuen.

Germain, Carel, and Alex Gitterman (1980). *The Life Model of Social Work Practice.* New York: Columbia University Press.

Gladstone, F. (1979). *Voluntary Action in a Changing World.* London: Bedford Square Press.

Gould, Ketayun (1987). "Life Model versus Conflict Model: A Feminist Perspective," *Social Work,* 32, 4: 346–51.

Gray, B. (1985). "Conditions facilitating interorganizational collaboration," *Human Relations,* 38, 10: 911–36.

Guberman, Nancy (1985). "Behind Recent Social and Fiscal Policy in Quebec: A Redefinition of Motherhood by the State," paper prepared for the Workshop on Motherwork, Val Morin, Quebec.

Guest, Dennis (1980). *The Emergence of Social Security in Canada*. Vancouver: UBC Press.

Gutierrez, Gustavo (1983). *The Power of the Poor in History*. New York: Orbis Books.

Hancock, Trevor (1986). "Lalonde and Beyond: Looking Back at 'A New Perspective on the Health of Canadians,'" *Health Promotion*, 1, 1: 93–100.

Hancock, Trevor (1987). "Perspective on Healthy Public Policy," *Health Promotion*, 2, 3: 257–62.

Hancock, Trevor (1989). "Where the rubber meets the road," in *Proceedings of the National Symposium on Health Promotion and Disease Prevention*. Victoria: B.C. Ministry of Health.

Hancock, Trevor (1990a). "From Public Health in the 1980s to Healthy Public Policy in Toronto 2000: The Evolution of Healthy Public Policy in Toronto," in A. Evers, W. Farrant, and A. Trojan, eds., *Local Healthy Public Policy*. Boulder, Colorado: Westview Press.

Hancock, Trevor (1990b). "The Toronto Story," unpublished paper.

Hancock, Trevor (1991). Personal communication.

Hancock, Trevor, and Leonard J. Duhl (1986). "Healthy Cities: Promoting Health in the Urban Context," background working paper for the Healthy Cities Symposium, Lisbon, Portugal.

Hancock, Trevor, and Fran Perkins (1985). "The Mandala of Health: A Conceptual Model and Teaching Tool," *Health Education* (Summer): 8–11.

Hayes, Michael V., and Sharon Manson Willms (1990). "Healthy community indicators: The perils of the search and the paucity of the find," *Health Promotion International*, 5, 2: 161–66.

Healthy City Office (1991). *The International Healthy City Movement*. Toronto.

Hillery, George, Jr. (1955). "Definitions of Community: Areas of Agreement," *Rural Sociology*, XX, 2.

Hudson, Peter (1980). *Report of the Preventive Services Project of the Family and Children's Service of Rainy River*. Winnipeg: University of Manitoba, School of Social Work.

Hudson, Peter, and Brad MacKenzie (1984). *Evaluation of Dakota Ojibway Child and Family Services*. Prepared for Dakota Ojibway Family Services and the Evaluation Branch of the Department of Indian Affairs and Northern Development.

Hume, Sharon (1991). "The Champagne/Aishihik Family and Child Services: A Unique Community Based Approach to Service Delivery," *The Northern Review*, 7 (Summer).

Johnston, Patrick (1983). *Native Children and the Child Welfare System*. Ottawa: Canadian Council on Social Development.

Johnston, Patrick (1990). Personal communication.

Jones, Andrew, and Leonard Rutman (1981). *In the Children's Aid*. Toronto: University of Toronto Press.

Kendall, Perry (1991). *Health Inequalities in the City of Toronto*. City of Toronto, Department of Public Health, Community Health Information Section.

Kickbusch, Ilona (1989). *Moving Public Health into the '90s*. Proceedings of the National Symposium on Health Promotion and Disease Prevention. Victoria: B.C. Ministry of Health.

Labonte, Ronald (1988). "Health Promotion: From Concepts to Strategies," *Healthcare Management* (Autumn): 24–30.

Labonte, Ronald, and Susan Penfold (1981). "Canadian Perspectives in Health Promotion: A Critique," *Health Education* (April): 4–9.

Lahti, Janet, Arthur Emlem, and Mary Troychak (1981). "Dissemination and Utilization of Permanent Planning Strategies for Children in Foster Care," *Children and Youth Services Review*, 3.

Laird, Joan (1985). "Working with the Family in Child Welfare," in Joan Laird and Ann Hartman, eds., *A Handbook of Child Welfare*. New York: The Free Press.

Lalonde, Marc (1974). *A New Perspective on the Health of Canadians*. Ottawa: Health and Welfare Canada.

Lane, Robert (1939). "The Field of Community Organization," in *Proceedings of the National Conference of Social Work*. New York: Columbia University Press.

La iere, Richard (1965). *Social Change*. New York: McGraw-Hill.

Lasswell, Harold, and Abraham Kaplan (1950). *Power and Society*. New Haven: Yale University Press.

Lecomte, Roland (1990). "Connecting Private Troubles and Public Issues in Social Work Education," in Brian Wharf, ed., *Social Work and Social Change in Canada*. Toronto: McClelland & Stewart.

Lemann, Nicholas (1988). "The Unfinished War," *The Atlantic*, 262, 6.

Leonard, Peter (1990). "Fatalism and the Discourse on Power: An

Introductory Essay," in Linda Davies and Eric Shragge, eds., *Bureaucracy and Community*. Montreal: Black Rose Books.

Lessing, Doris (1991). A public lecture at the University of Victoria, Victoria, B.C., quoted in *The Ring*, 12, 18.

Lewis, David (1972). *The Corporate Welfare Bums*. Toronto: James Lewis and Samuel.

Lindblom, Charles (1968). *The Policy Making Process*. Englewood Cliffs, N.J.: Prentice-Hall.

Lindblom, Charles (1979). "Still Muddling, Not Yet Through," *Public Administration Review* (Nov./Dec.): 517–26.

Lipsky, Michael (1980). *Street Level Bureaucracy*. New York: Russell Sage Foundation.

Lord, John, and Cheryl Hearn (1987). *Return to the Community. The Process of Closing an Institution*. Kitchener, Ont.: Centre for Research and Education in Human Services.

Maas, Henry, and Richard E. Engler, Jr. (1959). *Children in Need of Parents*. New York: Columbia University Press.

MacDougall, Heather (1990). *Activists and Advocates: Toronto's Health Department, 1883–1983*. Toronto: Dundurn Press.

Mackay and Associates (1986). *Final Report: Assessment of the Roles of Social Planning Agencies in Metropolitan Toronto*. Toronto.

Manson Willms, S., M.V. Hayes, and J.D. Hulchanski (1991). "Choice, voice and dignity: Social work's role in housing for persons with HIV infection," presentation to the Third Conference on Social Work and AIDS, New Orleans, May 29-June 1.

Marmot, M.G., and G.D. Smith (1989). "Why are the Japanese living longer?" *British Medical Journal*, 299: 1547–51.

Martin, Sharon (1991). Personal communication.

Mayo, M., ed. (1977). *Women in the Community*. London: Routledge and Kegan Paul.

McCarthy, Grace, and Chief W.M. Christian (1989). Original manuscript text of agreement between B.C. government and Spallumcheen band.

McDaniel, Susan A. (1987). "Implementation of abortion policy in Canada as a women's issue," *Atlantis*, 10, 2: 75–90.

McKeown, T. (1971). "An historical appraisal of the medical task," in McKeown, ed., *Medical History and Medical Care*. Oxford: Oxford University Press.

McKinlay, J.B., and S.M. McKinlay (1977). "The questionable contribution of medical measures to the decline of mortality in the United States in the twentieth century," *Health Sociology* (Summer): 405–28.

McKnight, John (1987). "Regenerating Community," *Social Policy* (Winter): 54–58.

McLaren, Angus, and Arlene Tigar McLaren (1986). *The Bedroom and the State: The Changing Practices and Policies of Contraception and Abortion in Canada, 1880–1980.* Toronto: McClelland and Stewart.

McLaughlin, Audrey (1990). "Canada reneging on promise to end child poverty," *Times Colonist*, Victoria, November 26.

McNiven, Christianne (1979). "The Vancouver Social Planning Department," in Brian Wharf ed., *Community Work in Canada*. Toronto: McClelland and Stewart.

McQuaig, Linda (1988). *Behind Closed Doors*. Toronto: Penguin Books.

Milowsky, Richard (1991). Personal communication.

Mishra, Ramesh (1984). *The Welfare State in Crisis*. Brighton: Wheatsheaf Books.

Montgomery, John (1979). "The Populist Front in Rural Development: or Shall We Eliminate Bureaucracies and Get On With the Job?" *Public Adminstration Review* (Jan./Feb.): 58–65.

Morris, Robert, and Robert Binstock (1966). *Feasible Planning for Social Change*. New York: Columbia University Press.

National Council of Welfare (1975). *Poor Kids*. Ottawa.

National Council of Welfare (1976). *The Hidden Welfare System*. Ottawa.

National Council of Welfare (1979). *In the Best Interest of the Child*. Ottawa.

National Council of Welfare (1990). *Poverty Profile*. Ottawa.

National Institute on Mental Retardation (1984). *Missing the Mark: An Analysis of the Ontario Government's Five Year Plan.* Downsview, Ont.

National Institute on Mental Retardation (1985). *Mandate for Quality: An Analysis of New Brunswick's Approach.* Downsview, Ont.

New Brunswick Telegraph Journal (1991). "Regular Schools Can't Handle Them," March 2.

Ng, Roxanna, Gillian Walker, and Jacob Muller, eds. (1990). *Community Organization and the Canadian State*. Toronto: Garamond Press.

Novick, Marvyn (1991). "National Family Policies: Endowments for Our Children," *Canadian Housing*, 8, 3: 22–26.

Novick, Marvyn, and Richard Volpe (1990). *Children at Risk*. A Review prepared for the Children at Risk Subcommittee of the Laidlaw Foundation. 2 vols. Toronto.

O'Brien, Dan (1979). "Documentation of Social Need, A Critical Planning Activity: Variations on an Old Theme," in Brian Wharf, ed., *Community Work in Canada*. Toronto: McClelland and Stewart.

Ottawa Charter for Health Promotion (1986). Ottawa: World Health Organization, Health and Welfare Canada, and the Canadian Public Health Association.

Pancoast, Diane L. (1981). "Finding and Enlisting Neighbors to Support Families," in James Garbarino *et al.*, eds., *Protecting Children from Abuse and Neglect*. San Francisco: Jossey Bass.

Parfit, Jessie (1986). *The Health of the City: Oxford 1770–1974*. Oxford: Amate Press.

Parker, Roy (1989). "Themes and Variations," in B. Kahon, ed., *Child Care: Research, Policy and Practice*. London: Hodder and Stoughton.

Pateman, Carol (1988). "The Patriarchal Welfare State," in Amy Gutmann, ed., *Democracy and the Welfare State*. Princeton, N.J.: Princeton University Press.

Pederson, Ann P., *et al.* (1988). *Coordinating healthy public policy – An analytic literature review and bibliography*. Ottawa: Health and Welfare Canada, Health Services and Promotion Branch Working Paper.

Pelton, Leroy (1981). "Child Neglect and Abuse: the Myth of Classlessness," in Pelton, ed., *The Social Context of Child Abuse and Neglect*. New York: Human Services Press.

Perlman, Robert, and Arnold Gurin (1972). *Community Organization and Social Planning*. New York: Wiley.

Pinchuk, R., and R. Clark (1984). *Medicine for Beginners*. London: Readers and Writers.

Porter, John (1965). *The Vertical Mosaic: An Analysis of Social Class and Power in Canada*. Toronto: University of Toronto Press.

Pressman, Jeffrey, and Aaron Wildavsky (1984). *Implementation.* Berkeley: University of California Press.

Pross, Richard (1975). *Pressure Group Behaviour in Canadian Politics.* Toronto: McGraw-Hill Ryerson.

Pullinger, Jan, and Dale Lovick (1990). "Statement to Nanaimo Regional General Hospital patient care committee," *Pro Abortion News* (Summer): 4, 8.

Rein, Martin, and S.M. Miller (1967). "The Demonstration Project as a Strategy of Change," in Mayer N. Zald, ed., *Organizing for Community Welfare.* Chicago: Quadrangle Books.

Repo, Marjaleena (1971). "The Fallacy of Community Control," in Gerry Hunnius, ed., *Participatory Democracy for Canada.* Montreal: Black Rose Books.

Report of the Provincial-Municipal Social Services Review (1990). Prepared for the Ontario Ministry of Community and Social Services by the Association of Municipalities of Ontario, Ontario Municipal Social Services Association, and the Ministry of Community and Social Services. Toronto.

Robinson, Elizabeth (1985). "Permanent Planning for Children in Care," in Kenneth Levitt and Brian Wharf, eds., *The Challenge of Child Welfare.* Vancouver: UBC Press.

Rooke, Patricia, and R.L. Schnell (1988). *No Bleeding Heart: Charlotte Whitton, a Feminist on the Right.* Vancouver: UBC Press.

Ross, Becki (1990). "The house that Jill built: Lesbian feminist organizing in Toronto, 1976–1980," *Feminist Review,* 35 (Summer): 75–91.

Ross, David (1987). "Income Security," in Shankar Yelaja, ed., *Canadian Social Policy.* Waterloo, Ont.: Wilfrid Laurier University Press.

Ross, Murray, with B.W. Lappin (1967). *Community Organization: Principles and Practice.* New York: Harper and Row.

Rothman, Jack (1974). "Three Models of Community Organization Practice," in Fred Cox et al., eds., *Strategies of Community Organization,* 2nd edition. Itasca, Illinois: Peacock Press.

St. Pierre, Paul (1985). *Stories of the Chilcotins.* Vancouver: Douglas and MacIntyre.

Schon, Donald (1980). "Framing and Reframing the Problems of Cities," in David Morley, Stuart Proudfoot, and Thomas Burns, eds., *Making Cities Work: The Dynamics of Urban Innovation.* London: Croom Helm.

Shragge, Eric (1990). "Community Based Practice: Political Alternatives or New State Forms?" in Linda Davies and Eric Shragge, eds., *Bureaucracy and Community.* Montreal: Black Rose Books.

Social Assistance Review Committee (1988). *Transitions.* Toronto: Queen's Printer.

Social Planning Council of Metropolitan Toronto (1976). *In Search of a Framework.* Toronto.

Social Planning Council of Metropolitan Toronto (1982). "The Underfunding of Social Assistance Programs in Ontario," *Social Infopac,* 1, 3 (July).

Social Planning Council of Metropolitan Toronto (1984). "The Adequacy of Welfare Benefits: Responding to the Recession," *Social Infopac,* 3, 4 (October).

Social Planning Council of Metropolitan Toronto (1986a). "Welfare Benefits. An Interprovincial Comparison, 1985," *Social Infopac,* 5, 1 (March).

Social Planning Council of Metropolitan Toronto (1986b). *Living on the Margin.* Toronto.

Social Planning Council of Metropolitan Toronto (1989). "The SARC Report: Investing in Ontario's Future," *Social Infopac,* 8, 1 (February).

Social Planning Council of Metropolitan Toronto (1988/89). *Annual Report.* Toronto.

Social Planning Council of Metropolitan Toronto (1990). "A Look at Poverty Lines," *Social Infopac,* 9, 2 (June).

Social Planning Council of Metropolitan Toronto and the Ontario Social Development Council (1981, 1983). *And the Poor Get Poorer.* Toronto.

Southern New Brunswick Mental Health Planning Study (1982). Fredericton.

Sower, Christopher, *et al.* (1957). *Community Involvement.* Glencoe, Illinois: The Free Press.

Splane, Richard (1965). *Social Welfare in Ontario, 1791–1893.* Toronto: University of Toronto Press.

Stachenko, S, and M. Jenicek (1990). "Conceptual differences between prevention and health promotion research implications for community health programs," *Canadian Journal of Public Health*, 81, 1: 53–59.

Statistics Canada (1991). *The Economic Observer*. Ottawa.

"Struggle for choice on Vancouver Island," *Healthsharing* (Spring, 1990).

Tester, Frank, and the Bearspaw Research Programme (1985). *After the Law*. A Report prepared for the Policy and Programme Development Branch, Ontario Ministry of Community and Social Services. 3 vols.

Thompson, Molly (1990). "Association between mortality and poverty," *B.C. Medical Journal*, 32, 8: 337–38.

Titmuss, Richard (1974). *Social Policy, An Introduction*. London: George Allen and Unwin.

Valpy, Michael (1990). "Politicians Won't See the Food Banks as a Crisis," *Globe and Mail*, October 16.

Vickers, Jill McCalla (1989). "Feminist Approaches to Women in Politics," in Linda Kealey and Joan Sangster, eds., *Beyond the Votes: Canadian Women and Politics*. Toronto: University of Toronto Press.

Vogel, Ursula (1986). "Rationalism and Romanticism: Two Strategies for Women's Liberation," in J. Evans *et al.*, eds., *Feminism and political theory*. London: Sage Publications.

Ward Richardson, Sir Benjamin (1876). *Hygeia: A City of Health*. London: Macmillan Company.

Warren, Donald (1981). "Support Systems in Different Types of Neighborhoods," in James Garbarino *et al.*, *Protecting Children from Abuse and Neglect*. San Francisco: Jossey Bass.

Warren, Roland (1971). "Types of Purposive Social Change at the Community Level," in Warren, ed., *Truth, Love and Social Change*. Chicago: Rand McNally.

Wharf, Brian (1989a). *Toward First Nation Control of Child Welfare: A Review of Emerging Developments in B.C.* Victoria: University of Victoria, Faculty of Human and Social Development.

Wharf, Brian (1989b). "Implementing Achieving Health for All," *Canadian Review of Social Policy*, 24: 42–48.

Wharf, Brian, ed. (1990). *Social Work and Social Change in Canada*. Toronto: McClelland & Stewart.

Wharf, Brian (1991). "Preventing Out of Home Placements," *Children Australia*, 16, 3: 15–24.

Wharf, Brian, and Marilyn Callahan (1984). "Connecting Policy and Practice," *Canadian Social Work Review*, Ottawa.

Whittaker, James K. (1983). "Mutual Helping in Human Services Practice," in James K. Whittaker and James Garbarino, eds., *Social Support Networks: Informal Helping in the Human Services*. New York: Aldine Publishing.

Wilkins, Russell (1986). "Health expectancy by local area in Montreal: A summary of findings," *Canadian Journal of Public Health*, 77: 216–20.

Wilkins, R., and O. Adams (1983). *Healthfulness of Life*. Montreal: The Institute for Research on Public Policy.

Williams, Walter (1980). *The Implementation Perspective*. Berkeley: University of California Press.

Wine, Jeri Dawn, and Janice L. Ristock, eds. (1991). *Women and social change: Feminist activism in Canada*. Toronto: James Lorimer.

Witty, David (1991). Personal communication.

Wolfensberger, Wolf (1973). *The Principle of Normalization in Human Services*. Downsview, Ontario: National Institute on Mental Retardation.

Working Committees on Urban Child Welfare and Urban Native G.A.I.N. and Rehab (1989). *Towards Improved Services in Child Welfare and G.A.I.N.* Vancouver.

World Health Organization (1981). *Global Strategy for Health for All by the Year 2000*. Geneva: WHO.

World Health Organization (1984). *The Concept and Principles of Health Promotion – A Discussion Document*. Copenhagen: WHO Regional Office for Europe.

World Health Organization (1986a). *Health Promotion: Concepts and Principles in Action, A Policy Framework*. Geneva: WHO.

World Health Organization (1986b). *Healthy Cities: Strategies for Health*. Promotion brochure. Copenhagen: WHO.

World Health Organization (1987). *Vienna Dialogue on "Healthy Policy and Health Promotion – Towards a New Conception of Public Health"*. Copenhagen: WHO Regional Office for Europe.

World Health Organization Healthy Cities Project (1990). *A Project becomes a movement – evaluation document*. Copenhagen: WHO Regional Office for Europe.

World Health Organization, Health and Welfare Canada, and the

Canadian Public Health Association (1986). *Ottawa Charter for Health Promotion*. Ottawa.

Yin, Robert K. (1984). *Case Study Research: Design and Methods*. Beverly Hills: Sage Publications.

Yukon Native Brotherhood (1973). *Together Today for Our Children Tomorrow*. Whitehorse: Whitehorse Star.

Zald, Mayer (1967). "Sociology and Community Organization Practice," in Zald, ed., *Organizing for Community Welfare*. Chicago: Quadrangle Books.

INDEX